IMAGES
of America

WEST HAVEN REVISITED

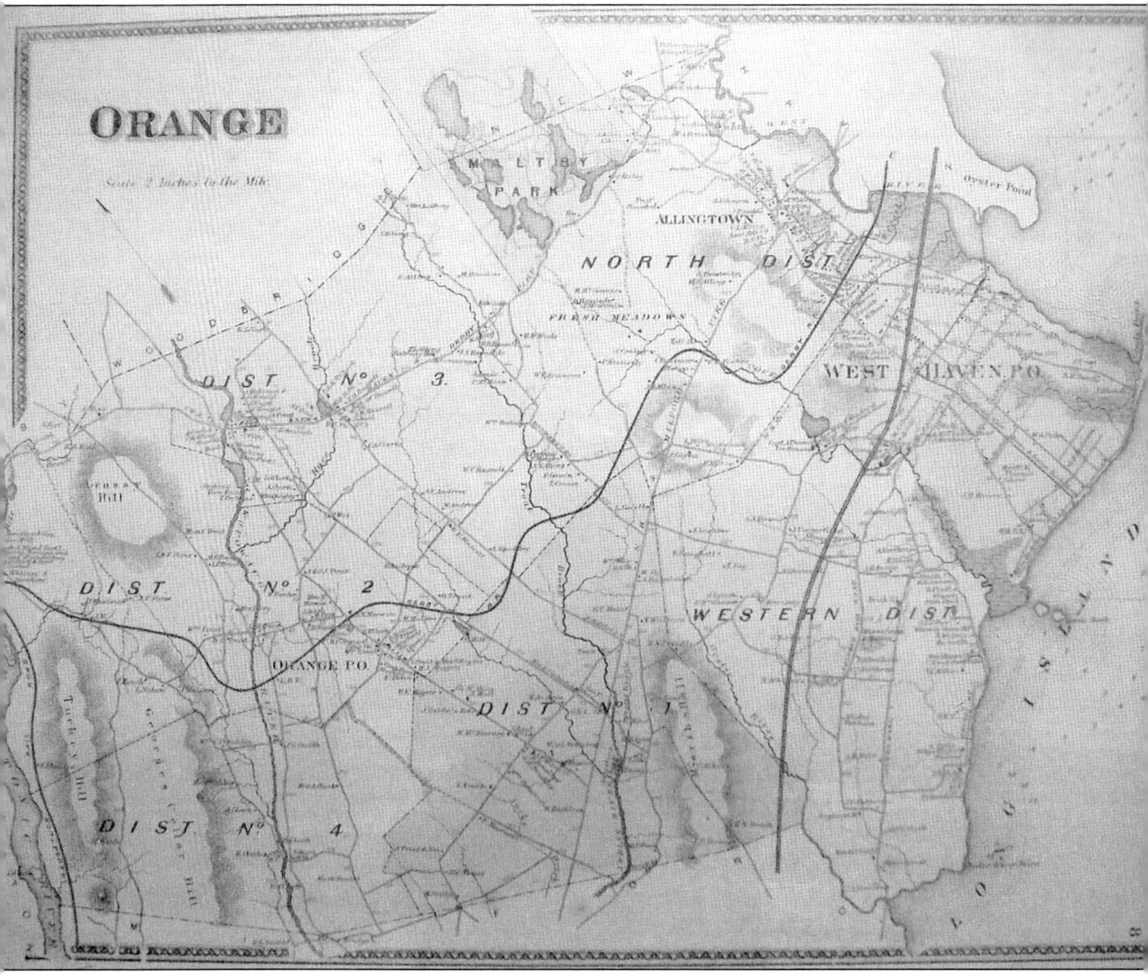

New Haven Colony grew to include West Haven and the Northern and Western Districts. In 1779, the British took advantage of the town's vulnerable position by landing there en route to destroy New Haven. (Courtesy of the West Haven Historical Society.)

On the Cover: Sea breezes from Long Island Sound were most welcome as dinner guests celebrated at a private party in late July 1920. (Courtesy of the West Haven Historical Society.)

IMAGES
of America

WEST HAVEN REVISITED

Carole A. Laydon McElrath

ARCADIA
PUBLISHING

ISBN 978-0-7385-7397-7

Published by Arcadia Publishing
Charleston SC, Chicago IL, Portsmouth NH, San Francisco CA

Printed in the United States of America

Library of Congress Control Number: 2010930263

For all general information contact Arcadia Publishing at:
Telephone 843-853-2070
Fax 843-853-0044
E-mail sales@arcadiapublishing.com
For customer service and orders:
Toll-Free 1-888-313-2665

Visit us on the Internet at www.arcadiapublishing.com

To Blanche Baldwin and Betty Roy, who quietly lit the path for other volunteers, clearing trails and traveling new roads in the ever-changing world of volunteerism.

Contents

Acknowledgments

Four years ago, the 56-year-old West Haven Historical Society made a bold decision to purchase the only remaining single-family home in the National Historic District on the Green in the center of West Haven. Aware that the estate property was considered endangered with the potential for its destruction, the membership voted to take on this enormous responsibility. The beautiful 1917 Dutch Colonial house now serves as the all-volunteer organization's headquarters, its museum, and home to its collections, exhibit space, and rooms for special events. This new, highly visible location has been the impetus for greater public involvement, and the community has become more involved in society activities, including the collection of all things relative to our 363-year-old city. The society's success is certainly due to the support of our community. The success of this book is most definitely due to the guidance, direction, and experience of my editors Hilary Zusman and Ashley McDonald, to the patience of our volunteer professional archivists, and to the technical production expertise of Ceren Laydon.

INTRODUCTION

West Haven Revisited is a compilation of images of some of the ephemera and artifacts donated by our local citizens. These precious documents, photographs, family and business memorabilia, and rare articles are being preserved by the West Haven Historical Society so that future generations may understand and appreciate our city's past. As I worked my way through the collections, I began to sense that this book should have been titled *Myths, Mysteries, and Majesties: Behind the Scenes Stories.* With every hour, the stories of West Haven and its people became increasingly more intriguing, woven into a vast play with a British governor, an Italian queen, the American Vaudeville Association, professional ball clubs, Eagle Scouts, orphans, and musicians becoming characters in a program with many acts.

West Haven Revisited touches on generally unknown or forgotten stories of people, places, incidents, and events of this small, southern Connecticut, coastal community, always with the idea that history is a story ever in the making. Over the centuries, our community was called West Farms, the Borough of West Haven, the Town of West Haven (1921), and finally, the City of West Haven (1961). We suffered several British invasions, had a grand maritime history, hosted a large Victorian-era amusement park, sustained a wartime industrial base, and boasted a wealthy economy. Through all the years, our citizens were progressive, accomplished, and often unique. It is that uniqueness, that special quality, which we try to share in this book.

While the first West Haven book concentrated on the chronological history of the city, this book attempts to tell the lesser-known, but equally fascinating, stories from those same times. It was certainly difficult to determine which images were to be incorporated herein, but the decision was made based on the number and types of inquiries we have at the historical society. Thanks to so many generous and/or curious people, the stories are here. Many thanks to donors Ken Berg; Ted Wolfe; Jon Purmont; Art Gilbert; Allison Sheahan; Frank Rully; Mary King; the Black Heritage Committee; Vaughn Grant; Chick Celentano; the Hentz, Sullivan, and Richards families; and each and everyone who has shared his or her personal treasures for you to enjoy.

The collections continue to grow, thanks to the hundreds of donors who understand the importance of the society's mission to preserve the history of the incidents, personalities, activities, and events that were so much a part of our city's history, as noted in the earlier Arcadia publication, *West Haven*. If you have a story to tell or items to share, please contact the West Haven Historical Society at P.O. Box 384, West Haven, Connecticut, 06516. Unless otherwise noted, all images appear courtesy of the West Haven Historical Society.

One

The Power of the Printed Word

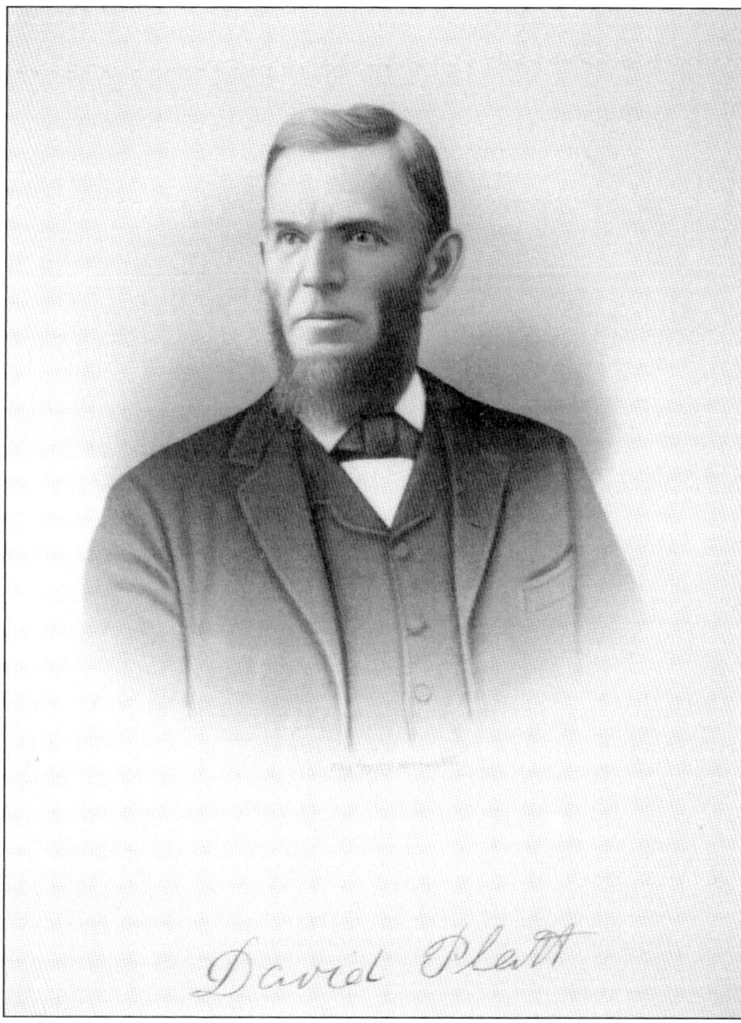

In the mid-19th century, David Platt purchased rolling land overlooking the Cove River. He built a handsome two-story country home, which still stands on the north-south avenue named after this well-known citizen.

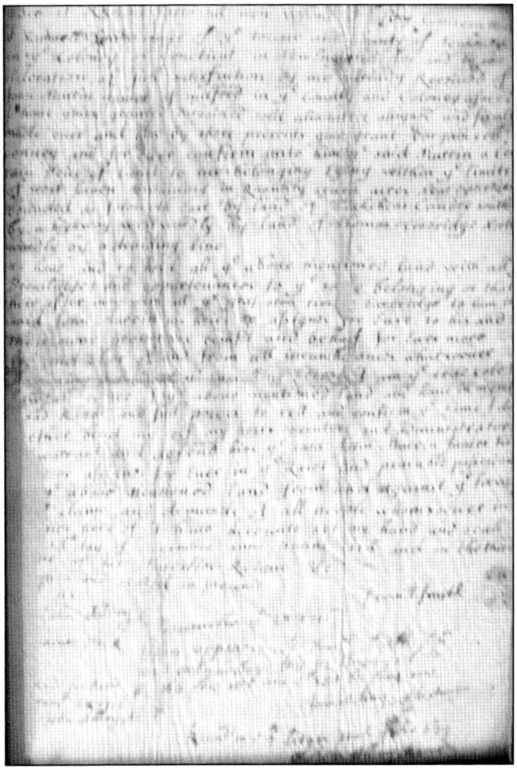

In his will of November 28, 1716, "in the town and county of New Haven in the Coloney of Coneticut in New England," Samuel H. Smith deeded his property at Oyster River to John Murrin Jr. Smith owned land adjacent to the Northrop-Merwin property on the Milford and West Haven line. The will, written in Smith's own handwriting, was witnessed by John Alling and Jonas Peck.

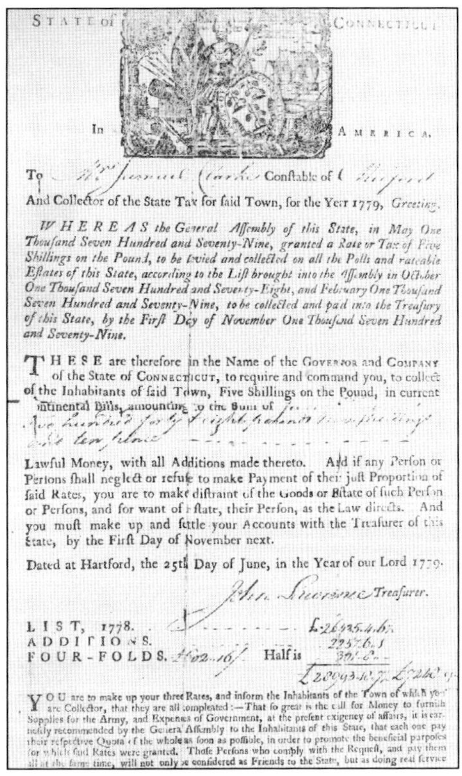

STATE of CONNECTICUT

In AMERICA.

To [illegible] Conftable of [illegible]

And Collector of the State Tax for faid Town, for the Year 1779, *Greeting.*

WHEREAS the General Affembly of this State, in May One Thoufand Seven Hundred and Seventy-Nine, granted a Rate or Tax of Five Shillings on the Pound, to be levied and collected on all the Polls and rateable Eftates of this State, according to the Lift brought into the Affembly in October One Thoufand Seven Hundred and Seventy-Eight, and February One Thoufand Seven Hundred and Seventy-Nine, to be collected and paid into the Treafury of this State, by the Firft Day of November One Thoufand Seven Hundred and Seventy-Nine.

THESE are therefore in the Name of the GOVERNOR and COMPANY of the State of CONNECTICUT, to require and command you, to collect of the Inhabitants of faid Town, Five Shillings on the Pound, in current Continental Bills, amounting to the Sum of [illegible]

Lawful Money, with all Additions made thereto. And if any Perfon or Perfons fhall neglect or refufe to make Payment of their juft Proportion of faid Rates, you are to make diftraint of the Goods or Eftate of fuch Perfon or Perfons, and for want of Eftate, their Perfon, as the Law directs. And you muft make up and fettle your Accounts with the Treafurer of this State, by the Firft Day of November next.

Dated at Hartford, the 25th Day of June, in the Year of our Lord 1779.

[illegible] *Treafurer.*

LIST, 1778. [illegible]
ADDITIONS. [illegible]
FOUR-FOLDS. [illegible] Half is [illegible]

YOU are to make up your three Rates, and inform the Inhabitants of the Town of which you are Collector, that they are all completed:—That fo great is the call for Money to furnish Supplies for the Army, and Expences of Government, at the prefent exigency of affairs, it is earneftly recommended by the General Affembly to the Inhabitants of this State, that each one pay their refpective Quota of the whole as foon as poffible, in order to promote the beneficial purpofes for which faid Rates were granted. Thofe Perfons who comply with the Requeft, and pay them all at the fame time, will not only be confidered as Friends to the State, but as doing real fervice

In 1779, Samuel Clark paid taxes to the State of Connecticut for land he owned in both West Haven and Milford. The tax bill was computed in British pounds.

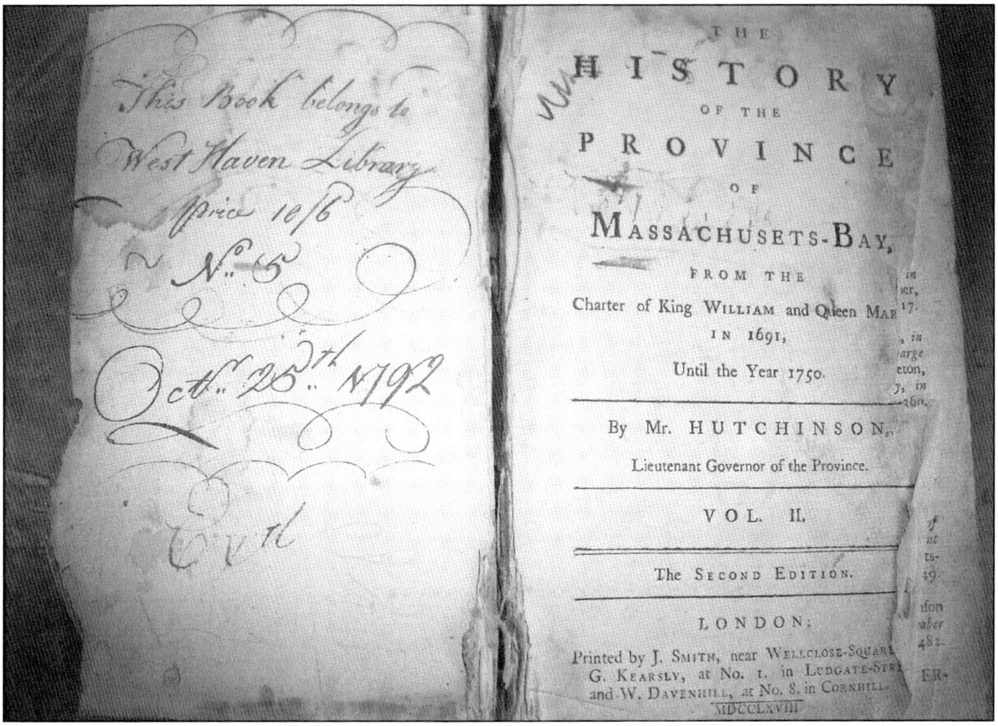

By 1792, a group of community leaders met to discuss the importance of a public education system and the need for a public library. Among the men pledging personal funds to support these endeavors were members of the Smith, Painter, and Kimberly families and Noah Williston of the Congregational Church, where the library would be housed. Books were to reflect the best of the sciences, history, theology, and philosophy. Interestingly, one of the books selected by these patriots of the American Revolutionary era was *The History of the Province of Massachusetts Bay* by the Honorable Lt. Gov. Thomas Hutchinson, the last English governor of Massachusetts, who retired to England after he was the target of the Boston uprising. The library also contained volumes on law, government, and theology.

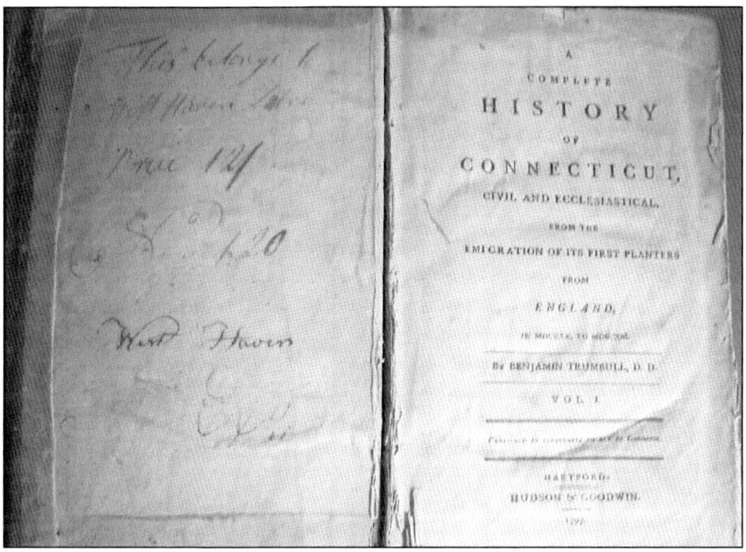

Another first library book, *The Complete History of Connecticut* (1797) was rescued from an early deaccessioning program more than 75 years ago. The book included an overview of Connecticut statutes.

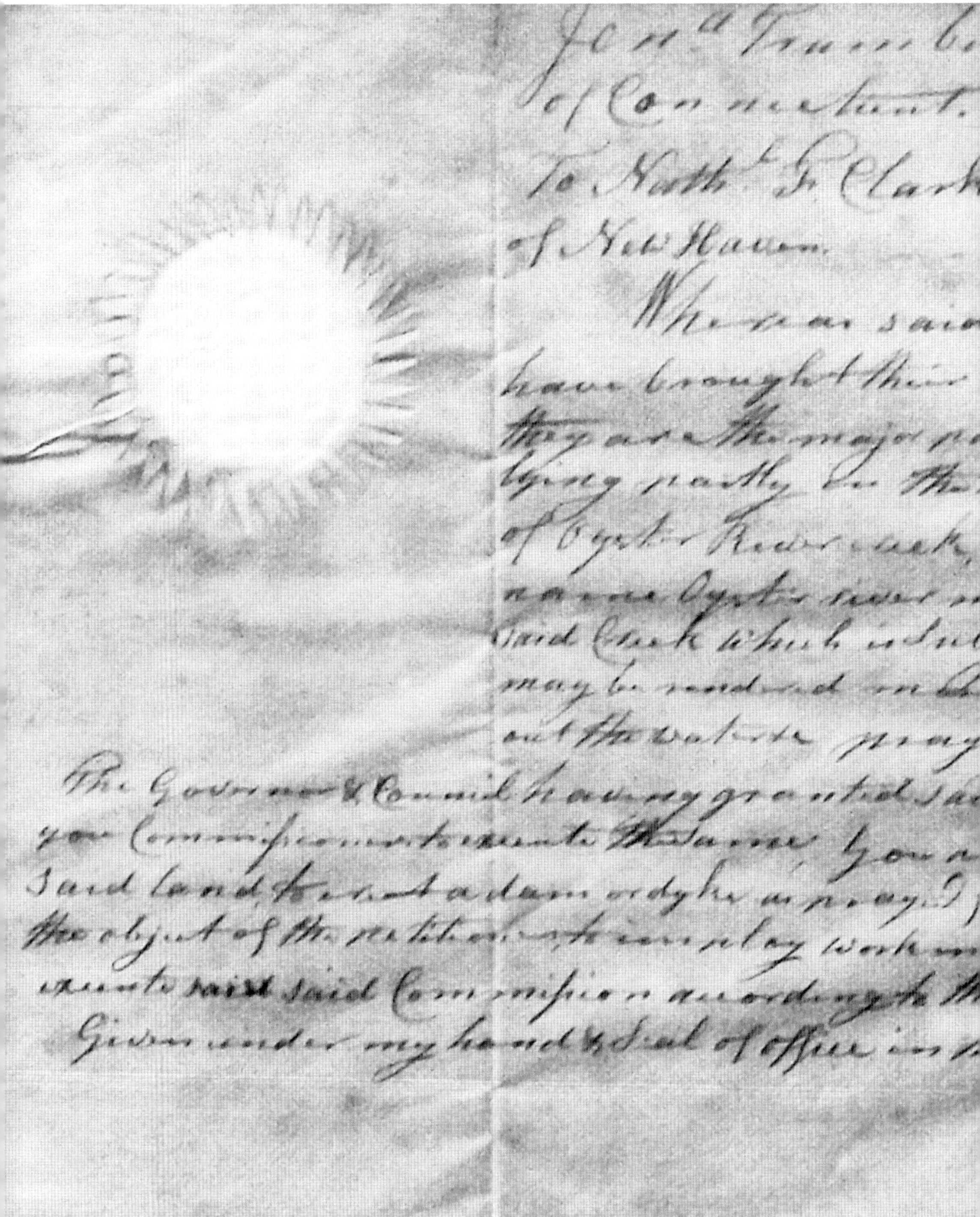

Jon^a Trumb
of Connecticut.
To Nathl G. Clark
of New Haven.
Whereas said
have brought their
they are the major pa
lying partly in the
of Oyster River creek
namely Oyster river
said Creek which is
may be
out the water pray
The Governor & Council having granted said
you Commissioners to execute the same you are
said land to erect a dam or dyke as prayed
the object of the petitioners
execute said Commission according to the
Given under my hand & Seal of office in

In October 1806, Federalist governor of Connecticut Jonathan Trumbull (1797–1809) affixed his signature to this document granting permission to the Clark, Platt, and Merwin petitioners to erect a dam or dyke at the mouth of the Oyster River, partly in the town of New (West) Haven

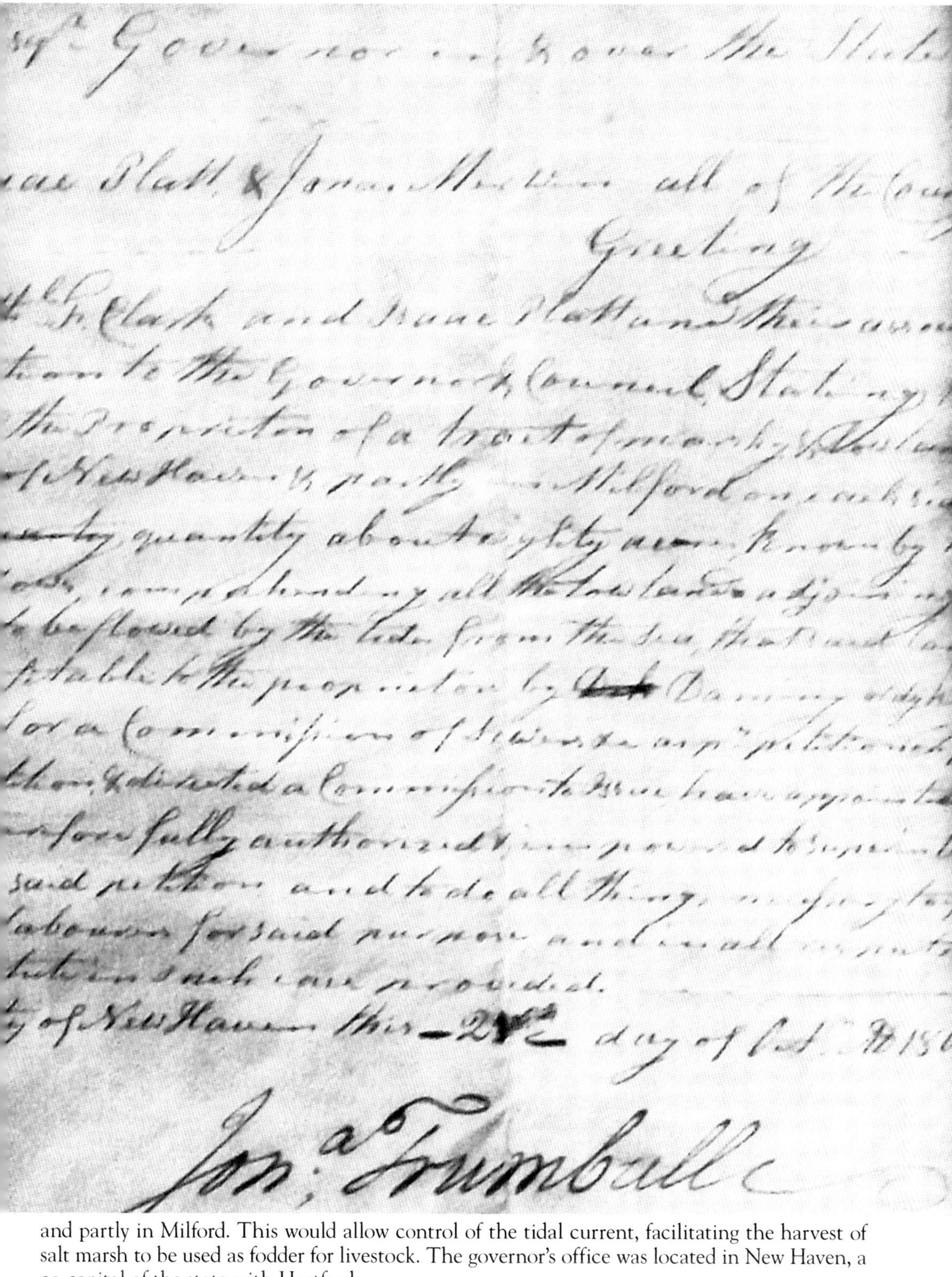

and partly in Milford. This would allow control of the tidal current, facilitating the harvest of salt marsh to be used as fodder for livestock. The governor's office was located in New Haven, a co-capital of the state with Hartford.

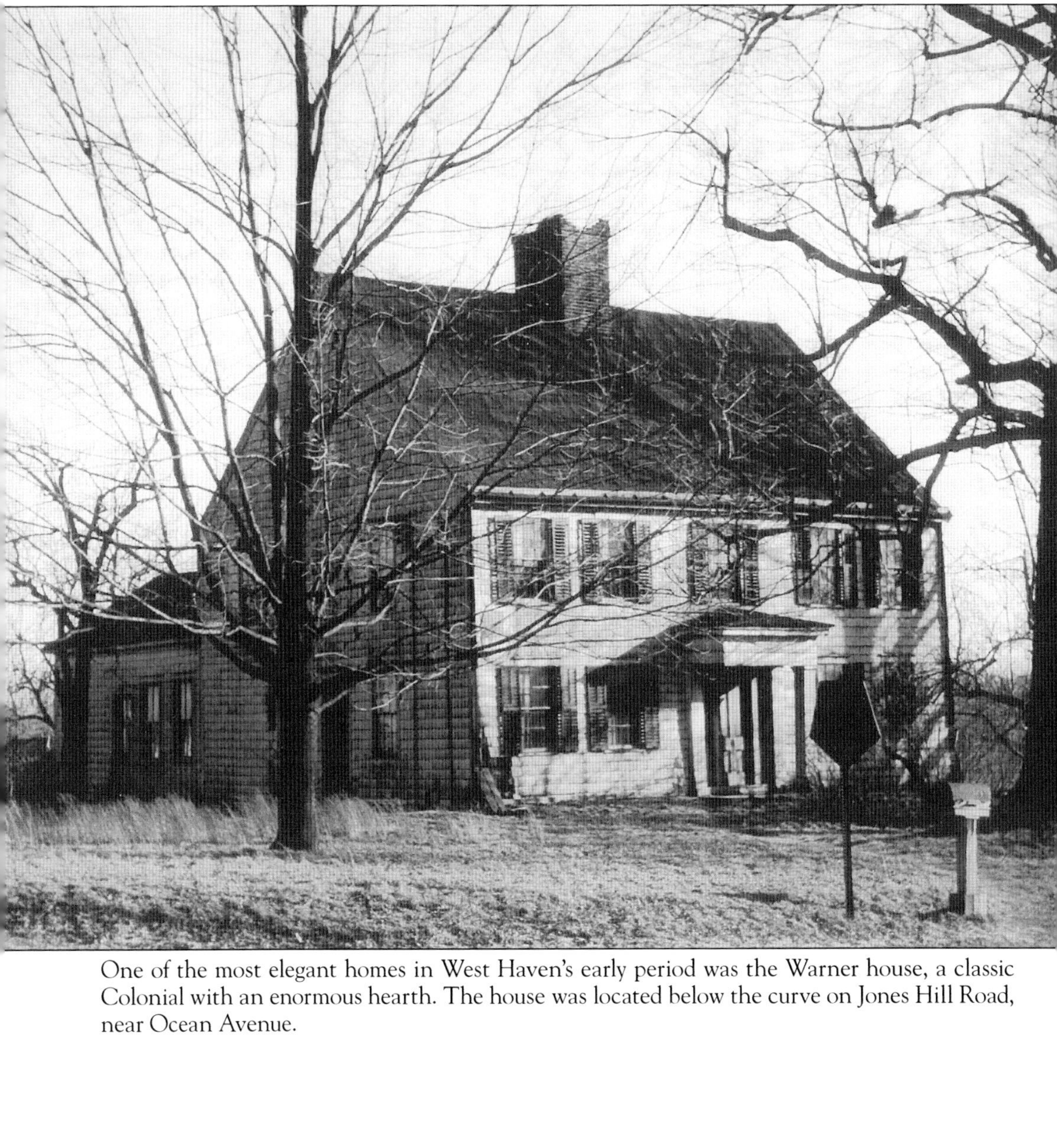

One of the most elegant homes in West Haven's early period was the Warner house, a classic Colonial with an enormous hearth. The house was located below the curve on Jones Hill Road, near Ocean Avenue.

Native lore tells that the land was covered with giant trees in some sections of West Haven, that the hunting was good, and the food abundant. This three-board drop leaf cherry table was made from a single tree in the late 1700s and was part of the estate of Martha Cartright, first wife of Jay Lord Northrop.

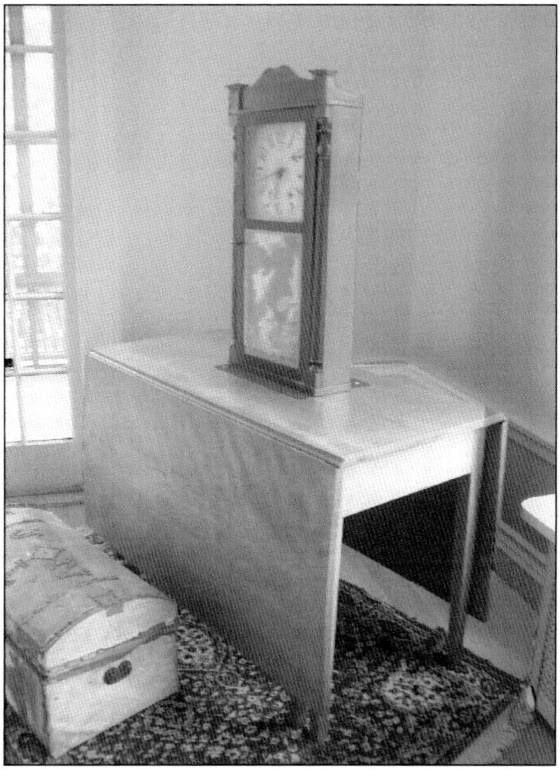

The clock and table are on permanent loan to the society from Ted Wolfe. The cherry table was a valued piece of family furniture, as attested to by its inclusion in this will.

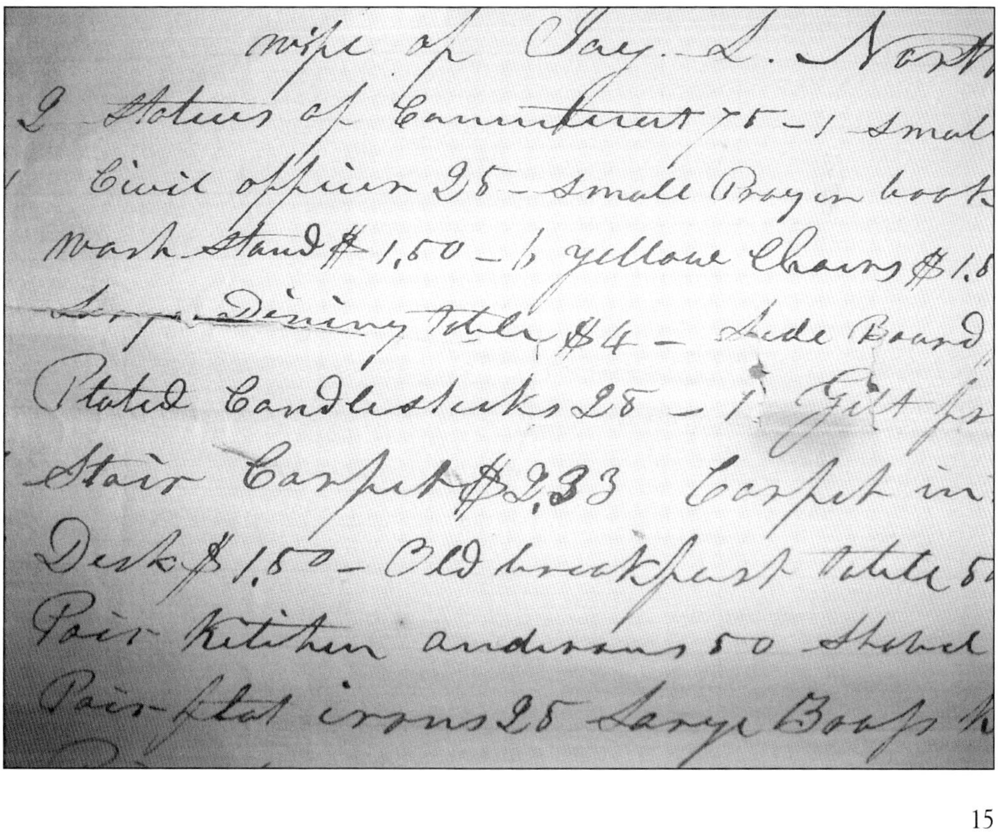

wife of Jay. L. North
2 Statues of Commandant 75 - 1 Smal
Civil officer 25 - Small Prayer book
Wash Stand $1.50 - 1/2 yellow Chairs $1.5
Dining table $4 - Side Board
Plated Candlesticks 28 - 1 Gilt fr
Stair Carpet $2.33 Carpet in
Desk $1.50 - Old breakfast table 5
Pair Kitchen andirons 50 Stand
Pair flat irons 25 Large Boxes

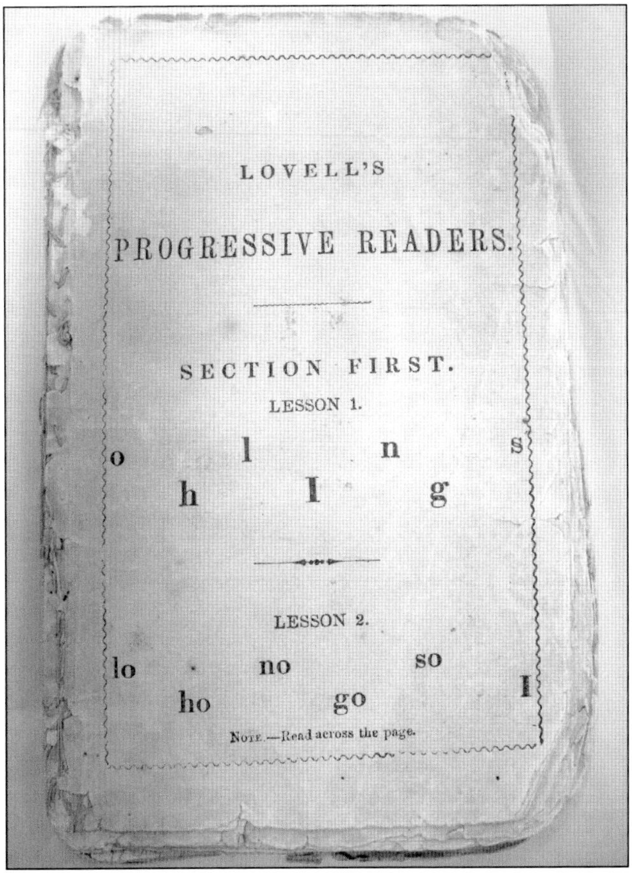

Lovell's primer was used by early readers and passed along to every family member.

All of the early documents in this chapter were kept intact in an old desk or in this trunk owned by Jay Lord Northrop. Northrop used this trunk to carry his belongings when he traveled to Texas each year to pay taxes on his holdings there.

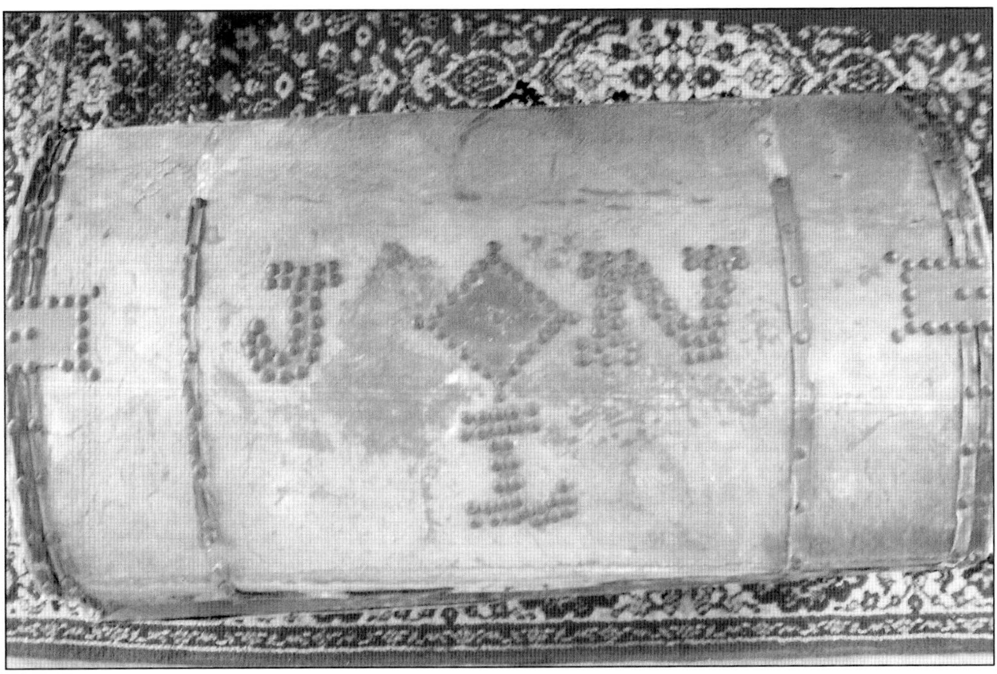

Next to the Bible, one of the standard publications found in homes was an almanac with all of the wisdom, recipes, and advertising of the day.

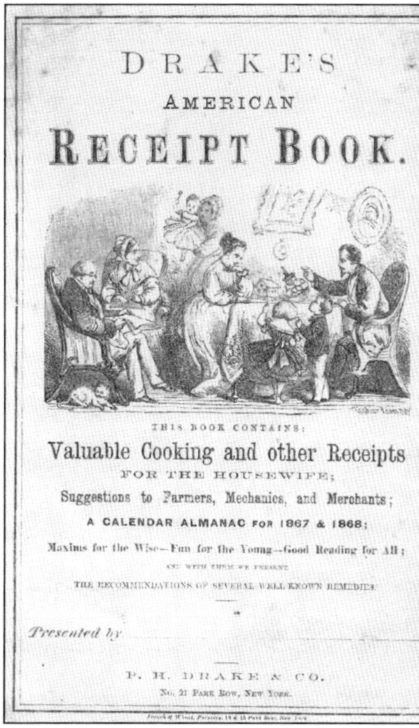

Drake's Almanac was popular because it helped the farmer and the housewife with everything from the ingredients for making shoe polish to the elimination of weevils.

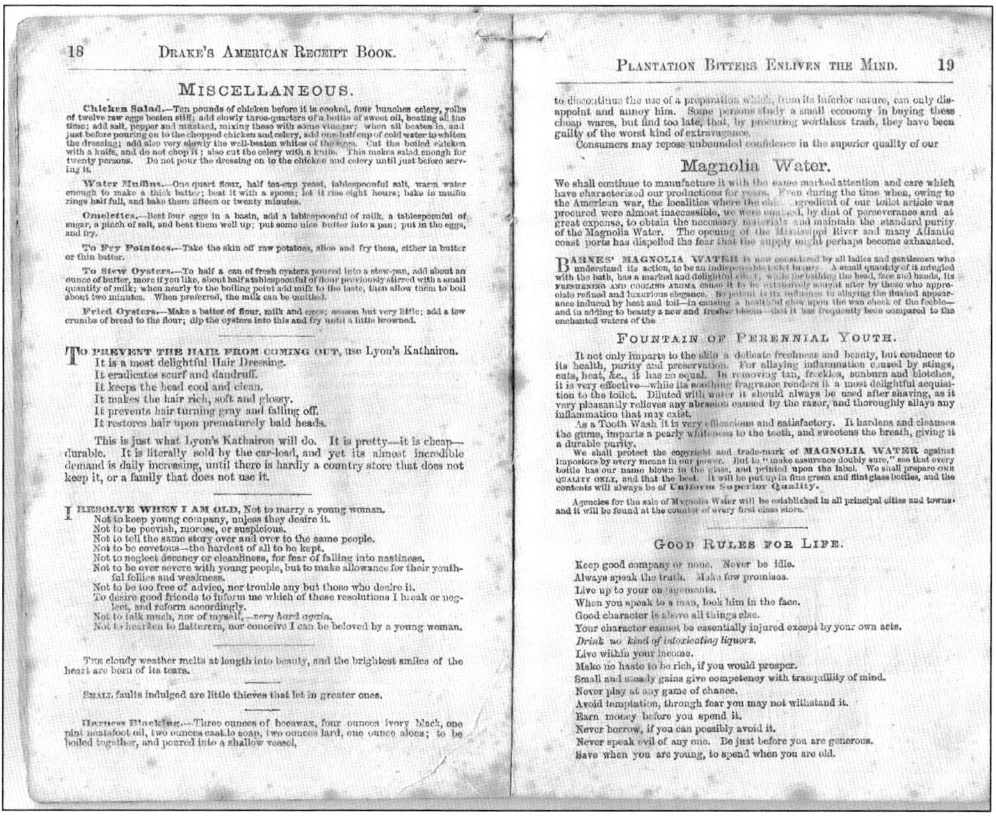

18 DRAKE'S AMERICAN RECEIPT BOOK.

MISCELLANEOUS.

Chicken Salad.—Ten pounds of chicken before it is cooked, four bunches celery, yolks of twelve raw eggs beaten stiff; add slowly three-quarters of a bottle of sweet oil, beating all the time; add salt, pepper and mustard, mixing these with some vinegar; when all beaten in, and just before pouring on to the chopped chicken and celery, add one-half cup of cold water to whiten the dressing; add also very slowly the well-beaten whites of the eggs. Cut the boiled chicken with a knife, and do not chop it; also cut the celery with a knife. This makes salad enough for twenty persons. Do not pour the dressing on to the chicken and celery until just before serving it.

Water Muffins.—One quart flour, half tea-cup yeast, tablespoonful salt, warm water enough to make a thick batter; beat it with a spoon; let it rise eight hours; bake in muffin rings half full, and bake them fifteen or twenty minutes.

Omelettes.—Beat four eggs in a basin, add a tablespoonful of milk, a tablespoonful of sugar, a pinch of salt, and beat them well up; put some nice butter into a pan; put in the eggs, and fry.

To Fry Potatoes.—Take the skin off raw potatoes, slice and fry them, either in butter or thin batter.

To Stew Oysters.—To half a can of fresh oysters poured into a stew-pan, add about an ounce of butter, more if you like, about half a tablespoonful of flour previously stirred with a small quantity of milk; when nearly to the boiling point add milk to the taste, then allow them to boil about two minutes. When preferred, the milk can be omitted.

Fried Oysters.—Make a batter of flour, milk and eggs; season but very little; add a few crumbs of bread to the flour; dip the oysters into this and fry until a little browned.

TO PREVENT THE HAIR FROM COMING OUT, use Lyon's Kathairon.
It is a most delightful Hair Dressing.
It eradicates scurf and dandruff.
It keeps the head cool and clean.
It makes the hair rich, soft and glossy.
It prevents hair turning gray and falling off.
It restores hair upon prematurely bald heads.

This is just what Lyon's Kathairon will do. It is pretty—it is cheap—durable. It is literally sold by the car-load, and yet its almost incredible demand is daily increasing, until there is hardly a country store that does not keep it, or a family that does not use it.

I RESOLVE WHEN I AM OLD, Not to marry a young woman.
Not to keep young company, unless they desire it.
Not to be peevish, morose, or suspicious.
Not to tell the same story over and over to the same people.
Not to be covetous—the hardest of all to be kept.
Not to neglect decency or cleanliness, for fear of falling into nastiness.
Not to be over severe with young people, but to make allowance for their youthful follies and weakness.
Not to be too free of advice, nor trouble any but those who desire it.
To desire good friends to inform me which of these resolutions I break or neglect, and reform accordingly.
Not to talk much, nor of myself,—*very hard again.*
Not to harken to flatterers, nor conceive I can be beloved by a young woman.

THE cloudy weather melts at length into beauty, and the brightest smiles of the heart are born of its tears.

SMALL faults indulged are little thieves that let in greater ones.

Harness Blacking.—Three ounces of beeswax, four ounces ivory black, one pint neatsfoot oil, two ounces castile soap, two ounces lard, one ounce aloes; to be boiled together, and poured into a shallow vessel,

PLANTATION BITTERS ENLIVEN THE MIND. 19

to discontinue the use of a preparation which, from its inferior nature, can only disappoint and annoy him. Some persons study a small economy in buying these cheap wares, but find too late, that, by procuring worthless trash, they have been guilty of the worst kind of extravagance.

Consumers may repose unbounded confidence in the superior quality of our

Magnolia Water.

We shall continue to manufacture it with the same marked attention and care which have characterized our productions for years. Even during the time when, owing to the American war, the localities where the chief ingredient of our toilet article was procured were almost inaccessible, we were enabled, by dint of perseverance and at great expense, to obtain the necessary materials and maintain the standard purity of the Magnolia Water. The opening of the Mississippi River and many Atlantic coast ports has dispelled the fear that the supply might perhaps become exhausted.

BARNES' MAGNOLIA WATER is now considered by all ladies and gentlemen who understand its action, to be an indispensable toilet luxury. A small quantity of it mingled with the bath, has a marked and delightful effect; while for bathing the head, face and hands, its FRESHENING AND COOLING AROMA cause it to be extensively sought after by those who appreciate refined and luxurious elegance. So potent is its influence in allaying the flushed appearance induced by heat and toil—in causing a healthful glow upon the wan cheek of the feeble—and in adding to beauty a new and fresher bloom—that it has frequently been compared to the enchanted waters of the

FOUNTAIN OF PERENNIAL YOUTH.

It not only imparts to the skin a delicate freshness and beauty, but conduces to its health, purity and preservation. For allaying inflammation caused by stings, cuts, heat, &c., it has no equal. In removing tan, freckles, sunburn and blotches, it is very effective—while its soothing fragrance renders it a most delightful acquisition to the toilet. Diluted with water it should always be used after shaving, as it very pleasantly relieves any abrasion caused by the razor, and thoroughly allays any inflammation that may exist.

As a Tooth Wash it is very efficacious and satisfactory. It hardens and cleanses the gums, imparts a pearly whiteness to the teeth, and sweetens the breath, giving it a durable purity.

We shall protect the copyright and trade-mark of MAGNOLIA WATER against impostors by every means in our power. But to "make assurance doubly sure," see that every bottle has our name blown in the glass, and printed upon the label. We shall prepare ONE QUALITY ONLY, and that the best. It will be put up in fine green and flint glass bottles, and the contents will always be of Uniform Superior Quality.

Agencies for the sale of Magnolia Water will be established in all principal cities and towns, and it will be found at the counter of every first class store.

GOOD RULES FOR LIFE.

Keep good company or none. Never be idle.
Always speak the truth. Make few promises.
Live up to your engagements.
When you speak to a man, look him in the face.
Good character is above all things else.
Your character cannot be essentially injured except by your own acts.
Drink no kind of intoxicating liquors.
Live within your income.
Make no haste to be rich, if you would prosper.
Small and steady gains give competency with tranquillity of mind.
Never play at any game of chance.
Avoid temptation, through fear you may not withstand it.
Earn money before you spend it.
Never borrow, if you can possibly avoid it.
Never speak evil of any one. Be just before you are generous.
Save when you are young, to spend when you are old.

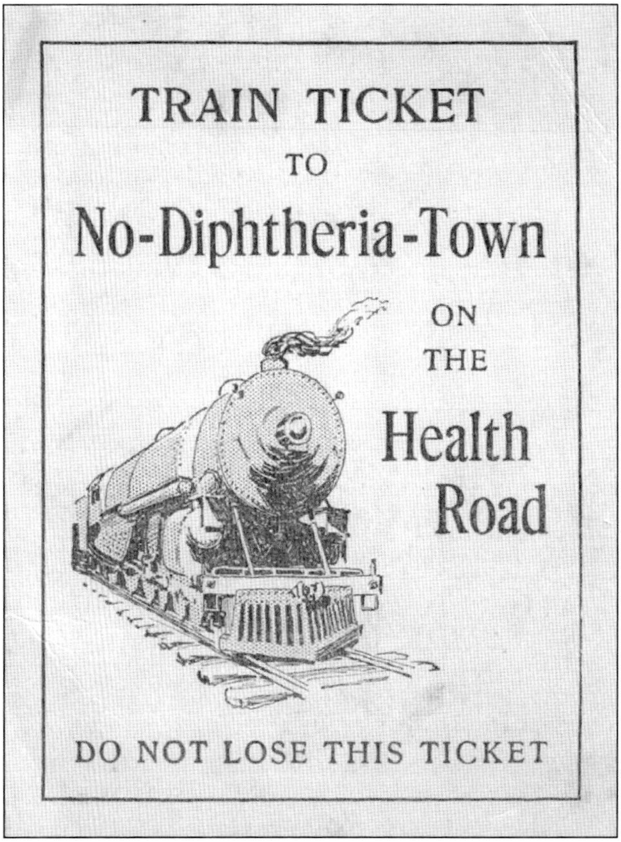

Children were inoculated against deadly diphtheria. This clever booklet not only records numerous visits to the doctor, but also encourages the child to take this "train trip" through the process, hopefully making it more palatable to the finish.

Reading was a lifetime pleasure and a social activity shared by Sarah Merwin Northrop (right) and her unidentified friend.

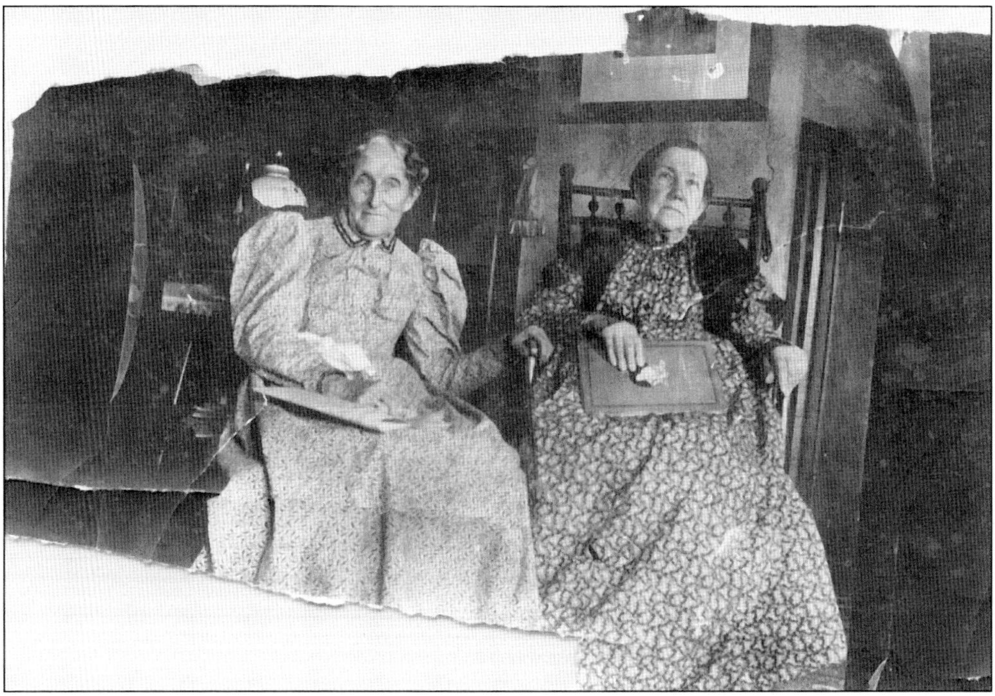

Students went from slates to penmanship books and primers, and there were several from which to choose.

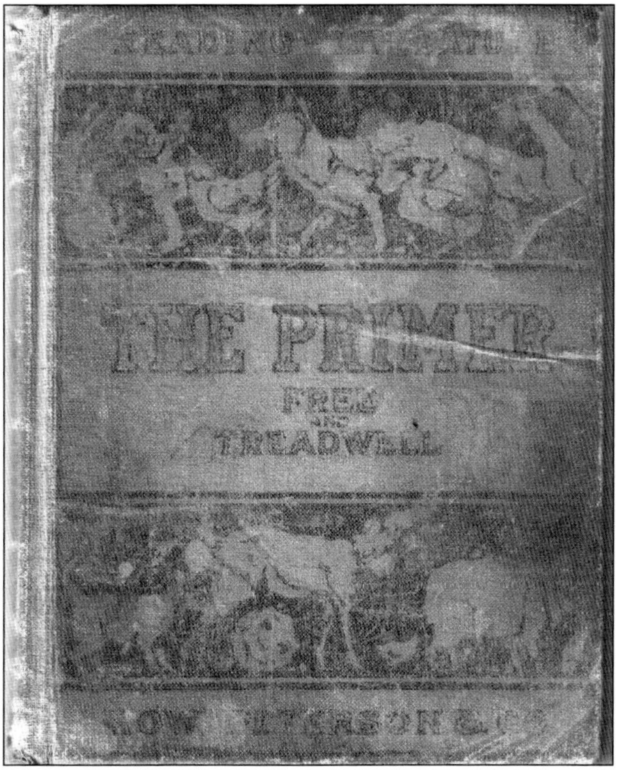

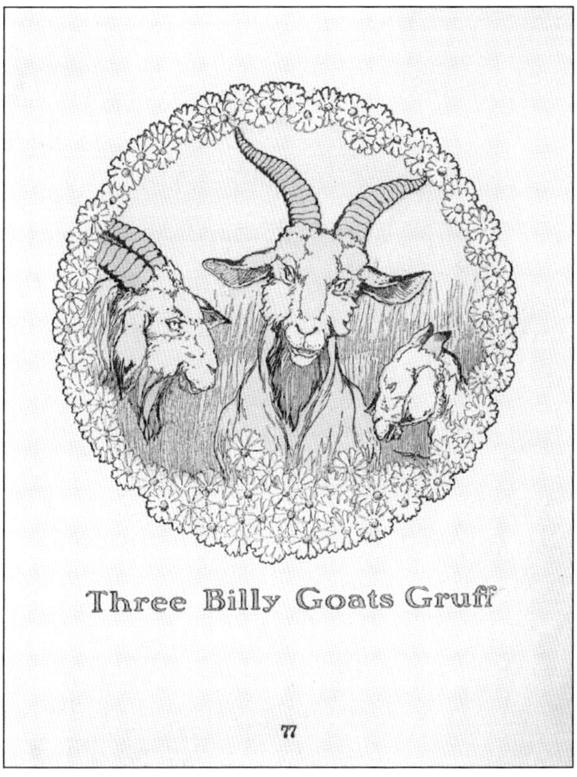
Three Billy Goats Gruff

77

By 1910, educators felt that students would learn to read more aggressively when provided with subjects of interest, thus the use of *The Primer* by Free and Treadwell featuring simple folk tales. This reader, with stories like "The Little Red Hen" and "Three Billy Goats Gruff," belonged to Anita Flannigan of Campbell Avenue.

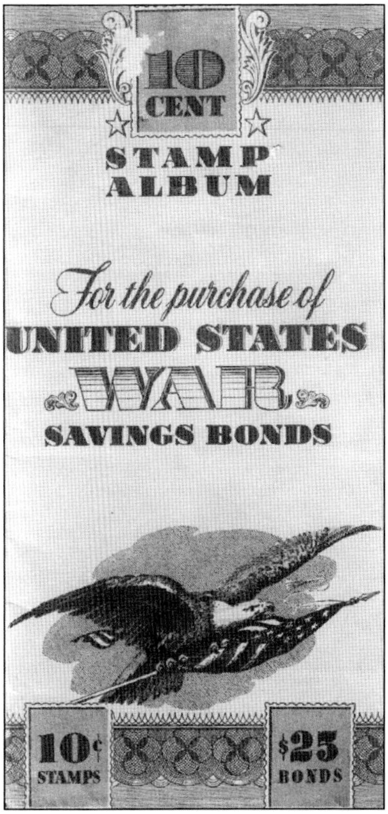

During World War II, the U.S. government guaranteed the repayment of principal and interest on the purchase of savings bonds. Stamps could be purchased for 10¢, 25¢, 50¢, $1, or $5. Schoolchildren had a weekly drive, usually purchasing one stamp at a time at smaller denominations.

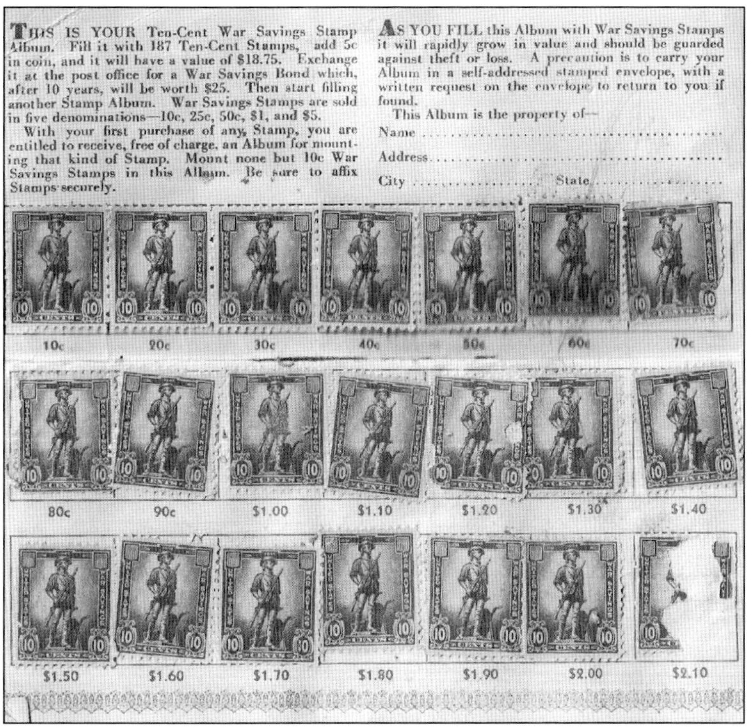

THIS IS YOUR Ten-Cent War Savings Stamp Album. Fill it with 187 Ten-Cent Stamps, add 5c in coin, and it will have a value of $18.75. Exchange it at the post office for a War Savings Bond which, after 10 years, will be worth $25. Then start filling another Stamp Album. War Savings Stamps are sold in five denominations—10c, 25c, 50c, $1, and $5.

With your first purchase of any Stamp, you are entitled to receive, free of charge, an Album for mounting that kind of Stamp. Mount none but 10c War Savings Stamps in this Album. Be sure to affix Stamps securely.

AS YOU FILL this Album with War Savings Stamps it will rapidly grow in value and should be guarded against theft or loss. A precaution is to carry your Album in a self-addressed stamped envelope, with a written request on the envelope to return to you if found.

This Album is the property of—

Name ....

Address ....

City .... State ....

Stamps were placed in the book, and when the book was filled it was turned in to the proper office. A 25¢ book filled at $18.75 brought a $25 return at maturity. Meanwhile, everyone was doing his or her share "towards the war effort" at an affordable scale.

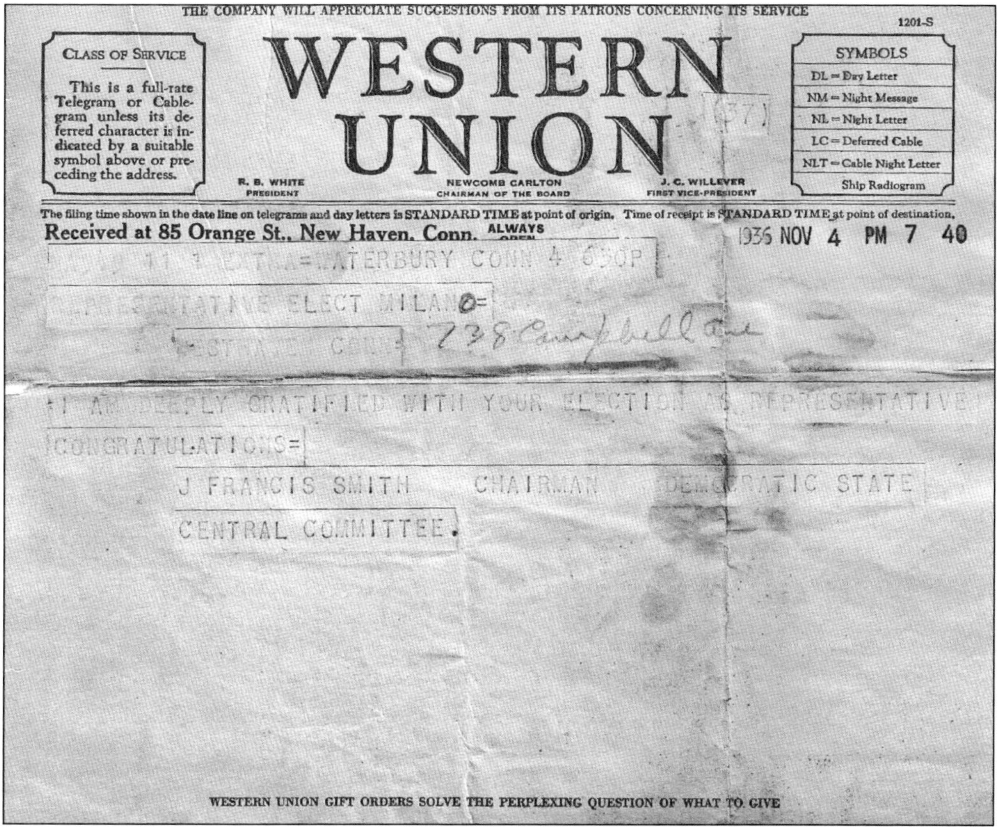

THE COMPANY WILL APPRECIATE SUGGESTIONS FROM ITS PATRONS CONCERNING ITS SERVICE

1201-S

CLASS OF SERVICE

This is a full-rate Telegram or Cablegram unless its deferred character is indicated by a suitable symbol above or preceding the address.

WESTERN UNION

R. B. WHITE, PRESIDENT — NEWCOMB CARLTON, CHAIRMAN OF THE BOARD — J. C. WILLEVER, FIRST VICE-PRESIDENT

SYMBOLS
DL = Day Letter
NM = Night Message
NL = Night Letter
LC = Deferred Cable
NLT = Cable Night Letter
Ship Radiogram

The filing time shown in the date line on telegrams and day letters is STANDARD TIME at point of origin. Time of receipt is STANDARD TIME at point of destination.

Received at 85 Orange St., New Haven, Conn. ALWAYS OPEN 1936 NOV 4 PM 7 40

WATERBURY CONN 4 630P

REPRESENTATIVE ELECT MILANO=

738 Campbell Ave

WEST HAVEN CONN

I AM DEEPLY GRATIFIED WITH YOUR ELECTION AS REPRESENTATIVE CONGRATULATIONS=

J FRANCIS SMITH CHAIRMAN DEMOCRATIC STATE CENTRAL COMMITTEE.

WESTERN UNION GIFT ORDERS SOLVE THE PERPLEXING QUESTION OF WHAT TO GIVE

Telegraphs and telegrams had been a major source of long-distance communication for almost a century when this congratulatory message was sent on November 4, 1940, from Waterbury to West Haven's newly elected Representative Milano from J. Francis Smith, chairman of the Democratic State Central Committee.

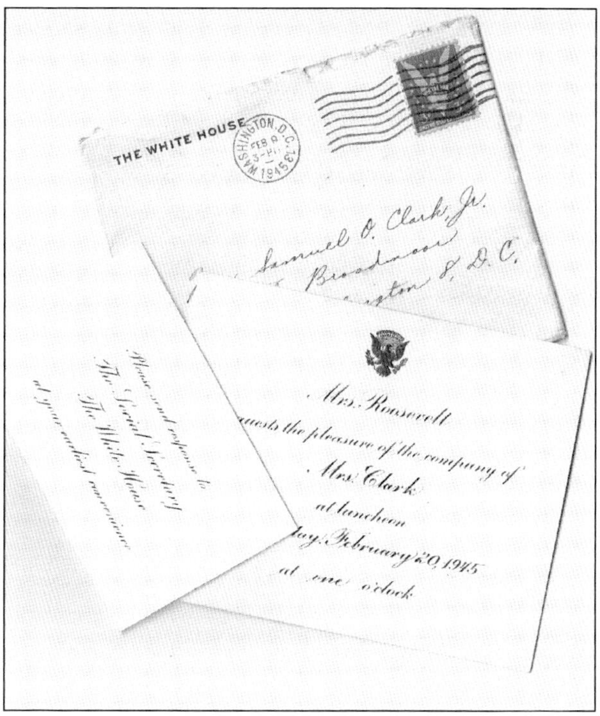

The U.S. mail still held an important seat when it came to personal communications. This invitation addressed to Mrs. Samuel Clark Jr. was sent by Eleanor Roosevelt in February 1945. It was at a later social attended by Clark, her sister Esther Wolfe, and their mother that Roosevelt politely excused herself, having just learned of her husband Franklin's death.

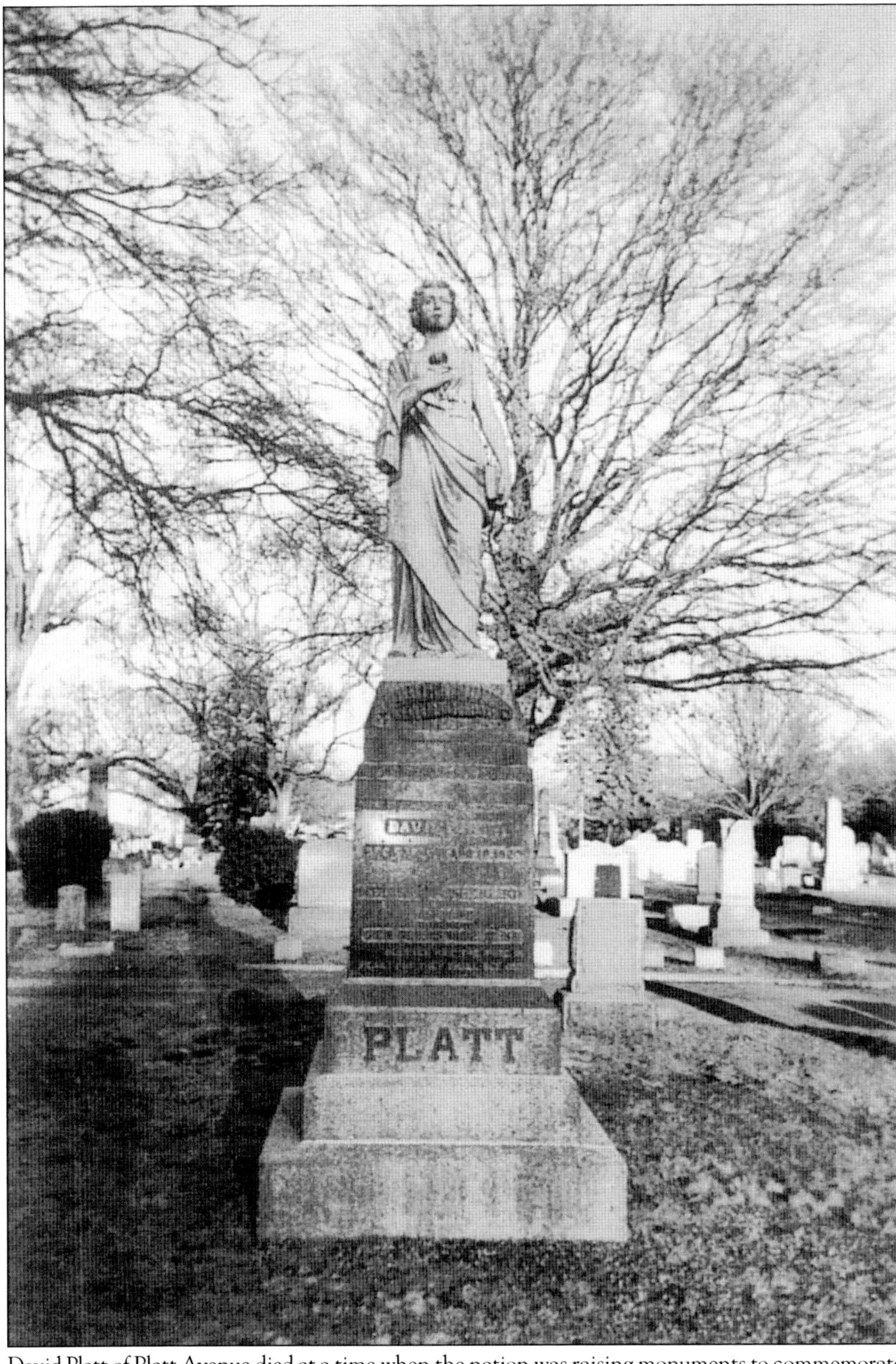

David Platt of Platt Avenue died at a time when the nation was raising monuments to commemorate its centennial and burial sites were marked with equal splendor, as his reflects.

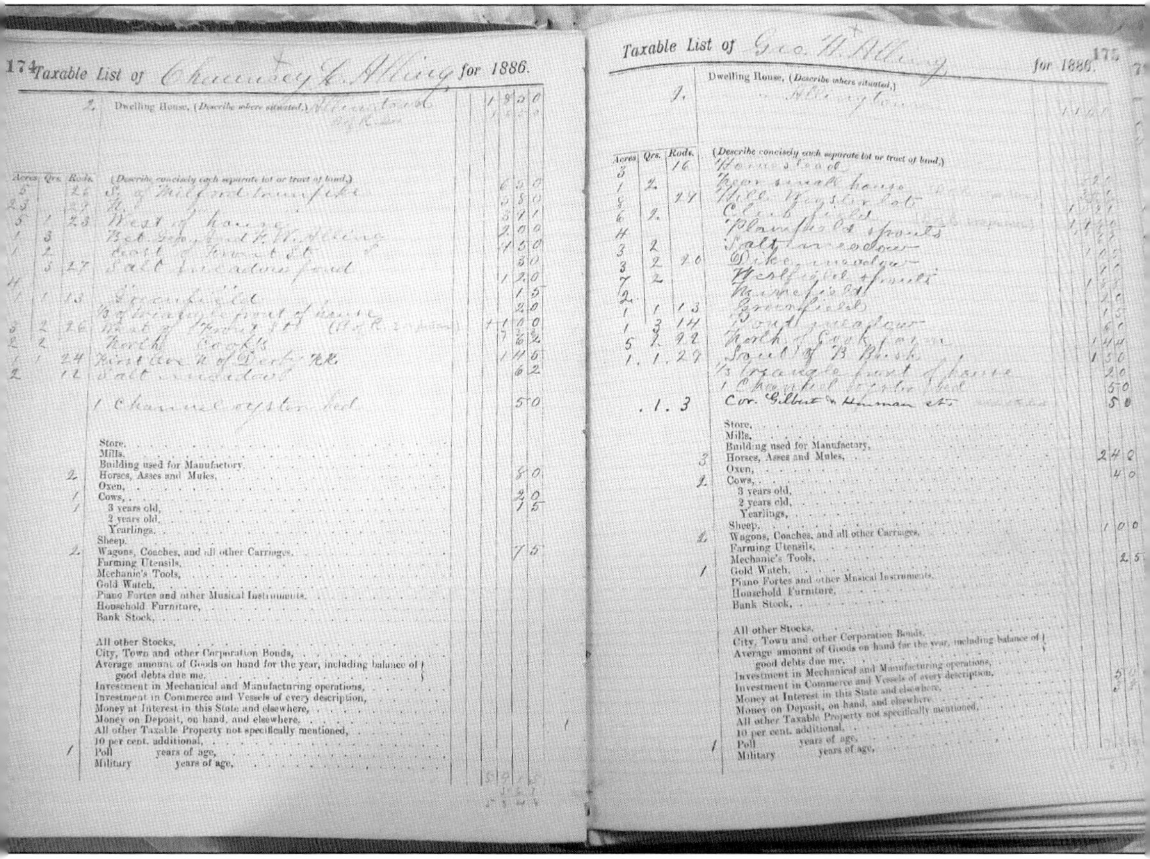

Residing in a borough of the town of Orange, West Haven residents were taxed accordingly. They were assessed on land, buildings, livestock, oyster beds, and anything else that could be considered property.

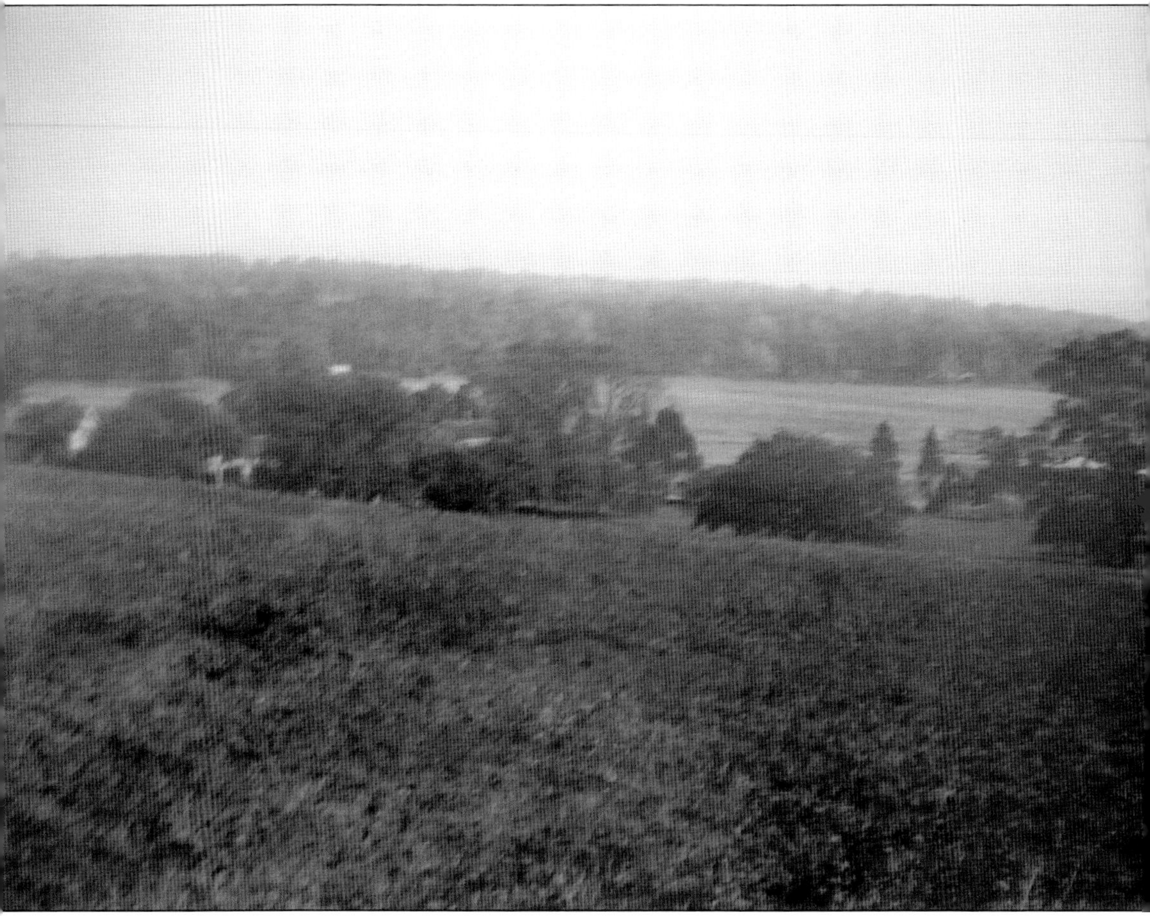

It is easy to understand why David Platt selected this site for his homestead. In this rare, two-part *c.* 1865 photograph, the Cove River winds its last quarter mile toward Long Island Sound.

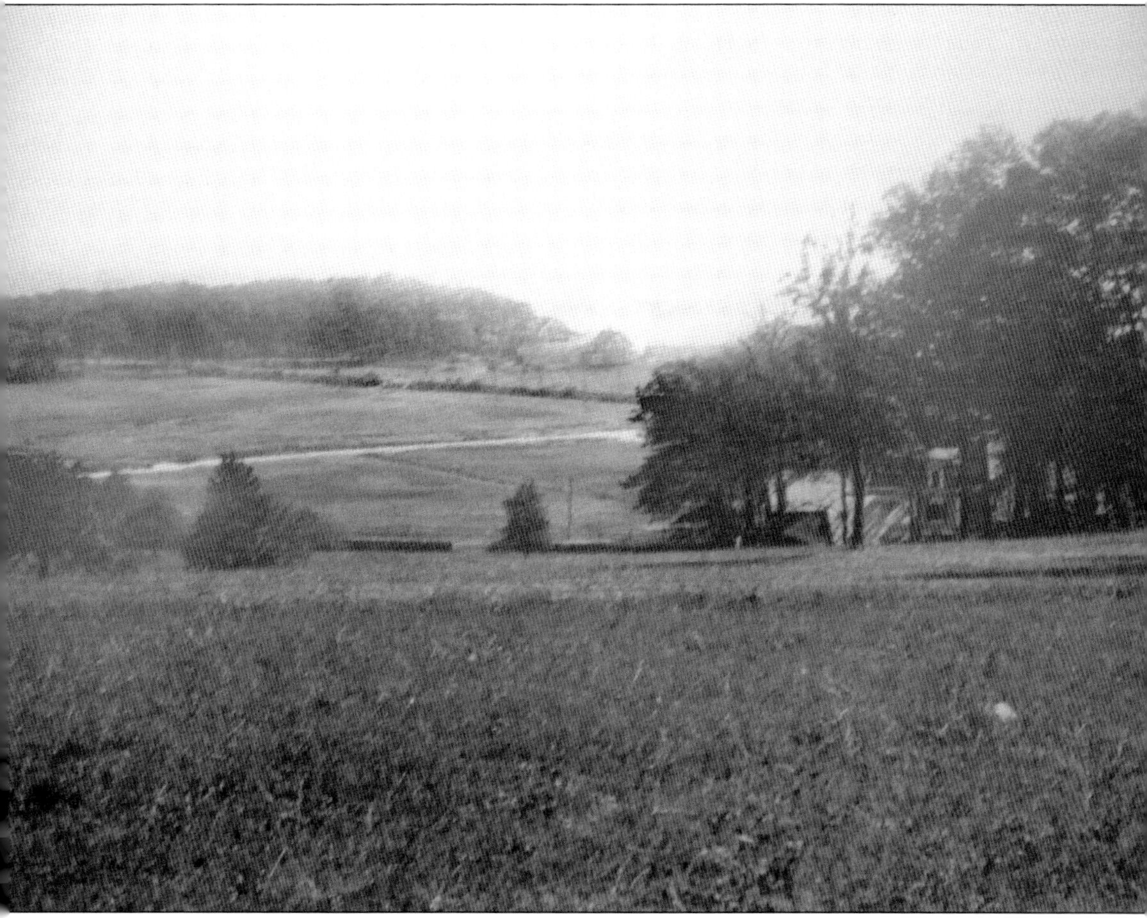

The Savin Rock Hotel, which opened its doors before the Civil War, may be seen in the far upper right, near the shore of Long Island Sound.

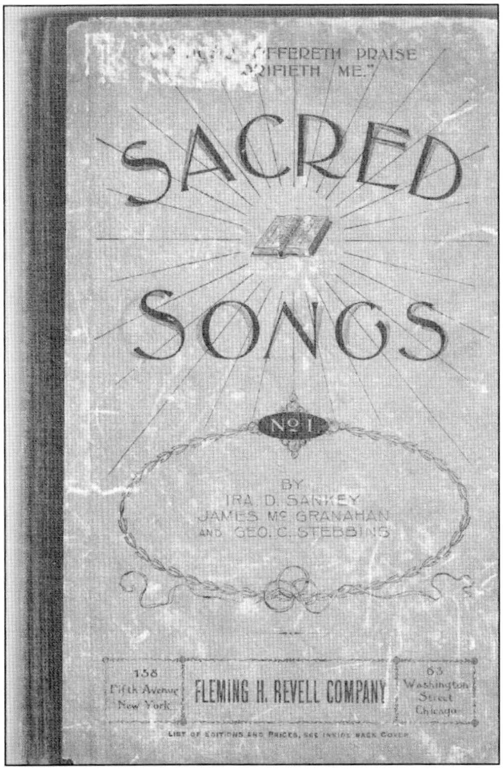

The so-called "Stebbins hymnal" was widely used in the Congregational Church community, of which Stebbins was a well-known member.

Native American tribes were known to summer along the three tributaries leading to Long Island Sound, taking advantage of the freshwater and saltwater habitat, the fertile soil, and the abundant wildlife, for more than 7,000 years. Settlers traded goods with the Natives and learned skills from them like seeding and maintaining oyster beds and farming. This is one of the magnificent baskets from the Oyster River area. Today the area is wooded and densely populated, making it difficult to see the river.

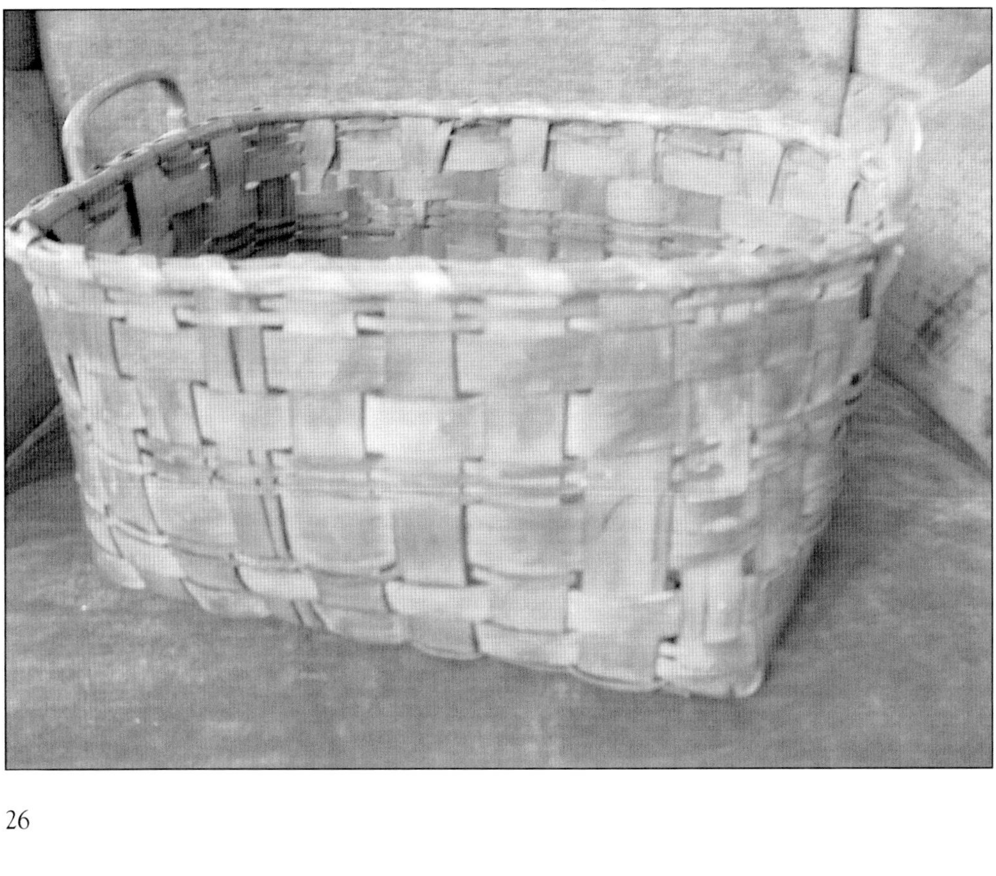

Two

Sportsmen Find Their Mark

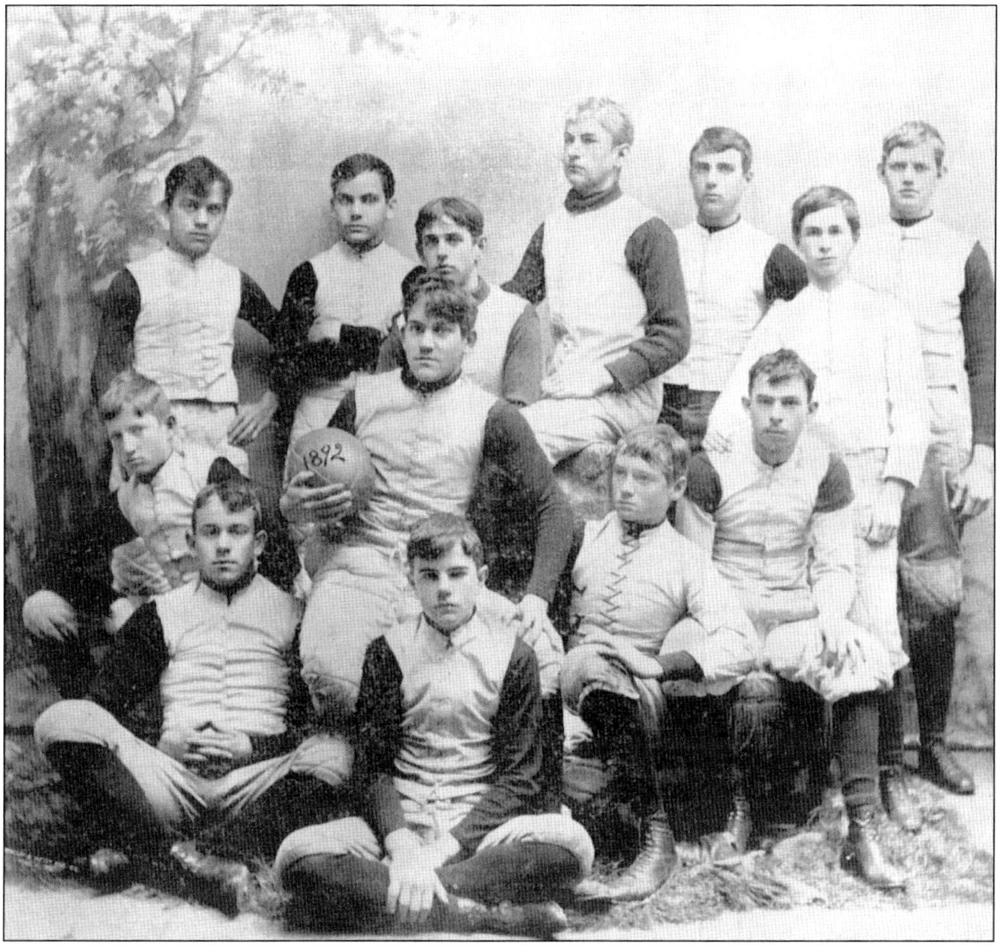

Hubert Aimes (fourth from rear right) played center on the 1892 Gunnery football team. While the team seemed to be generally successful in the prep school circuit, they suffered an overwhelming defeat against the Torrington (Connecticut) YMCA team. The explanation given for the loss was the bigger and more experienced opposition, which led to a final score of 64-0.

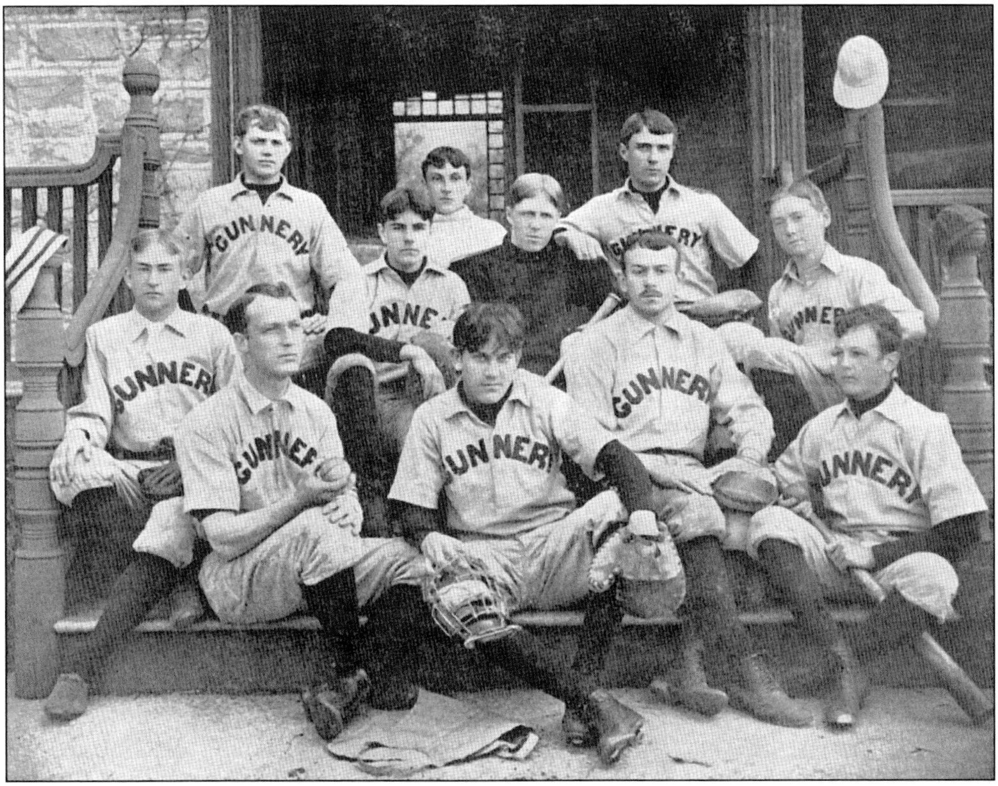

Young Hubert H. Aimes proved to be both a serious scholar and an avid athlete while at the Gunnery School in Washington, Connecticut. Aimes, seen here seated on the far left with his 1893 team, covered third base and had a batting average of .345.

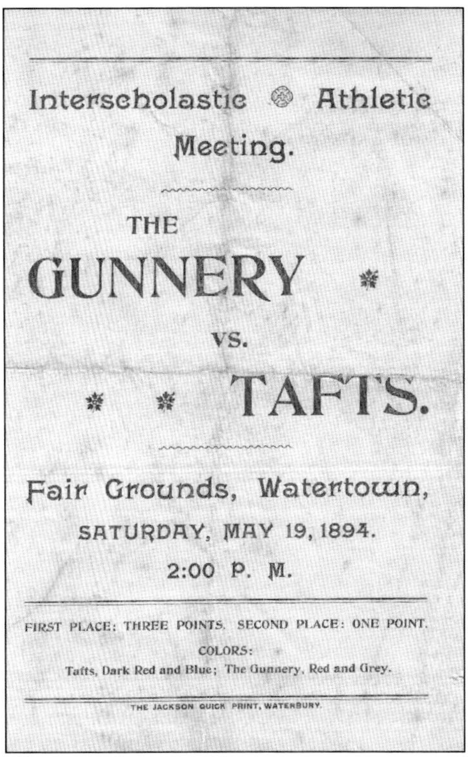

Interscholastic Athletic Meeting.

THE

GUNNERY

vs.

TAFTS.

Fair Grounds, Watertown,

SATURDAY, MAY 19, 1894.

2:00 P. M.

FIRST PLACE: THREE POINTS. SECOND PLACE: ONE POINT.

COLORS:

Tafts, Dark Red and Blue; The Gunnery, Red and Grey.

THE JACKSON QUICK PRINT, WATERBURY.

One of the greatest rivalries between private boarding schools over the years was that of Gunnery versus Tafts, and this 1894 track and field event was no exception. Wearing the Gunnery School team colors of red and gray, Aimes competed in the 12-pound shot put, standing broad jump, and the 12-pound hammer throw.

The 1893 athletic achievement of Hubert Aimes and his teammates is recorded for posterity.

STRAY SHOT. May 1893 199

Athletic Notes.

Baseball practice is now in full swing.

C. F. Neergaard has been elected manager of first nine in place of J. J. West resigned.

The schedule of games for this season so far as arranged is as follows:

May 5,	Gunnery	vs.	Hotchkissville at Hotchkissville.
" 13,	"	"	Woodbury at Washington.
" 20,	"	"	Hotchkissville at Washington.
" 30,	"	"	Gunnery Alumni at Washington.
June 3,	"	"	E. A. C. at Watertown.
" 10,	"	"	Woodbury at Woodbury.
" 17,	"	"	E. A. C. at Watertown.

We have four nines this year.

The first nine has been chosen; the positions will be occupied as follows: Pitchers, Perkins and Palmer, Catchers, A. Sanchez, Phelps, Phelps. In-fielders, Compton, Palmer, Barney, Perkins, A. Sanchez. Out-fielders, West, Aimes,(Capt.) P. Sanchez. Subs. Holter, Neergaard.

Quite a few improvements have been made on the ball grounds. The vicinity of first base has been leveled and some ugly rocks taken out of the out field. There is lots of room for improvement yet.

It is rumored that Compton is going to Chicago. His absence from the Nine will be severely felt.

The Base Ball Nine and the two Batteries had their pictures taken on May 9.

Aimes has been elected in place of Perkins resigned.

The Gunnery base ball team opened their season at Hotchkissville on May 9, receiving a defeat at the hands of the home team by the score of 14 to 8. The team was rather disabled as several of the players were ill. There was a great weakness in batting and base running displayed, but the fielding was fair considering the condition of the field. The battery, Palmer and Phelps, were at a great disadvantage, Palmer never having pitched under the new rules before and Phelps never having caught in a game before. The batting was poor till the last inning when the Gunnery boys developed a batting streak and scored five runs. Perkins pitched one inning.

The Score.

GUNNERY.

	A.B.	R.	B.H.	S.H.	P.O.	A.	E.
A. Sanchez, 2b. c.f.	4	2	2	1	2	2	0
Phelps, c.	3	1	1	2	7	4	4
Aimes, 3b.	5	2	3	0	1	1	0
West, l. f.	3	0	0	2	0	0	0
Perkins, c. f. p.	5	0	2	0	1	0	0
Palmer, p. 2b.	4	0	0	0	0	4	1
Barney, s. s.	4	1	0	0	2	5	1
Holter, r. f.	3	1	0	0	1	0	0
Compton, 1b.	4	1	1	0	13	0	1
	35	8	9	5	27	16	7

HOTCHKISSVILLE.

	A.B.	R.	B.H.	S.H.	P.O.	A.	E.
F. Smith, 2b.	5	3	1	0	1	3	2
Cowles, s. s.	2	3	1	1	0	3	2
Holmes, 1b.	4	1	0	0	13	0	1
G. Cam, c.	5	2	2	0	8	3	0
Wells, p.	4	0	0	1	0	5	2
C. Smith, 3b.	4	2	0	0	3	0	1
France, l. f.	4	0	0	1	1	0	0
Pearson, c. f.	5	2	1	0	0	0	0
Foster, r. f.	3	1	1	0	0	0	0
	36	14	6	3	*26	14	8

*Aimes declared out.

Bases on balls, off Palmer 11, off Perkins 1, off Wells 1. Struck out, by Palmer 9, by Perkins 1, by Wells 7. Left on bases, Hotchkissville 12, Gunnery 6. Double plays, France, F. Smith and Holmes, Barney and Sanchez. Hit by pitcher, Wells and Foster. Passed balls, Phelps 6, Cam 1. Wild pitches, Palmer 6, Wells 1.

If the members of the nine who have had the misfortune to be taken with the mumps recover in time it is hoped that by practise a good team may be developed.

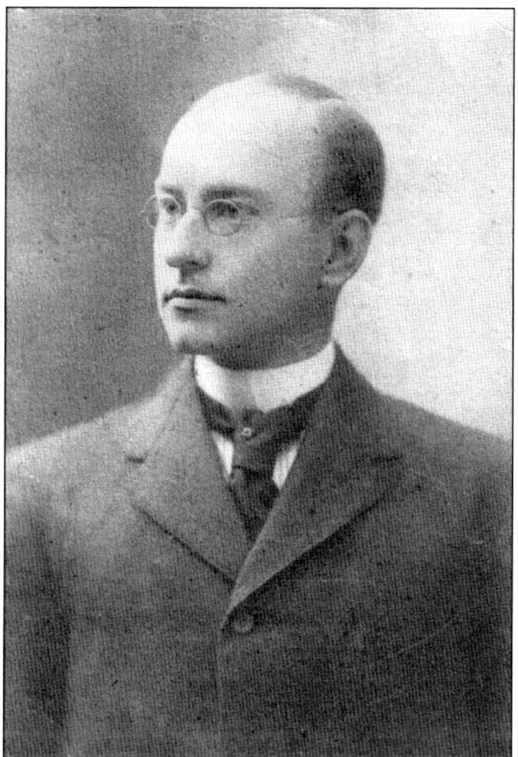

Aimes went on to Yale University, earned a doctorate, and became internationally known for his publication *The History of Slavery in Cuba*.

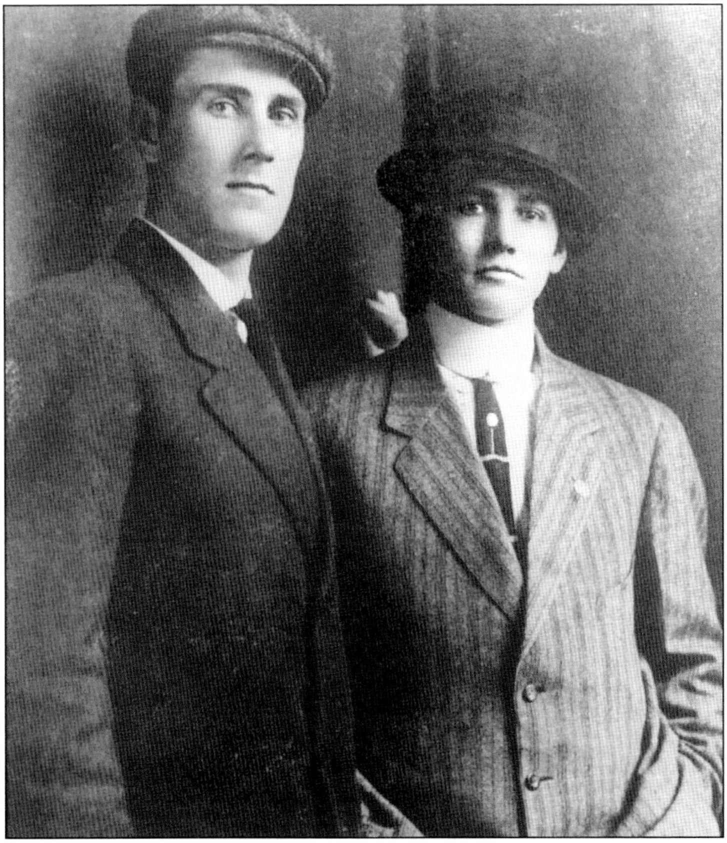

For a brief period between 1923 and 1942, West Haven was home to Howard Ellsworth "Smokey Joe" Wood (left), winning pitcher for the 1912 Boston Red Sox, while he was coaching baseball at Yale. Wood's performance was considered the best ever of any Boston athlete. His nomination to the National Baseball Hall of Fame states that he and Babe Ruth were the only two players to ever have played two positions in two World Series. The man standing with Wood in this photograph is unidentified.

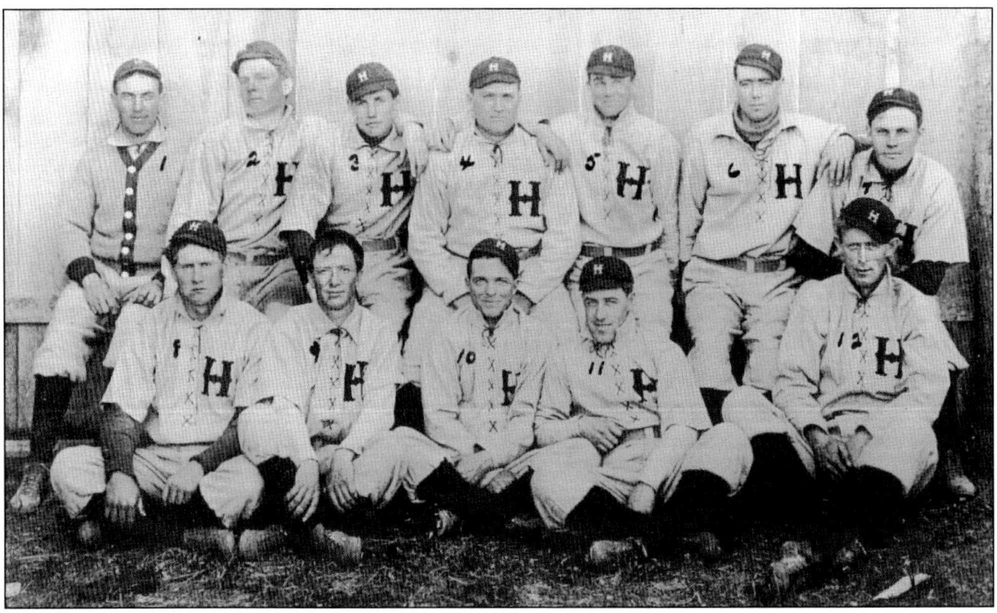

The first professional team that Wood (third from left, second row) played for was the Hutchinson, Kansas, team of the Western Association in 1907. The nickname "Smokey Joe" came from an opposing pitcher several years later, when Wood's amazingly fast pitch could not be matched.

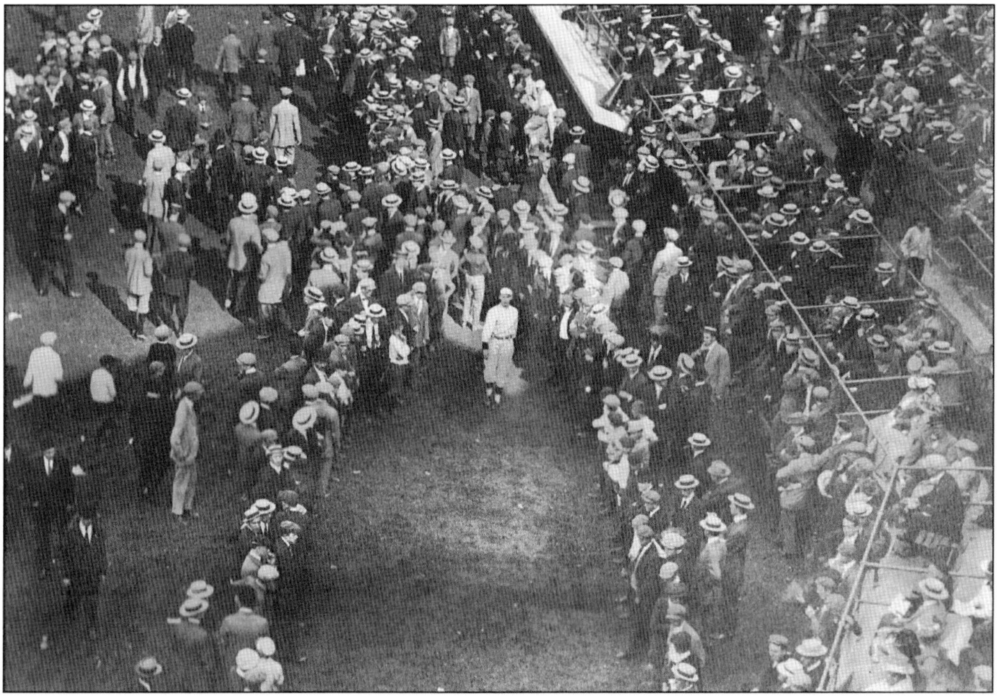

Admiring fans surrounded Wood in Boston as he warmed up before going to the mound, as there was no separate bull pen for him to practice. Wood's professional career spanned many years and several teams before it ended with an injury, but even today statistics show that he was one of the best.

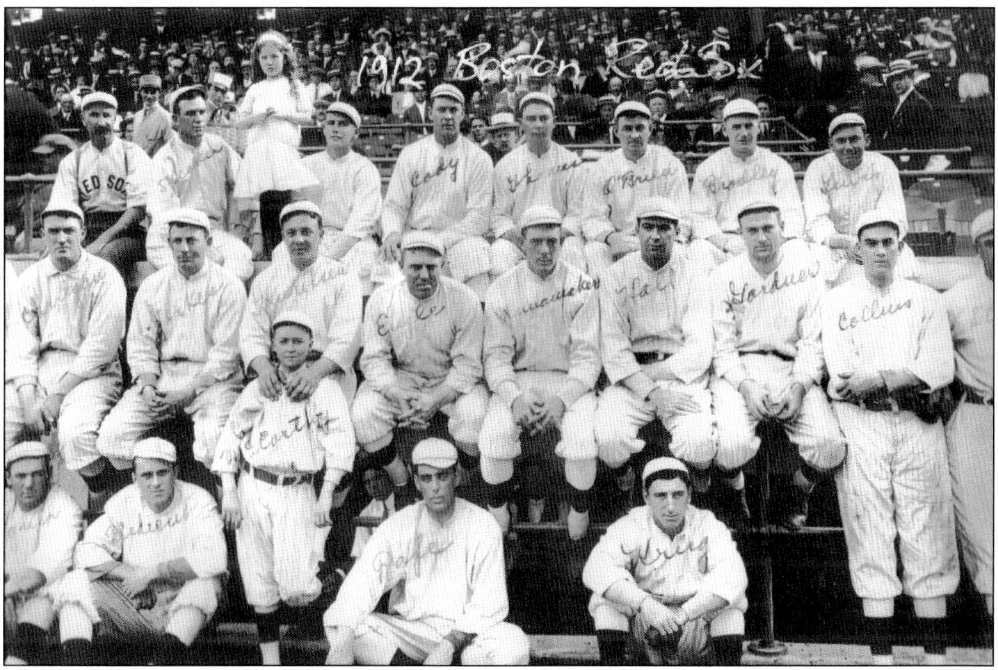

Wood (third row, fourth from left) poses with his 1912 Boston Red Sox team before a gathering crowd at Fenway Park. Wood resided in West Haven at the time of his death in 1985.

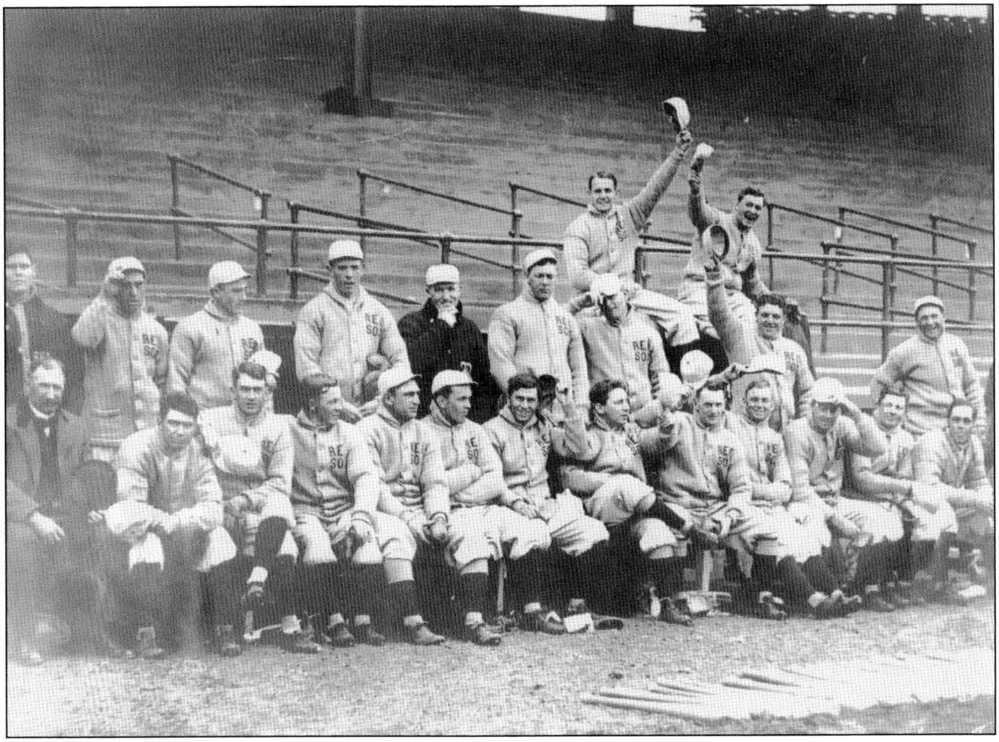

Practice made perfect, but occasionally the 1912 Red Sox Team took a break.

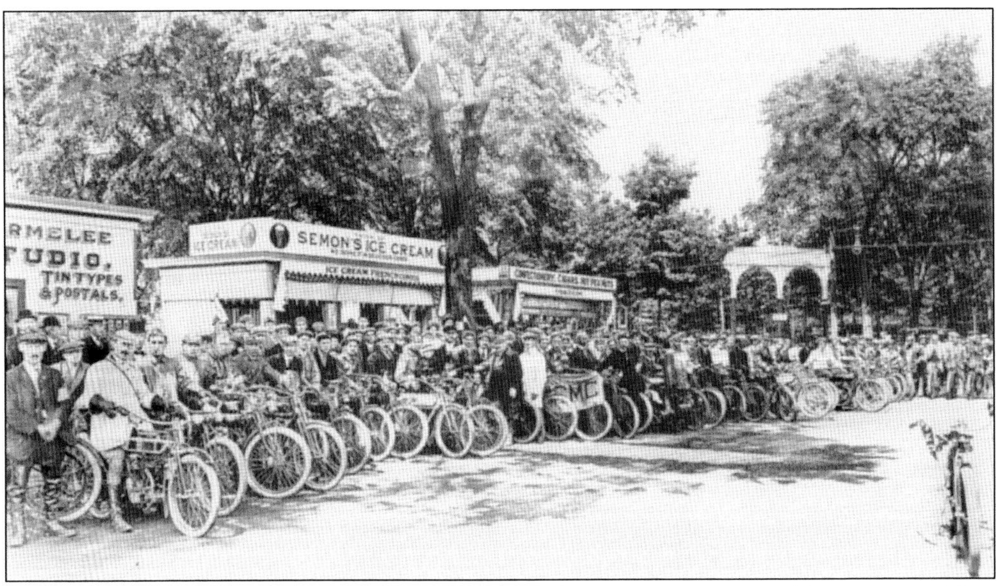

Bicycling was still a popular sport and one in which the average person could participate. Here cyclists line up for the final call on Beach Street in Savin Rock.

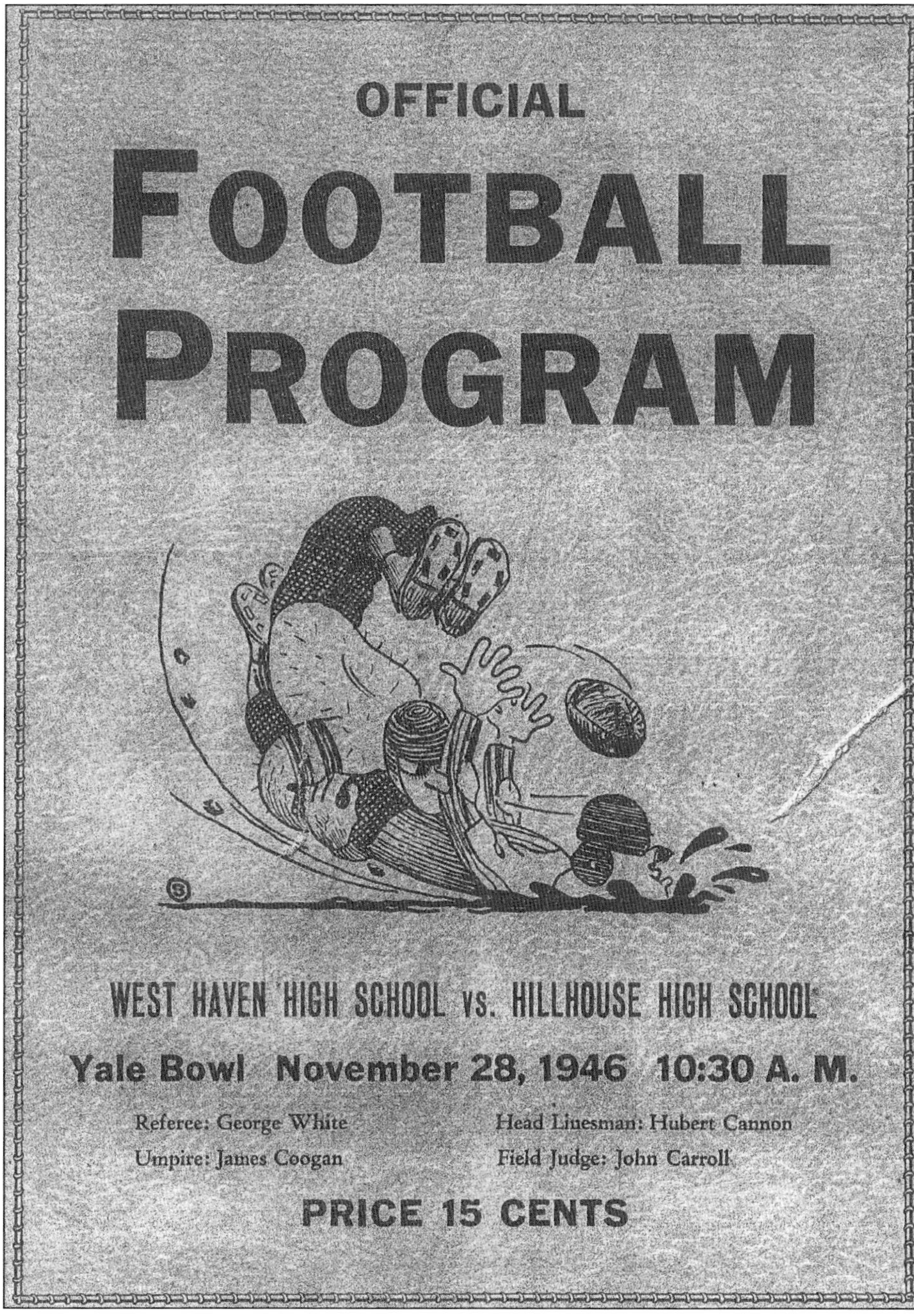

There was no greater local competition than that of the Thanksgiving Day games between West Haven and the Acs (Academics) of New Haven's James Hillhouse High School. Thousands of fans attended the contest—the high school equivalent of the Yale-Harvard game—at the Yale Bowl. West Haven coach John "Whitey" Piurek was a collegiate basketball star at Holy Cross, where he played three sports. He also played professional ball with the St. Louis Cardinals. Coach Edward Bennett was tri-captain at the University of Richmond, served in the U.S. Navy during World War II, and coached at King's Point Merchant Marine Academy before coming to West Haven.

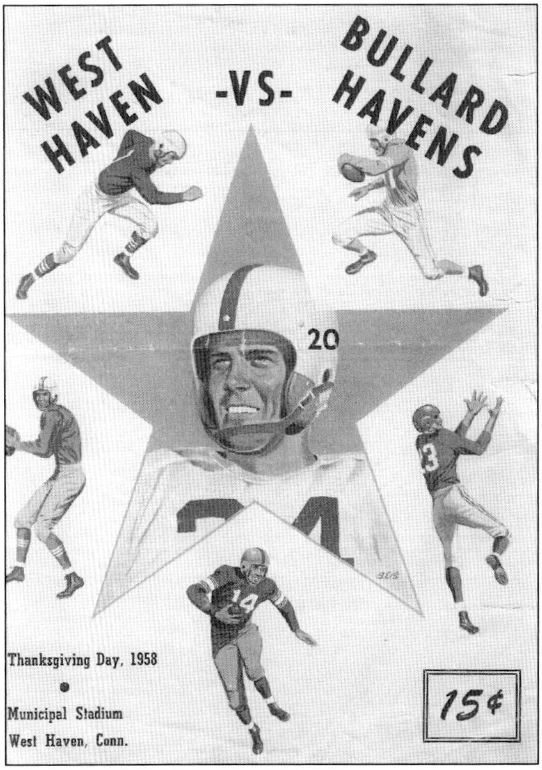

By 1958, Bullard-Havens High School had replaced Hillhouse High School, and Municipal Stadium was the venue for the big game against West Haven.

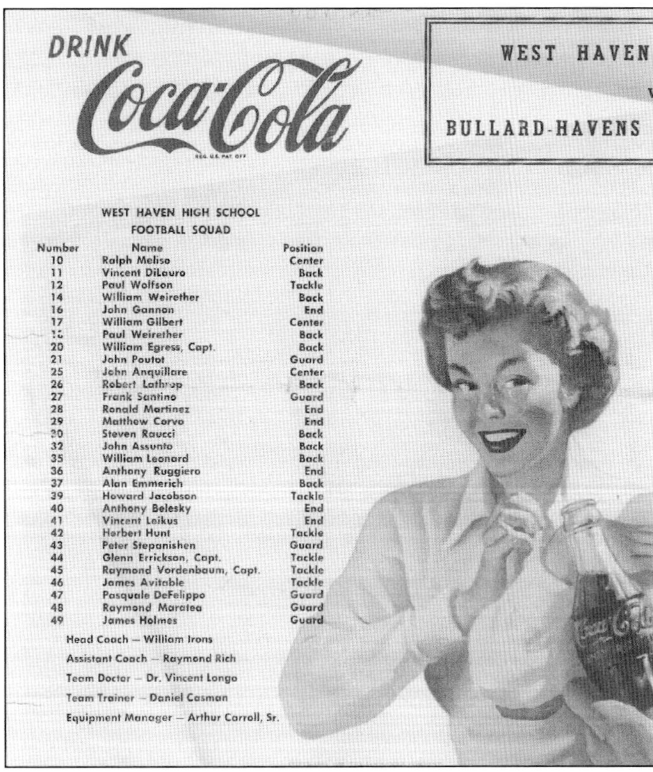

WEST HAVEN HIGH SCHOOL
FOOTBALL SQUAD

Number	Name	Position
10	Ralph Meliso	Center
11	Vincent DiLauro	Back
12	Paul Wolfson	Tackle
14	William Weirether	Back
16	John Gannon	End
17	William Gilbert	Center
[illegible]	Paul Weirether	Back
20	William Egress, Capt.	Back
21	John Poutot	Guard
25	John Anquillare	Center
26	Robert Lathrop	Back
27	Frank Santino	Guard
28	Ronald Martinez	End
29	Matthew Corvo	End
30	Steven Raucci	Back
32	John Assunto	Back
35	William Leonard	Back
36	Anthony Ruggiero	End
37	Alan Emmerich	Back
39	Howard Jacobson	Tackle
40	Anthony Belesky	End
41	Vincent Leikus	End
42	Herbert Hunt	Tackle
43	Peter Stepanishen	Guard
44	Glenn Errickson, Capt.	Tackle
45	Raymond Vordenbaum, Capt.	Tackle
46	James Avitable	Tackle
47	Pasquale DeFelippo	Guard
48	Raymond Maratea	Guard
49	James Holmes	Guard

Head Coach — William Irons

Assistant Coach — Raymond Rich

Team Doctor — Dr. Vincent Longo

Team Trainer — Daniel Casman

Equipment Manager — Arthur Carroll, Sr.

Many players on the 1958 football squad were all-around athletes, and some went on to compete at higher levels. Outstanding center John Anquillare became a professional baseball player, spent many years with the Raybestos Brakettes, and enjoyed a coaching career at the University of New Haven.

Three

Music Makes the World Go Round

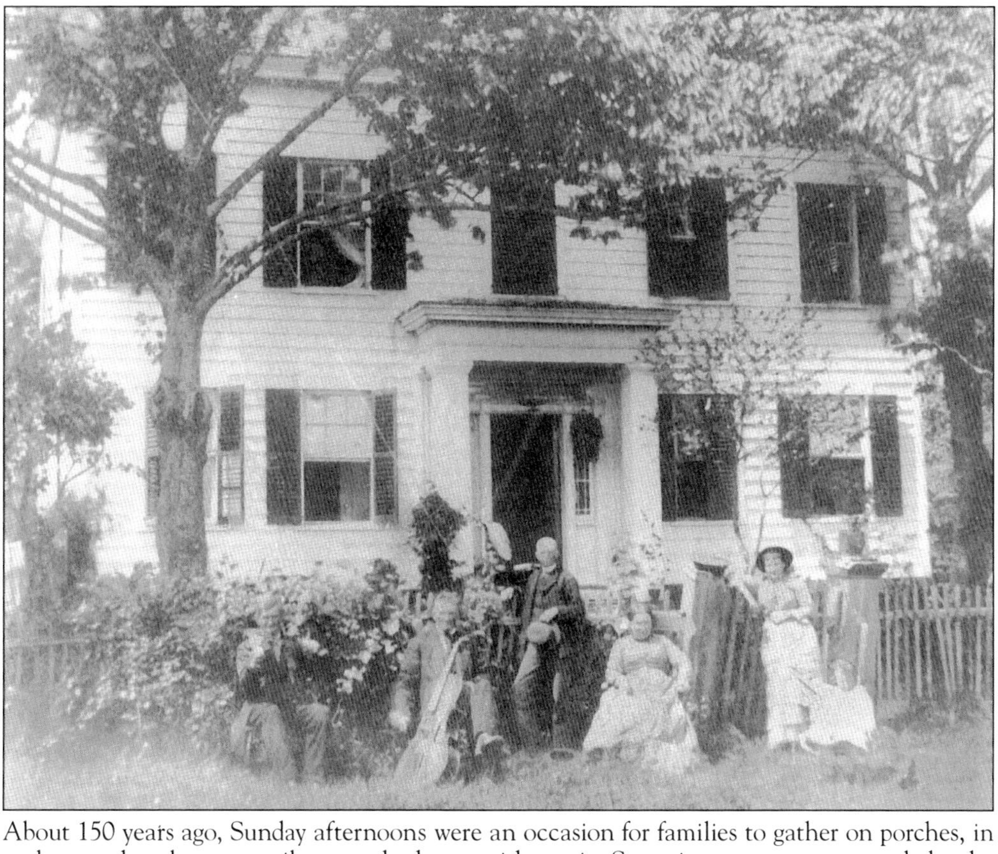

About 150 years ago, Sunday afternoons were an occasion for families to gather on porches, in parlors, and on lawns to wile away the hours with music. Some instruments were made by the musician, such as this cello belonging to Jay Lord Northrop, who is hosting the Atwill family of New York City.

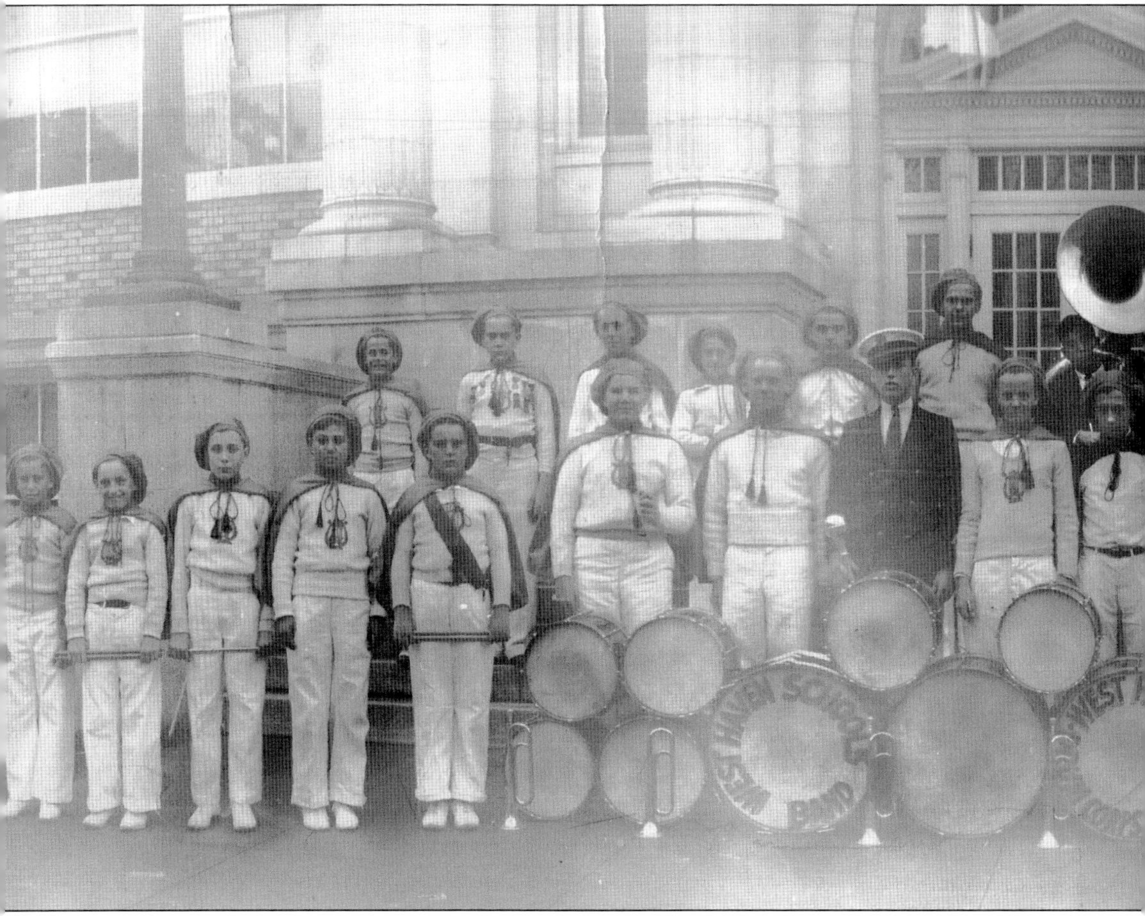

Music played an important role in the lives of West Haven residents, and young people especially enjoyed marching bands. The West Haven High School band was formed shortly after the opening

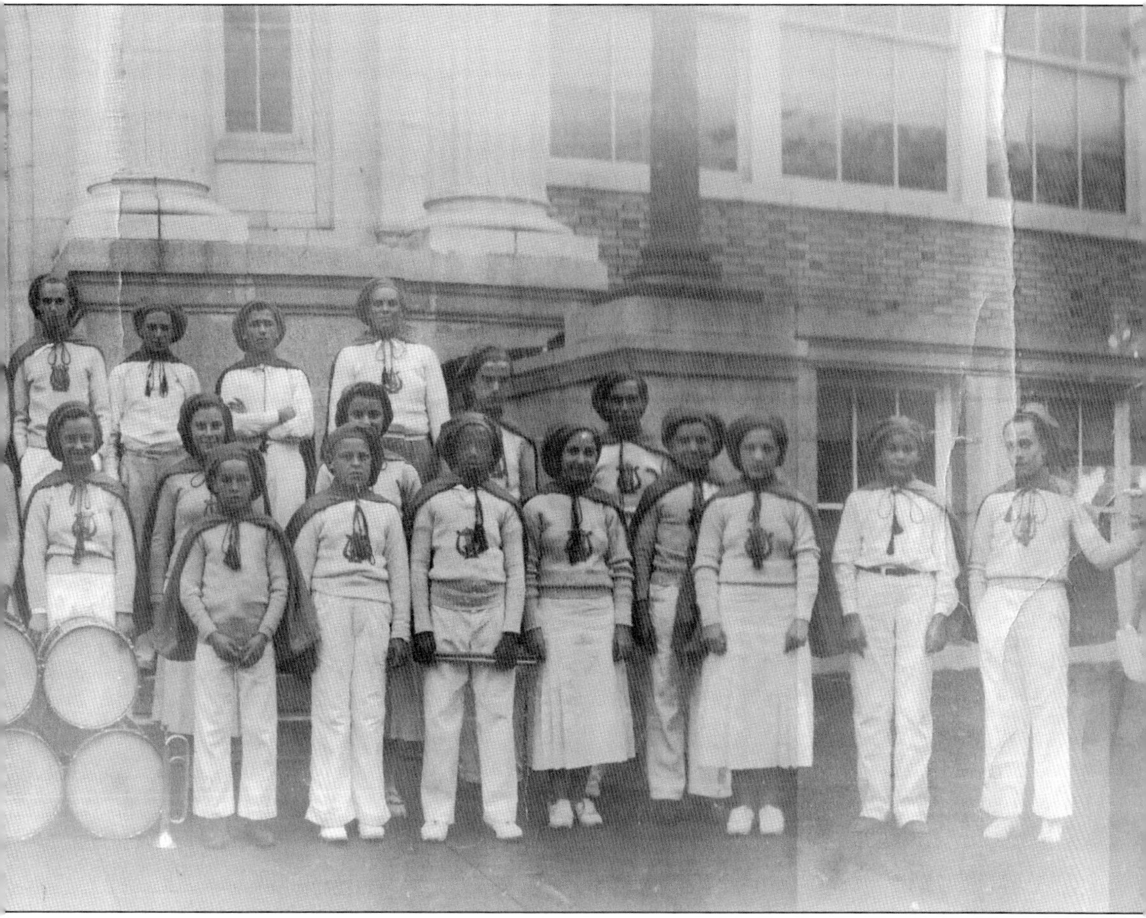

of the new Main Street building in 1927. With the construction of a newer high school some years ago, this building was converted into apartments.

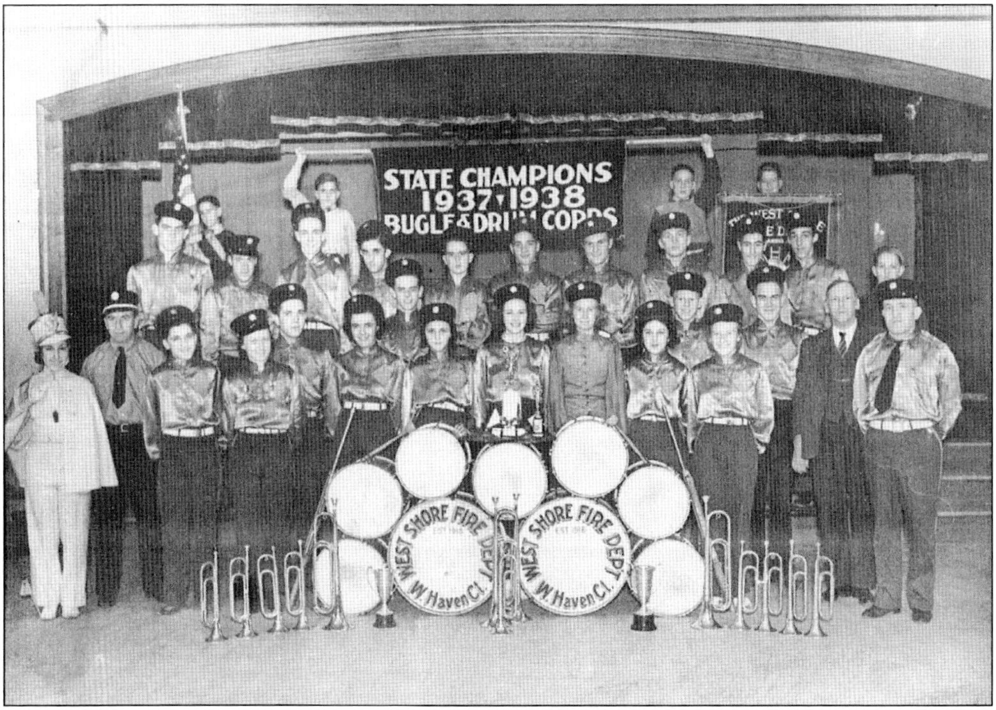

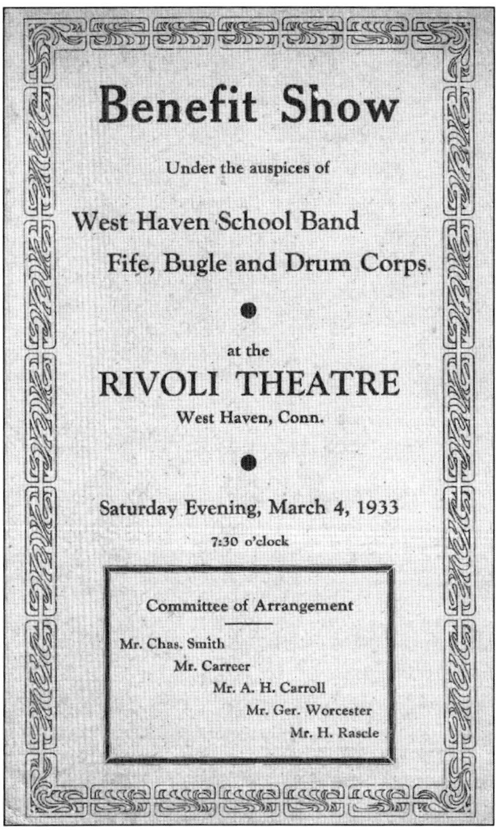

Benefit Show

Under the auspices of

West Haven School Band

Fife, Bugle and Drum Corps

●

at the

RIVOLI THEATRE

West Haven, Conn.

●

Saturday Evening, March 4, 1933

7:30 o'clock

Committee of Arrangement

Mr. Chas. Smith
Mr. Carreer
Mr. A. H. Carroll
Mr. Ger. Worcester
Mr. H. Rascle

The drum and bugle corps of the West Haven Fire Department held the 1937–1938 state championship title. This was quite a feat at a time when it was not unusual for 100 units to be in an area competition.

Drum and bugle corps popularity increased during the 1930s, and it was standard to have a group performing at special functions. On March 4, 1933, the West Haven School Band and Fife, Bugle, and Drum Corps performed in a benefit at the Rivoli Theatre, along with Mickey Mouse, a newsreel, and the film *Hot Pepper*. These events supported milk drives, unemployment funds, and other public needs in the post-Depression years.

The award-winning Cpl. (Arthur H. Jr.) Carroll Drum Corps of Our Lady Of Victory Church participated in the dedication of the Seth G. Haley School on June 3, 1962.

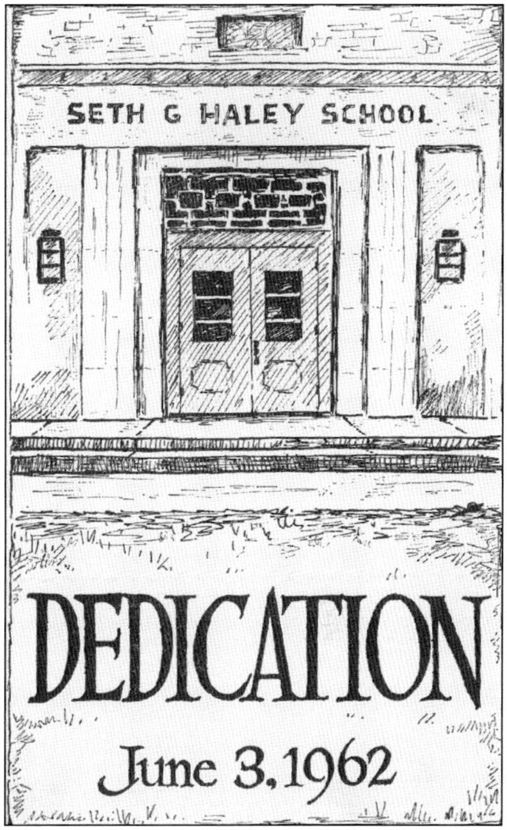

Parents and friends joined educators in the event dedicating the new state-of-the-art school.

SETH G. HALEY SCHOOL

Dedication Program

June 3, 1962

WELCOME .... Mary Finnegan, *Principal*

INVOCATION .... The Reverend James Lambert

PRESENTATION OF COLORS .... Local Scout Groups
Bernard Weiner, *Leader*

PLEDGE OF ALLEGIANCE .... Paul McManus

NATIONAL ANTHEM .... Helen Jamieson, *Accompanist*

PRESENTATION OF HONORED GUESTS
Geraldine Abbatello, *Chairman*

DEDICATION PRAYER .... The Reverend Charles Olsen

DEDICATION .... Dr. Melvin E. Wagner
Superintendent of Schools

MUSICAL SELECTION .... Corporal Carroll Drum Corps of Our Lady of Victory Church

ADDRESS .... Honorable Gregory Morrissey
Mayor of the City of West Haven

ADDRESS .... Francis Gebauer
President of the Board of Education

SCRIPTURE READING .... The Reverend Arthur Robertshaw

PRESENTATION .... Rita Graberek
President of Seth G. Haley Parent Teacher Association

ACCEPTANCE .... Seth G. Haley
Former Superintendent of Schools

MUSICAL SELECTION .... Corporal Carroll Drum Corps

CLOSING .... Geraldine Abbatello

BENEDICTION .... Rabbi Leon Mitsky

* Cover Art — Richard Hodes

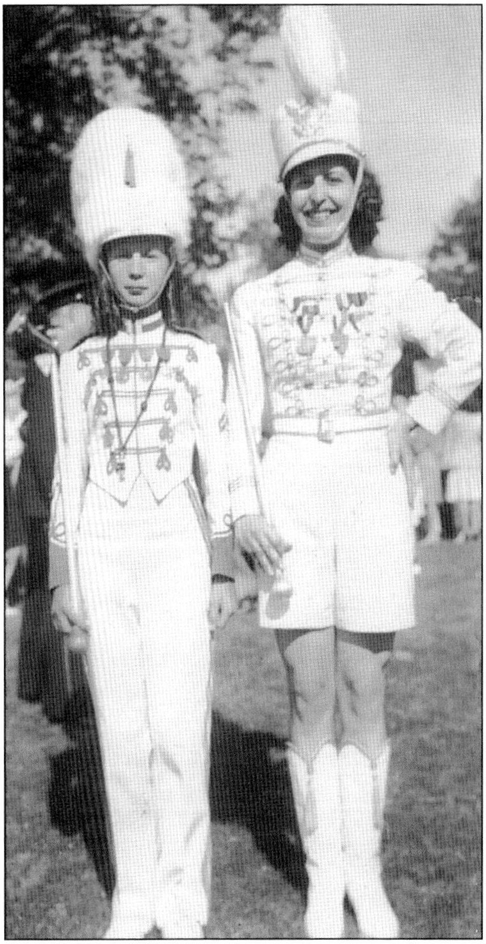

Every marching band had majorettes, and Virginia Vollenwelder (right) was considered the best. Vollenwelder, a graduate of the Weylister Junior College of Milford, was the ace majorette with the West Shore Drum and Bugle Corps in the 1940s.

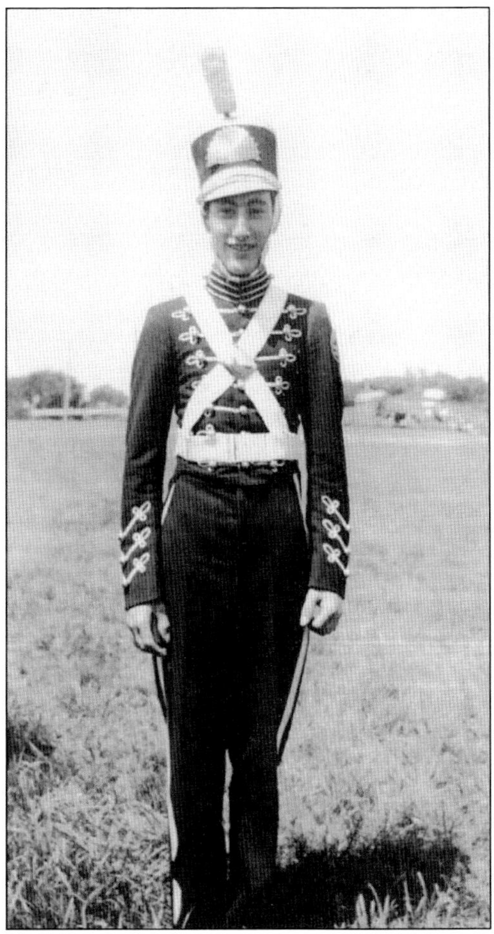

Local band member Louis DelGudice shows off his handsome uniform. Marching bands spent many hours practicing patterns and routines, earning members the right to stand tall in their attractive outfits.

For a while after the Great Depression, unemployment statistics remained high. There were no national social services like those that exist today. Consequently, the community worked together to aid the families. The School Milk Fund benefit targeted food provision.

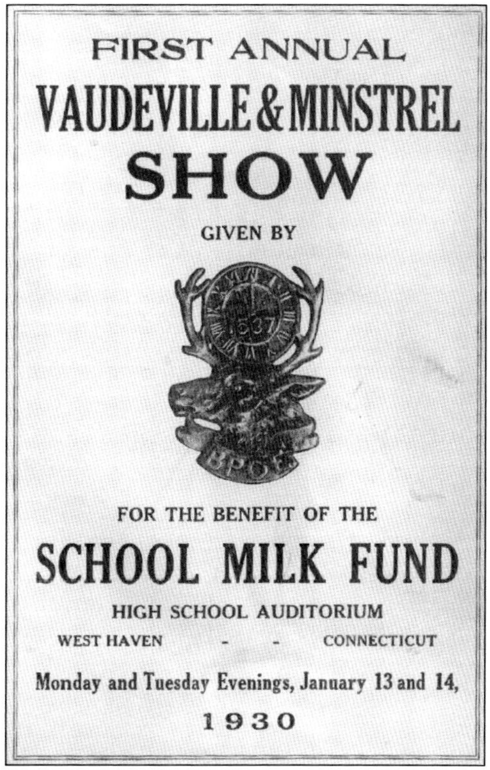

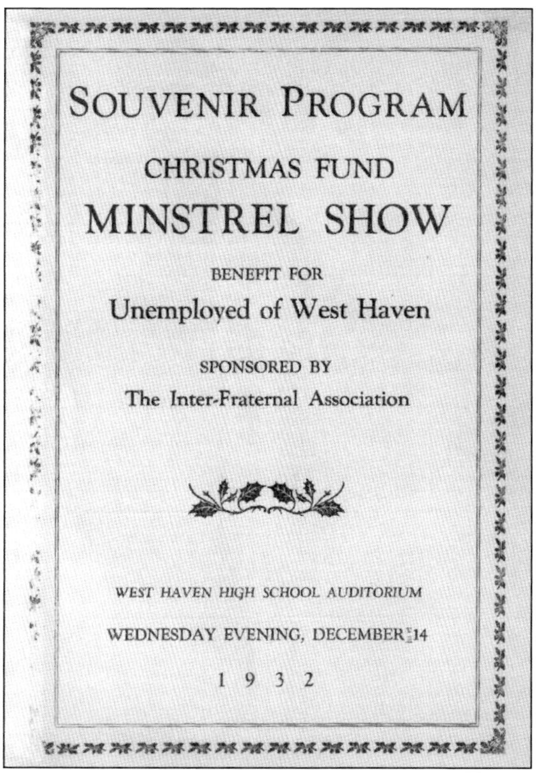

West Haven unemployed were the beneficiaries of a Christmas Eve minstrel show in 1932. Performers were members of the Savin Rock Progressive League and the West Haven High School Orchestra.

We Are Grateful to These Friends Who Made This Program Possible

R. FARQUHARSON
S. J. CONDON
F. L. McDERMOTT
JAMES J. CONWAY
ROY MacLEOD
FRANK B. WALSH
JOHN J. BLAKE
JOHN ANDERSON
THE A. D. PERKINS CO. W. B. Shroff
HENRY P. LYNCH
DR. A. F. GAFFNEY
A. J. McSHERRY
TOM'S PUBLIC MARKET
MAYFLOWER RESTAURANT
COOLEY'S BARBER SHOP
GIORDANO BROS. Monuments
F. TORELLO & SON Allingtown Garage
F A T E R ' S Allingtown Center
ROBT. GREENE Groceries and Meats
BREAKWATER HOTEL
J. J. HOWARD
WEST SHORE CLEANERS
DONALD D. NOEL
THOMAS P. HARKIN
CONN. IRON WORKS 87 Eddy St., New Haven
SALLY OLIVER Cement Work Contractor 5 Bassett Court, West Haven

KACEY KNIGHT KAPERS

1932 EDITION

JOHN MURPHY, Director — JAMES CONWAY, Chairman

Auspices of

Knights of Columbus Building Association

HARUGARI HALL, WEST HAVEN

Friday and Saturday, April 1 and 2, 1932

BOOSTER PROGRAM

WM. PEACOCKE *and* ALFRED CREAMER

Masters of Ceremony

SCENE 1—Boat Leaving for Havana
Opening Chorus—J. Conway, Jr., J. Onofrio; Misses Clark, Bowe and Moore Sisters and Entire Company

"Home" .... Gregory Morrissey

SCENE 2—Pullman Train Leaving New York for New Orleans
Messrs. R. MacLeod, Brereton and Reynolds

Military Dance .... Buddy Cadwell

SCENE 3—Cotton Field Down South
"River Stay 'Way from My Door" .... C. Finnigan
"Down By the Barnyard Gate" .... E. True
"Oh! Susanna!" .... C. Finnigan

"Mandalay" .... Thos. Kennedy
Connecticut's Foremost Police Baritone

SCENE 4—Harlem Speakeasy
Messrs. Walsh, Conway and MacLeod

SCENE 5—Tyler City Station
Messrs. Morrissey, Quigley and Onofrio
Misses Reynolds, Hunihan, Quigley and Baby Toots

SCENE 6—Havana; An Open Air Cabaret
Troubadours .... Rocco and Vito Manzari
"Neapolitan Night" .... Rocco Danieli
Solo and Comedy Dance— S. Oliver and L. Lantimonaco
"Time On My Hands" .... Miss Barney
"Won't You Promise?" .... John Walsh
"Down By the Old Swimming Pool" James Conway, Sr.
"Jig, Jig, Jigolo" .... Roy MacLeod
(*Assisted by* Miss Mary O'Brien)
Acrobatic Dance .... Baby Toots
"My Daddy's Lullaby" .... Wm. Peacocke
Billy Welch's Rhythmic Trio
James Conway, Jr., Marguerite Clark, Ruth Bowe
"Lulu Belle" .... Marion Conway
"Cuban Love Song" .... Joe Panza
Concetta DiCerbo and Girls of Rose Ballet
Nancy Kirby, Mary O'Brien, Marguerite Clark and Ruth Bowe

CLOSING CHORUS .... Entire Company

CHORUS—Geo. Heather, J. Walsh, Jr., Frank Cull, E. Batchelder, George Schrader, J. Rourke, C. Sanzo, R. McKay, Edw. Bates, G. Carr.

We Are Grateful to These Friends Who Made This Program Possible

HOWARD CLEANERS
CENTRAL FRUIT & VEGETABLE MARKET
THOMAS RUSSELL
J. H. WOOD Hardware
WM. H. SILVER
CENTRAL BARBER SHOP
LOUIS H. WARNER
HENRY F. HART
GEORGE CHARMEN
E. C. BATES
T. DUFFY
H. O'NEIL
A. J. CREAMER
LYNN REYNOLDS
EDWARD C. CROWLEY
JOHN J. CULL
FRANK CULL
ED. T. BRERETON
JOHN J. McQUIGGAN Florist
M. F. WALKER & SONS
DAN'S BARBER SHOP
BARNEY & CLARK, Inc.
MARY HELEN BEAUTY SHOP
ULIZIO'S HEALTH GYM Fox-Poli Bldg.

The Kaycees of the Knights of Columbus did their share to help alleviate the hunger and poverty by holding a program of their own.

"On The Canadian Border"

A Drama in Five Acts by

LEWIS L. FIELD

TOWN HALL, WEST HAVEN, CONN.

Presented by the

UNION MUSICAL ASSOCIATION

Thursday and Friday Evenings, May 5th and 6th, 1910

ADMISSION, 25c. **RESERVED SEATS, 35c.**

OVER

This ticket was for admission to *On the Canadian Border*, a five-act theater piece.

Before the days of television, people looked to entertainment outside the home, and almost every organization had a musical group or program. The Stevens Heights Community Club held its seventh-annual Minstrel and Dance Show at its Collis Street clubhouse on May 3–4, 1940. The program included jitterbug, buck and wing, acrobatics, skits, and many popular songs of the day.

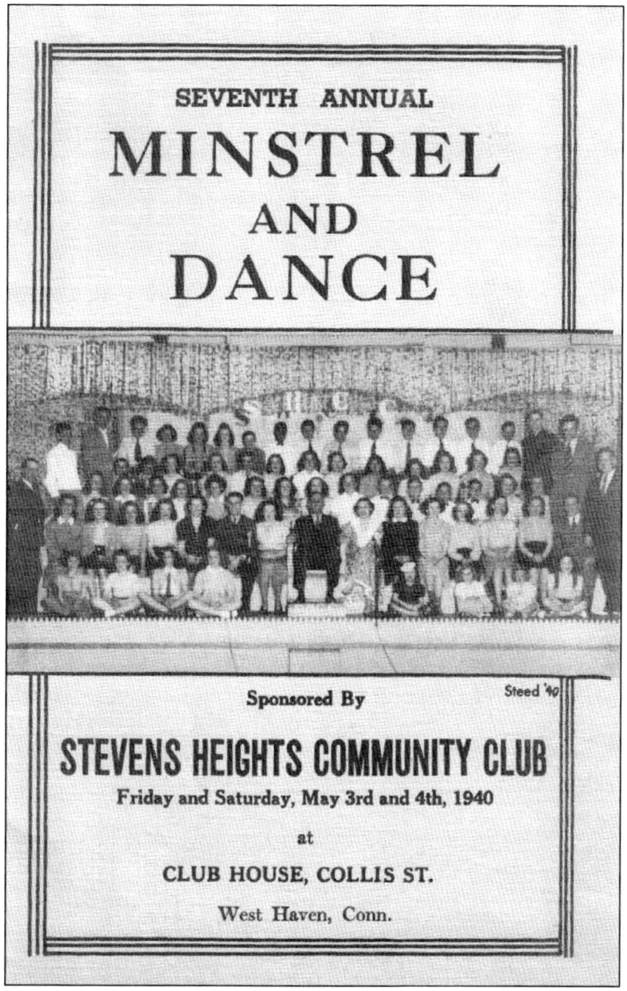

Before the Depression, popular dances included the Charleston, tango, and Black Bottom, but these gave way to the Big Band sound by groups like Barney Rapp and his New Englanders.

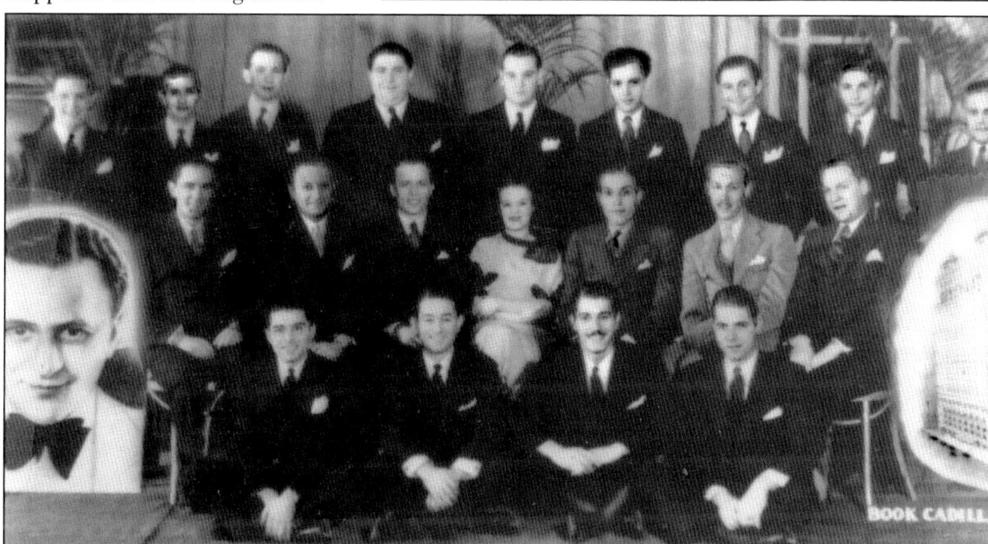

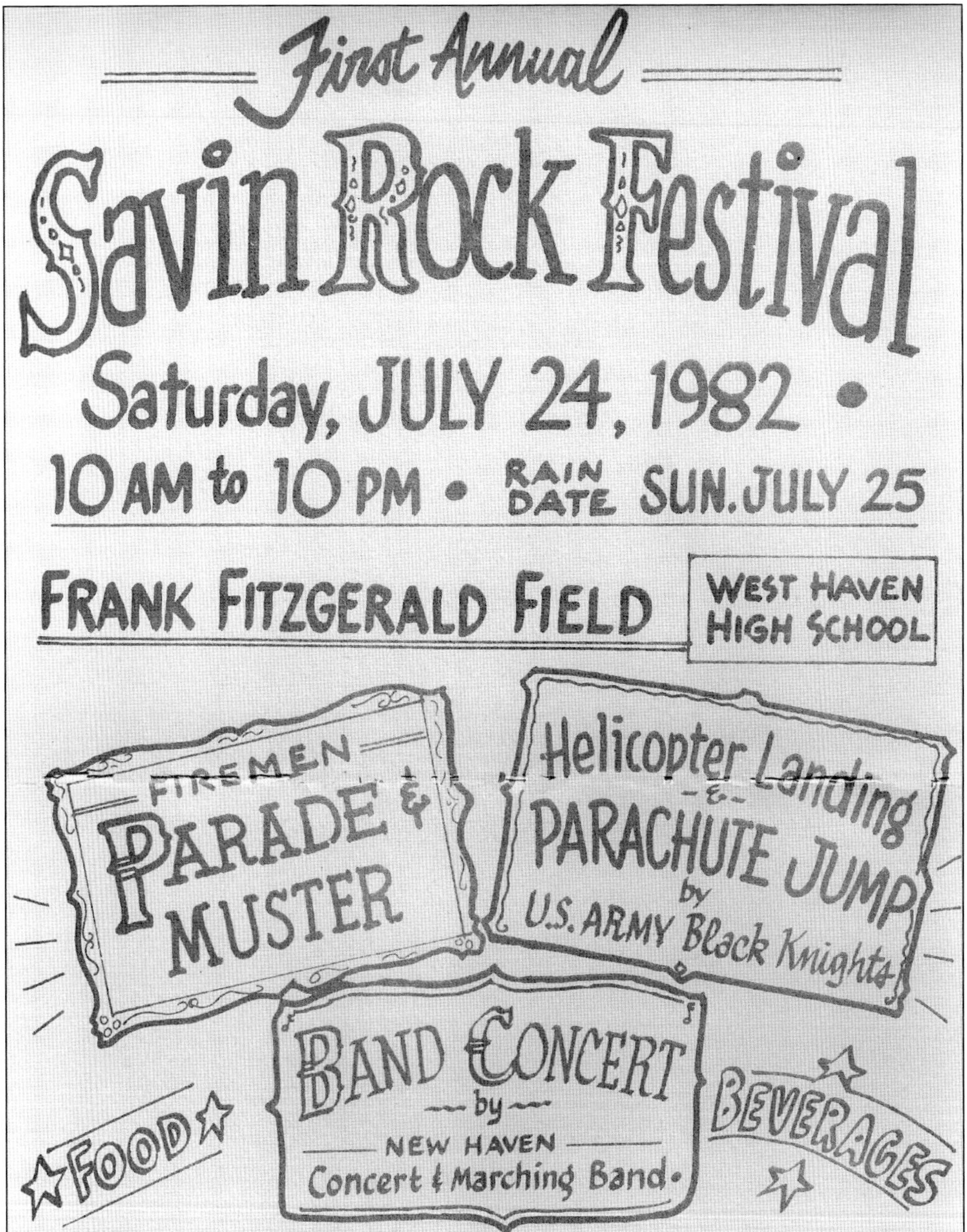

One of the main features of the first Savin Rock Festival, held on July 24, 1982, was a performance by the New Haven Concert and Marching Band.

Four

At Home in the Town of Cranberry

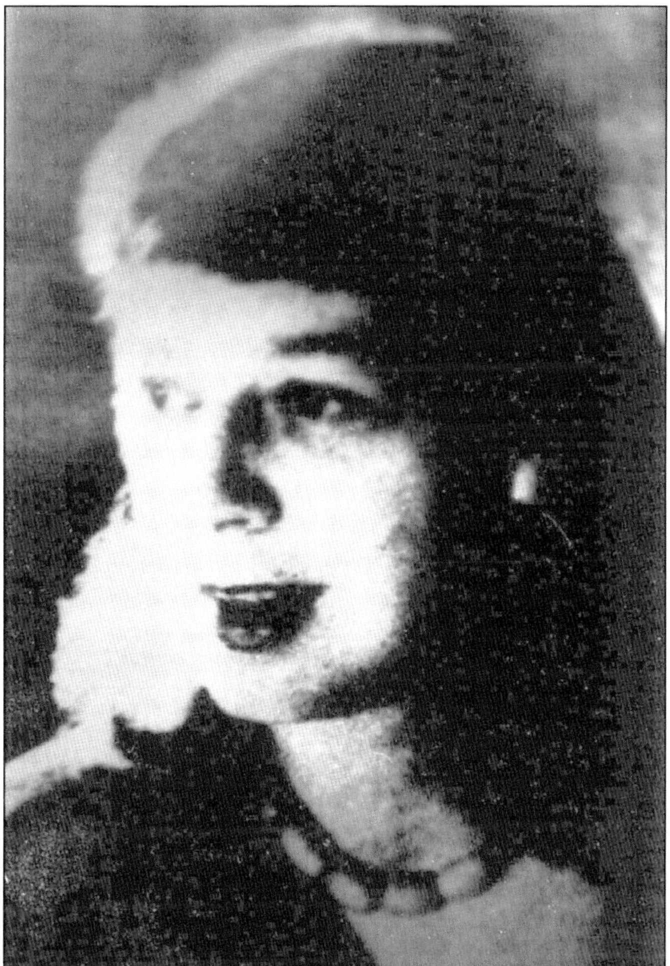

A young Eleanor Estes, storyteller and writer, shared her youthful experiences in the "town of Cranberry" (her native West Haven) in her Moffat series children's books.

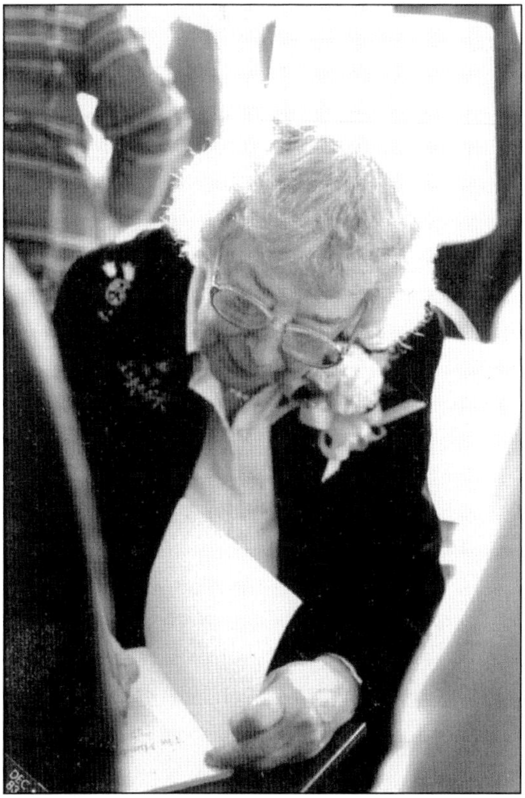

The City of West Haven honored native Eleanor Estes for her life's work at a reception in the main library. Estes, recipient of the 1952 Newbery Medal for her book *Ginger Pye*, gracefully signed copies of her award-winning book for her many readers.

Estes renamed favorite, familiar places in Cranberry, but her readers knew well where they were. Each of the Moffat series books was based on her real-life experiences, including an episode in her third book where her brother spent all day in the library trying to get a library card.

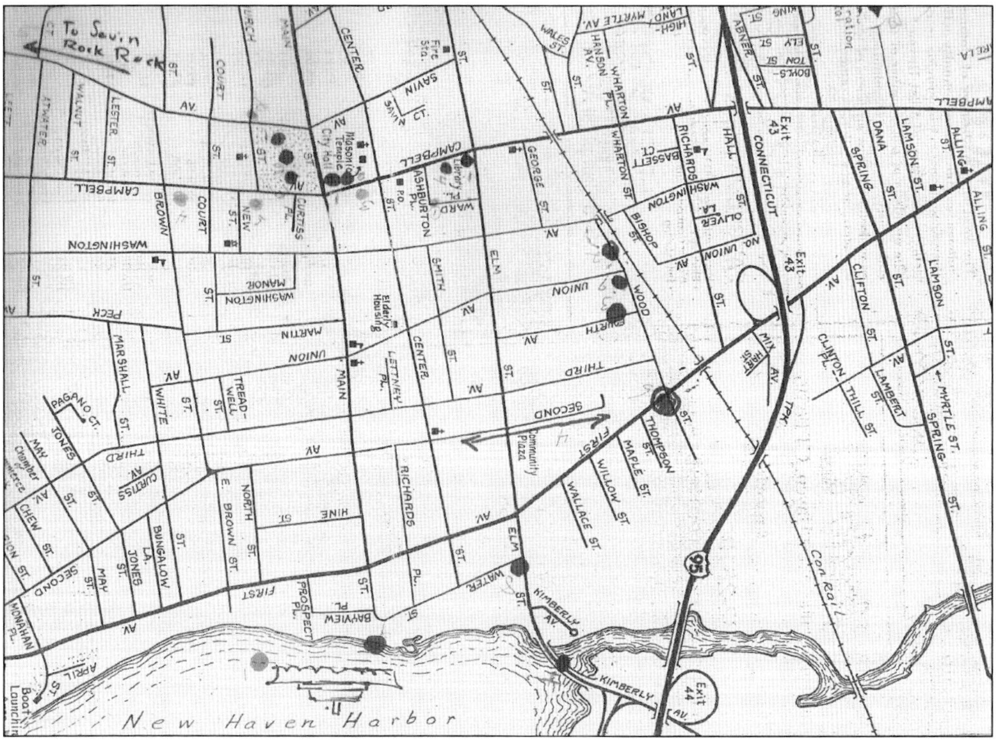

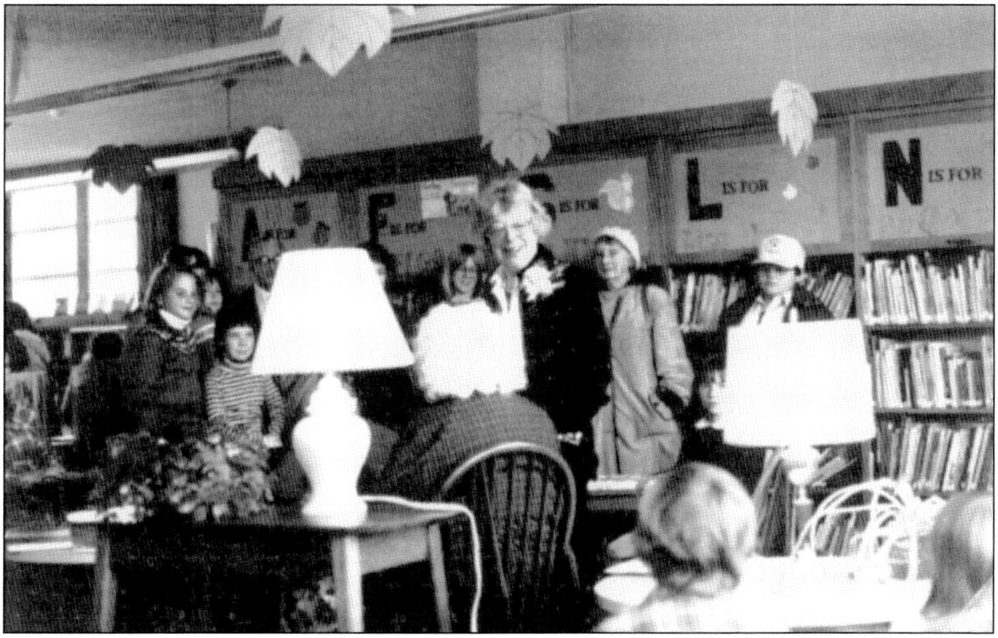

Estes's love of children's literature was well known. She worked many years as children's librarian in the New York Public Library system and was well-known as a storyteller.

Locations identified by Book and Page in
Moffat Books

"The Moffats"

Page No.
2. Town Hall
2. Shingle Hill
3. New Dollar Street (Fourth Avenue)
4. Trolley (Second Avenue).
34. Deli with hidden box
51. Brooney's Deli
68. Horse Trough, and the West Haven Green
108. Brown wooden school on Wood Street.
137. Coal Barge
185 Sandy Beach.

"Rufus M."

13. Public Library
22. Railroad Station (Soldiers and washcloth incident)
37. Soldiers leaving town
116. Settlement House for Veterans (West Haven Veterans' Hospital)
121. Kimberly Avenue Bridge (called Cumberland Bridge)
170. Flying Horses.
171. Savin Rock (Plum Beach)
174. Great White Way (White City, Savin Rock)
176. Old Mill, Jolly Olga (laughing lady-Savin Rock).

"Moffat Museum"

55. Granite Church facing Green (Christ Church)
111. Church Street and Christ Church.
162. Carbarn, corner of Court St. and Campbell Ave.
185 Wilcox's Pier Restaurant.

"Middle Moffat"

15. Green and Fireworks
132. Town Hall
175. Gym at First Congregational Church, Church St.
218. Illustration of Public Library

"Pinky Pie"

20 Liner "Richard Peck."

As West Haven residents recognized Estes's favorite places, they relived experiences that they had when the city was still a town. Historical society researchers Mary Lee Neale, Peggy Mayer, and Betty Roy identified 28 sites in the four Moffat books, as well as one in *Pinky Pye*. A reader could easily trace the route that the Moffats followed in their adventures.

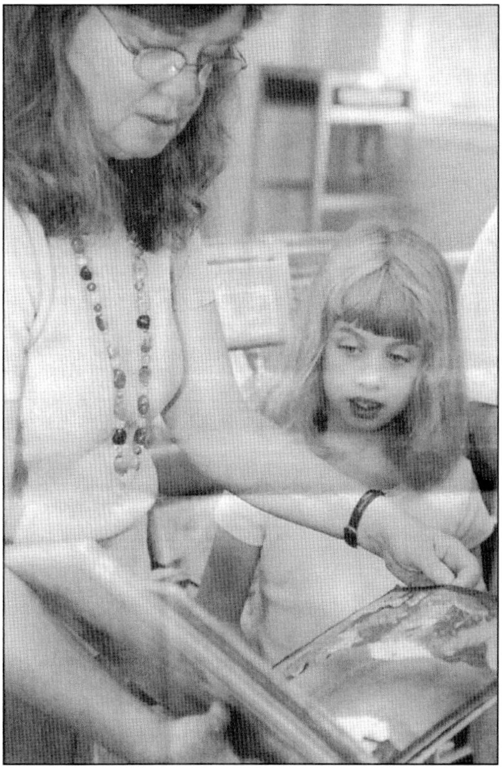

Daughter Helena Estes inherited the love of books and her career from her father and mother, both librarians. She describes her mother's books as having "a universal quality." Here she shares a favorite story with a young reader.

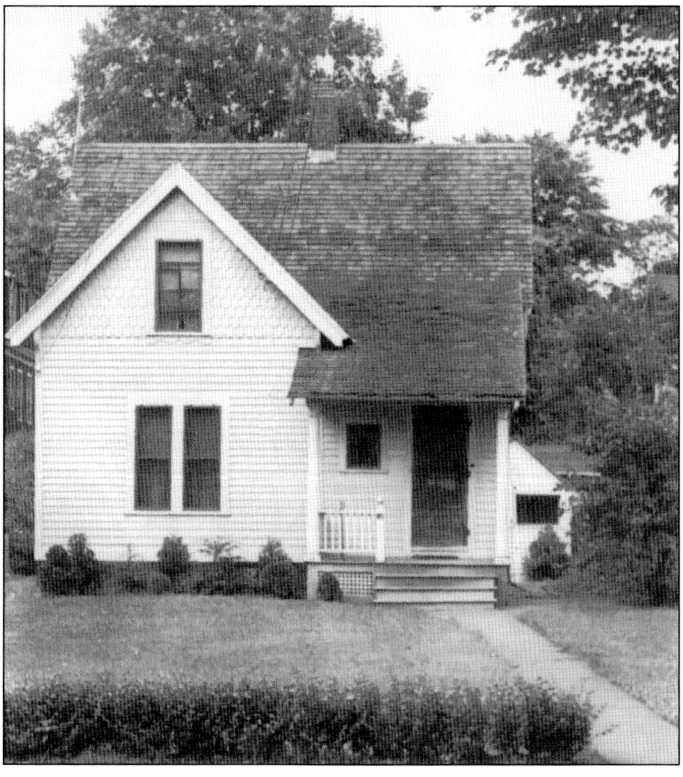

Estes developed tuberculosis, and it was during her home confinement in this cottage that she began to write the memories of her childhood, which became prize-winning works.

Five

From County Home to Maxey Hall

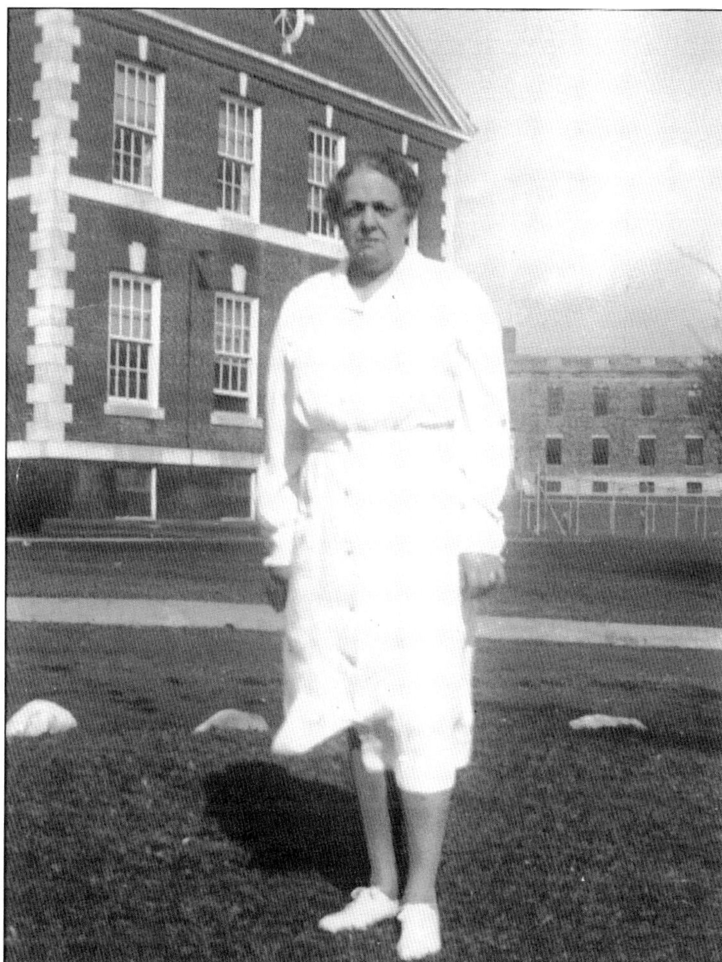

Esther Isbel Northrop Wolfe became superintendent of the New Haven County Home for Children during the most difficult economic times, yet her vision changed the lives of hundreds of youngsters.

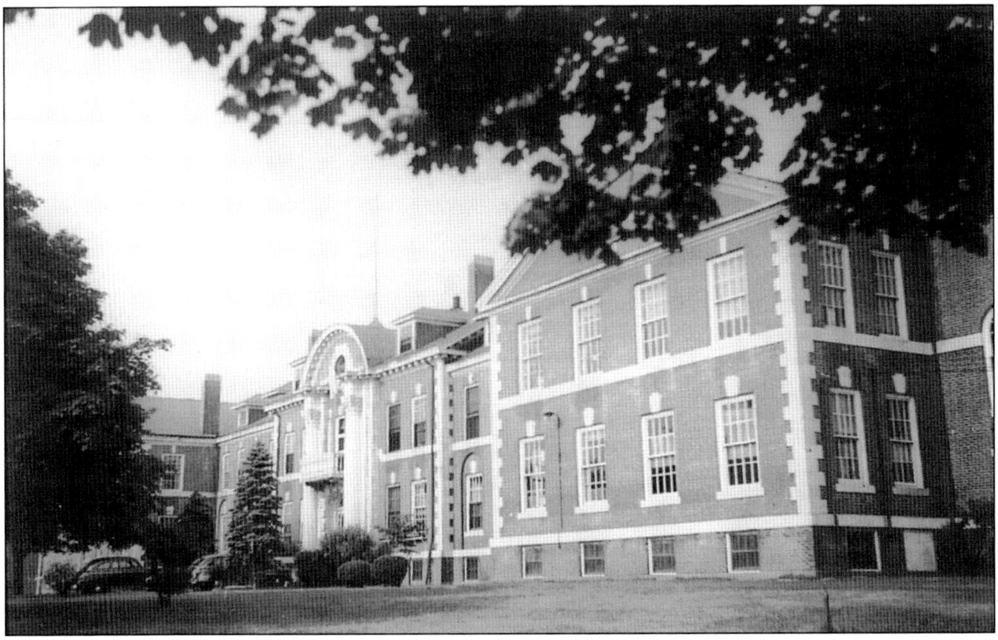

Recognized today as Maxey Hall, the administrative building at the University of New Haven in the Allingtown section of West Haven was originally the New Haven County Home for Children (orphans and the needy and neglected). Not long after Esther Isbel Northrop Wolfe became superintendent, she had another group of children to care for—those whose families could not support them because of the impact of the Great Depression. It was not unusual for such families to place some children in facilities while keeping others at home.

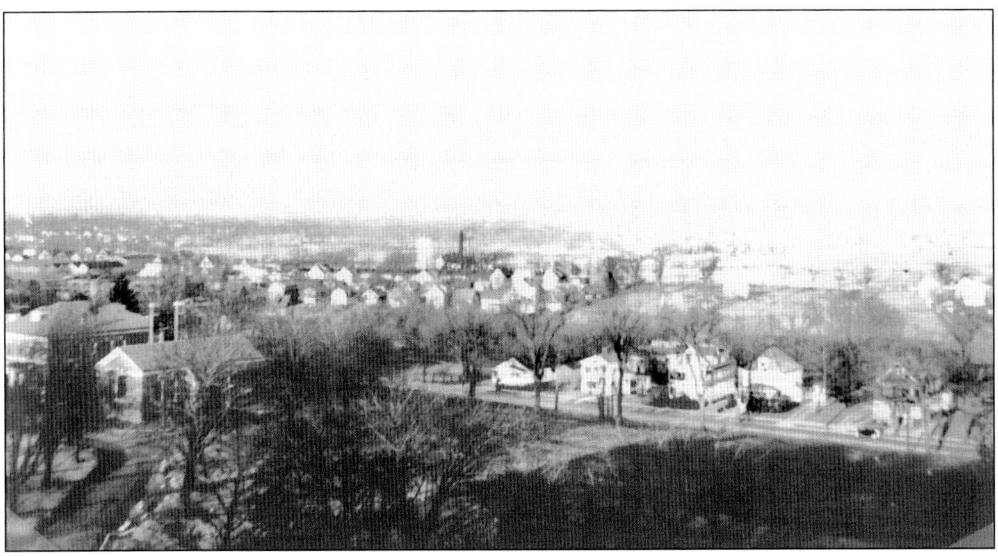

With an unbroken view of New Haven, the County Home sat high on a hill above the main intersection of the Boston Post Road and the north end of Campbell Avenue. A testimony to the fact that the hill was believed to be a healthier environment was evident in the selection of a nearby site for a tuberculosis sanitarium, later the Veterans Administration hospital.

Seen here with their working mother on Easter Sunday 1940, the Wolfe family includes, from left to right, Harold, John, Edward "Ted," an unidentified staff member, Esther, Marjorie "Midge," and the family dog, Hi-Boy (Midge and Ted are twins.) In later years, Ted would say that their mother was occupied around the clock with the massive responsibility of running the state facility.

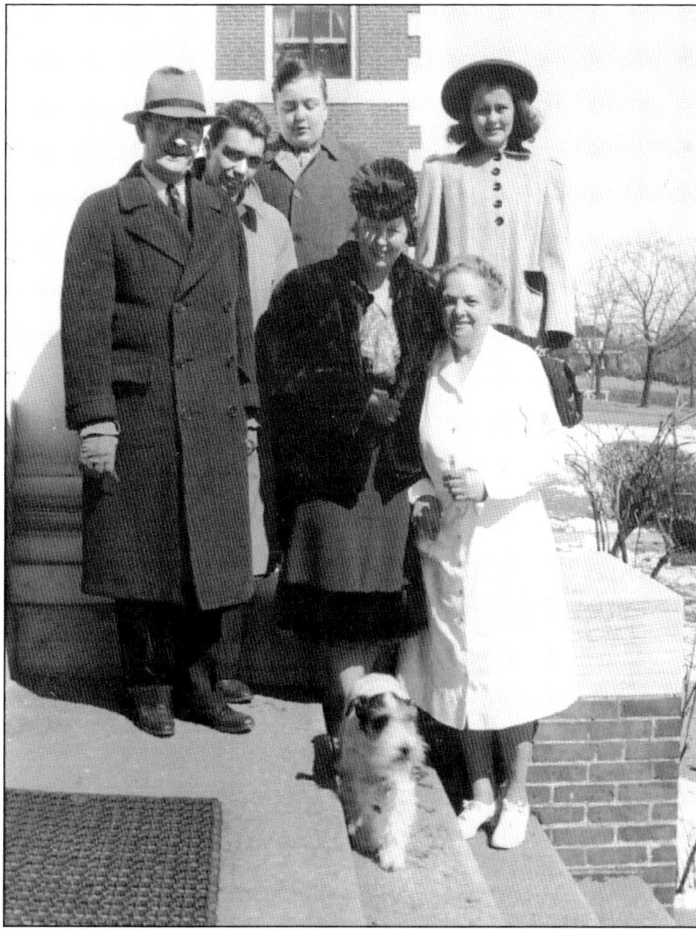

The Wolfe family's quarters were located in Maxey Hall, along with classrooms, dormitories, dining rooms, a gymnasium, and a library.

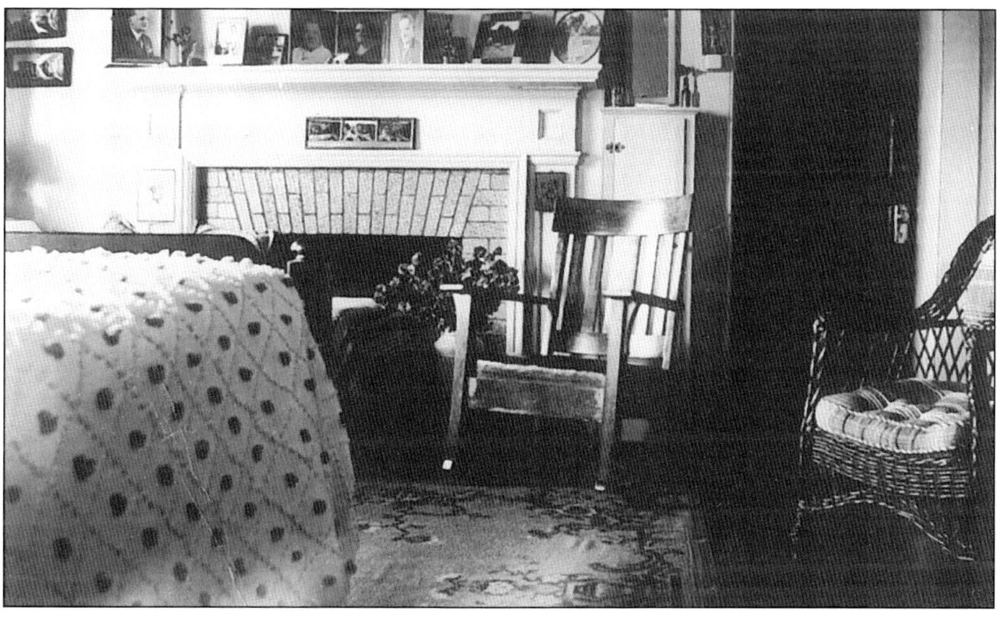

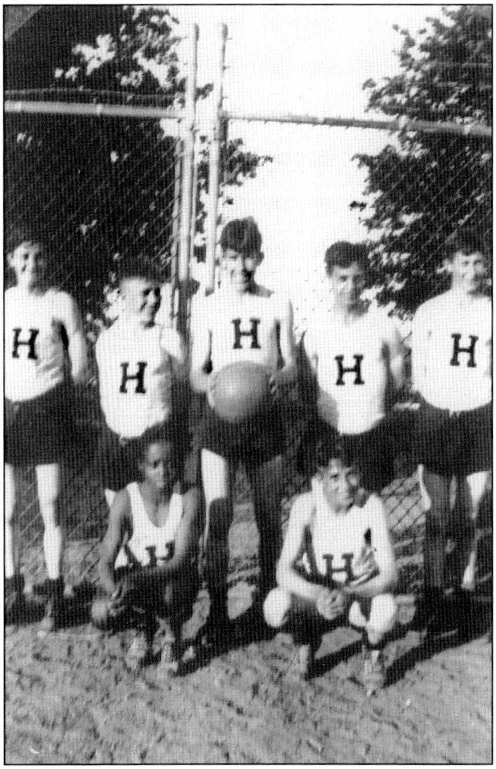

Superintendent Wolfe encouraged youngsters to participate in after-school sports programs, and before long, the Hilltoppers were teams to be given a second look. Local businesses sponsored uniforms, and the Hilltoppers were ready for action on the court or on the field.

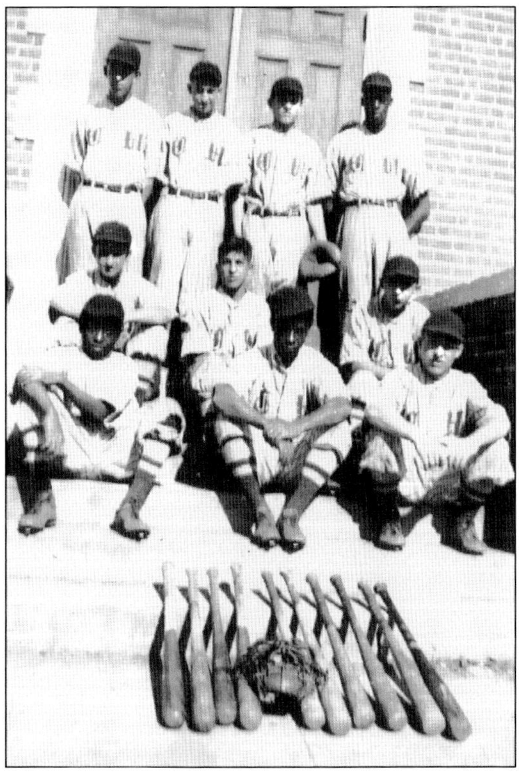

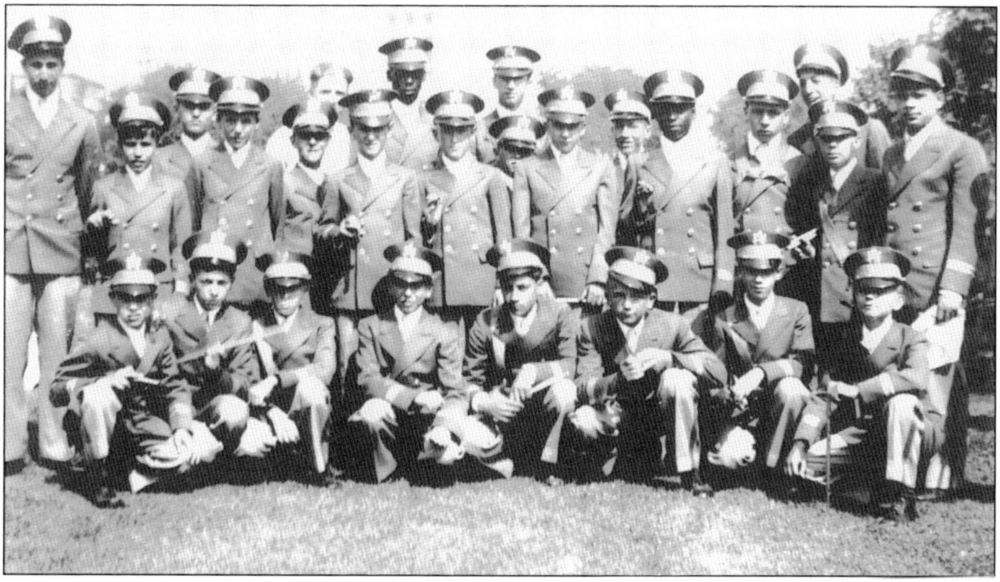

Wolfe made certain that youngsters had the opportunity to participate in something that interested them, and in the days when bands were popular, it did not take long for a group to form.

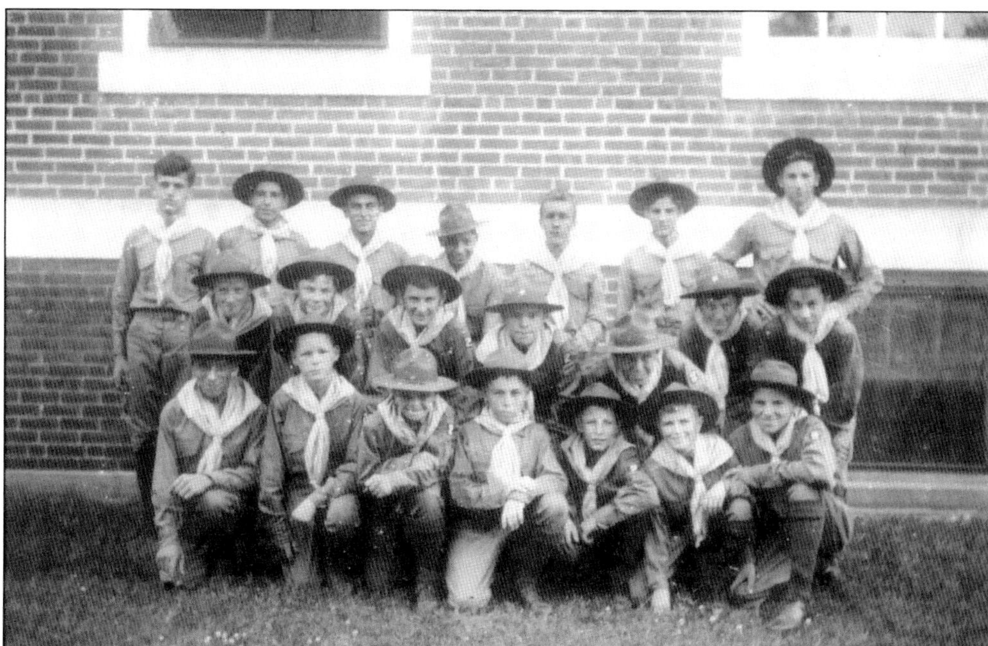

Boy Scouts was another challenging and rewarding outlet for the children, and one which took them out of the confines of the facility.

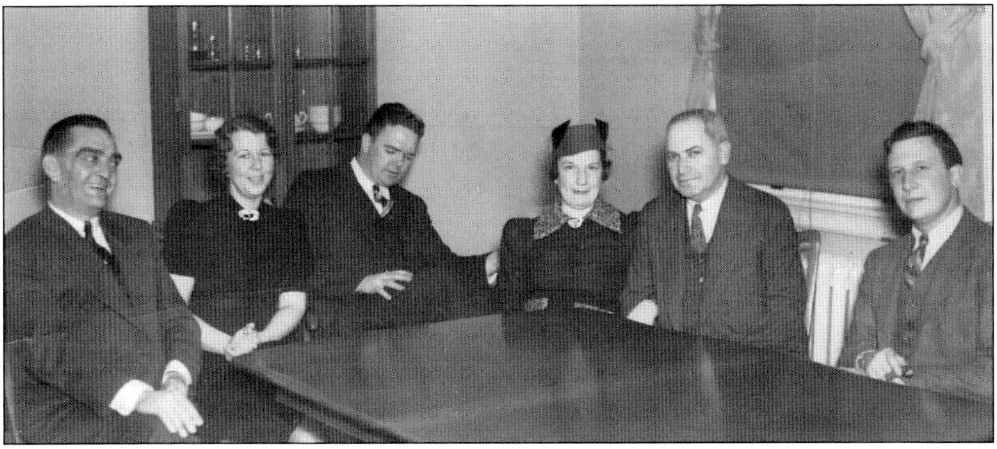

Under Superintendent Wolfe, directors and staff kept an eye on the operation and programs of the County Home, with the goal that each child be self-sufficient and able to carry on when he or she left the protection of the home.

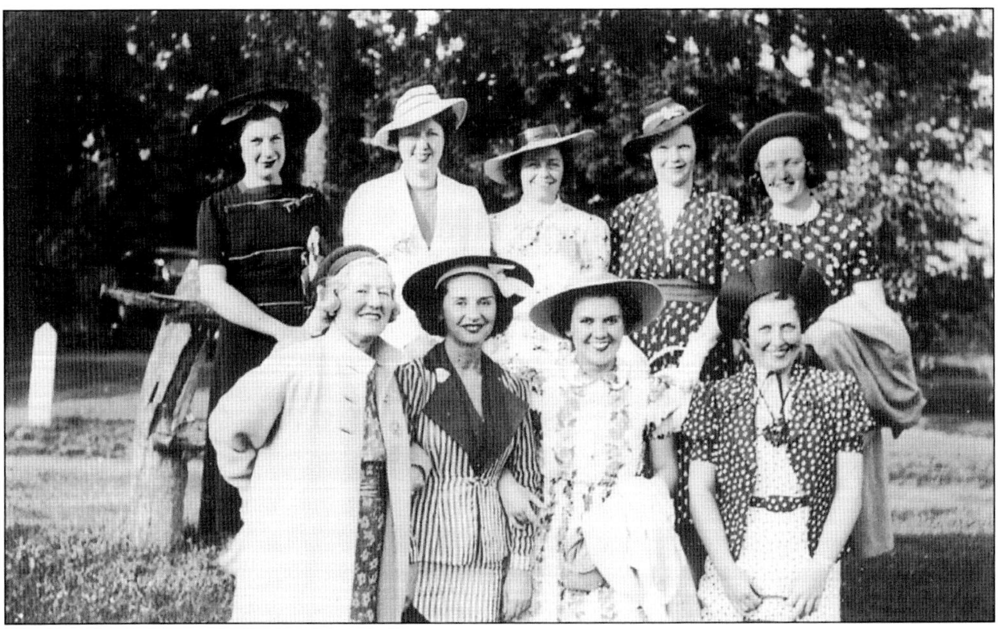

The caring and supportive staff poses in their Sunday best for this group photograph.

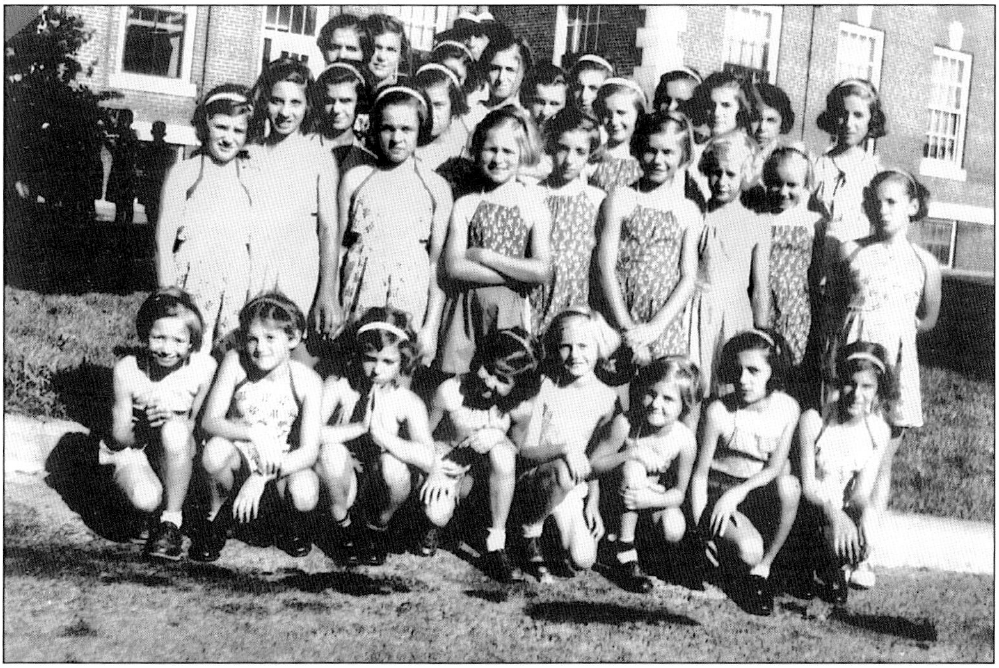

With the stigma of bowl haircuts and uniforms gone, boys and girls proudly pose in front of Maxey Hall. Wolfe often visited friends and associates in the New York City Garment District to gather clothing donations for the children.

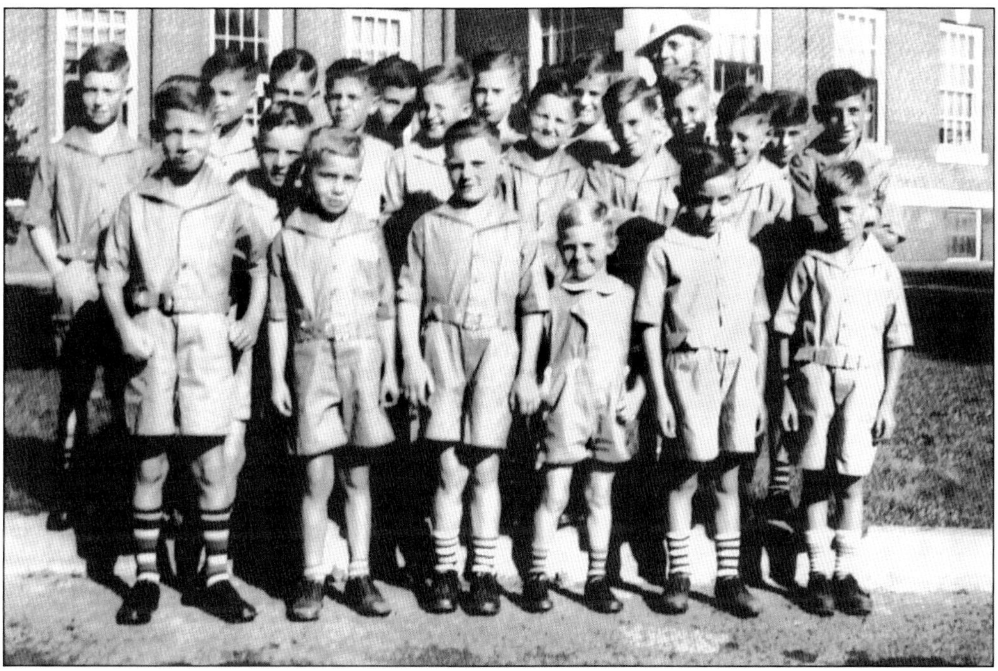

Gym outfits were the only uniforms allowed, and these youngsters are prepared for that class.

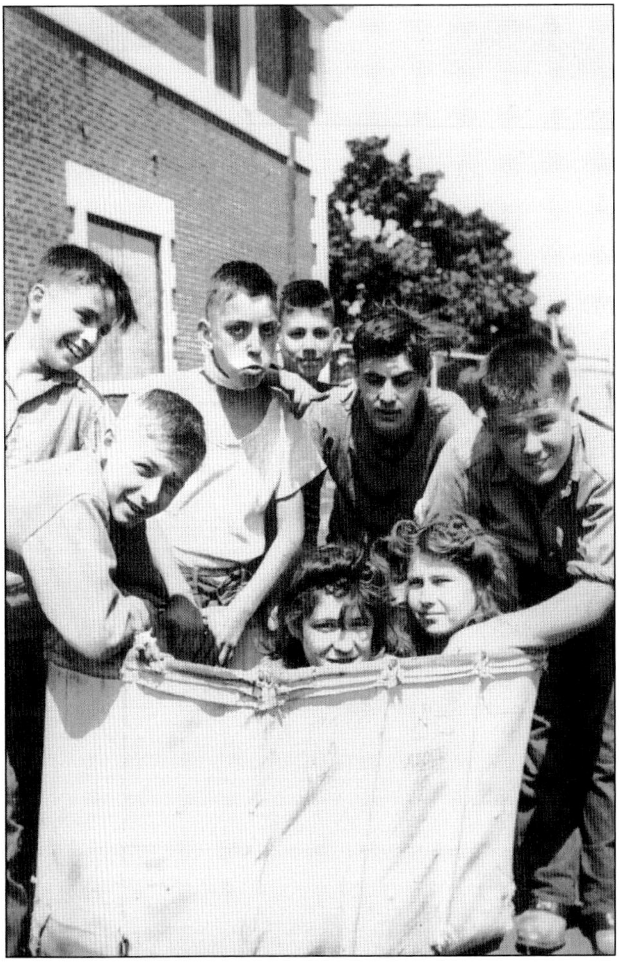

It was not all work and no play at the County Home. While the children did have their responsibilities and chores, they also had free time for some horseplay.

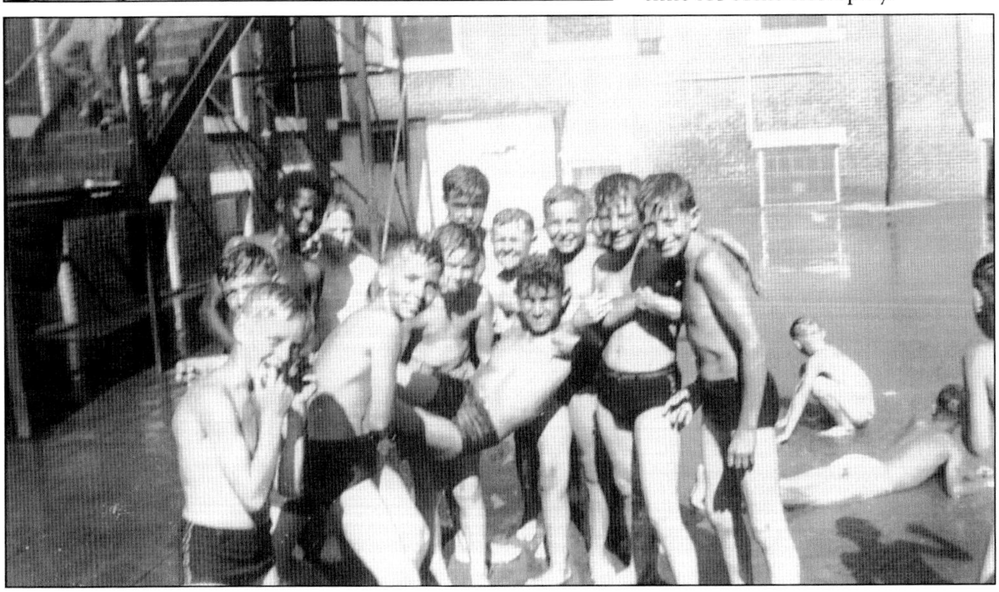

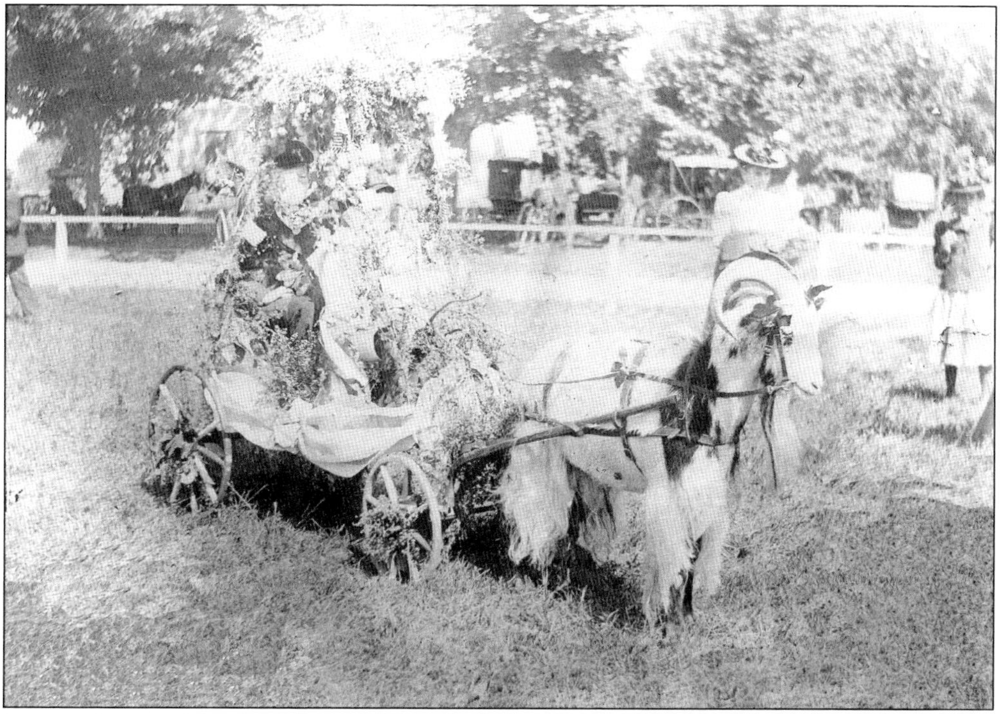

Having their mother work as superintendent of the County Home was a far cry from the days when Ted and Midge were able to ride in the goat cart at Grandpa Northrop's house.

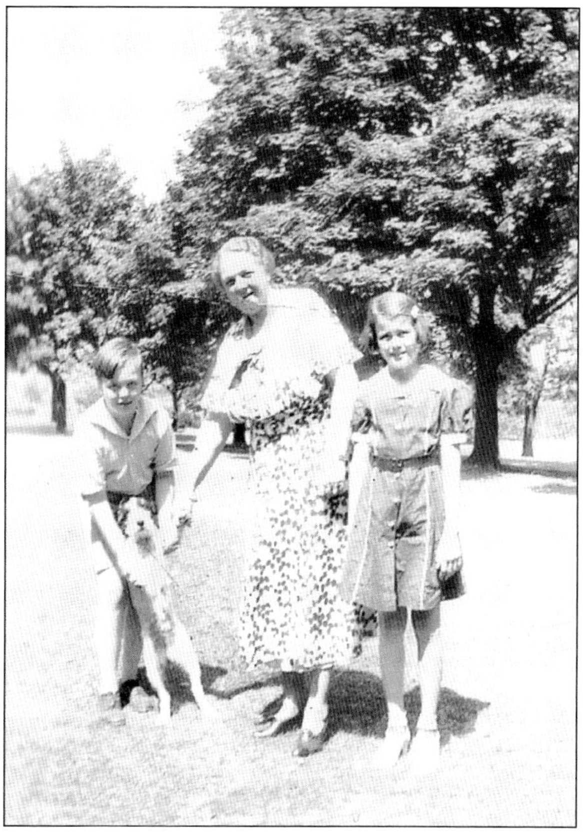

Hi-Boy became the center of attention at every opportunity. Here he is seen with the twins, Ted and Midge, and their mother, Esther.

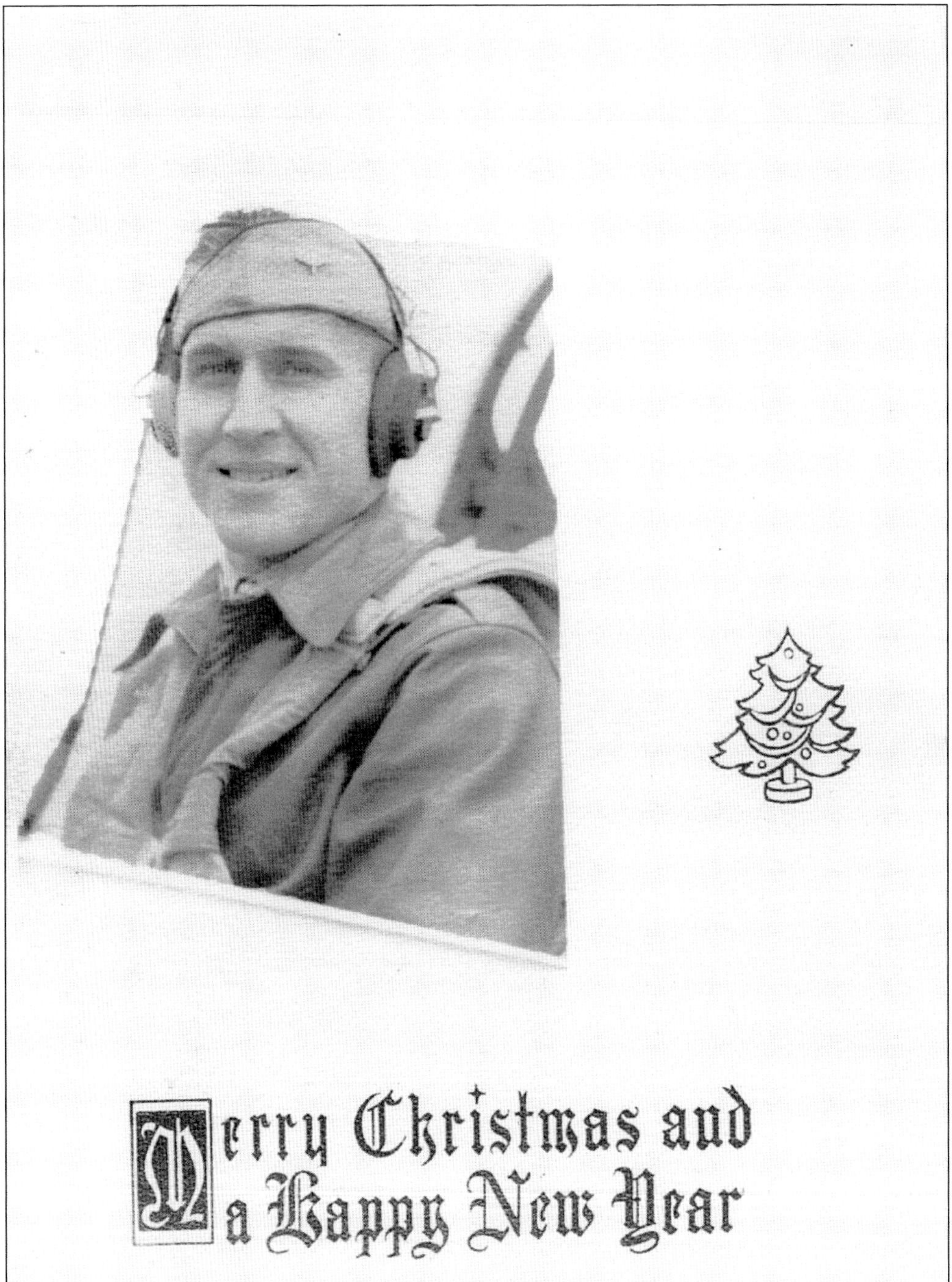

Joe Yurovish kept in touch with the Wolfe family after he joined the Army Air Corps in World War II. Yurovish was a dedicated student throughout his school years, as were many of his friends. He continued to Fordham University, where the Wolfe family attended his graduation.

The Reverend Robert "Bob" Martin was a young man at the Yale Divinity School when he was recruited by Wolfe to serve as chaplain at the County Home. Martin remained in West Haven, where he became curator of the historical Christ Episcopal Church in 1944 and rector in 1949.

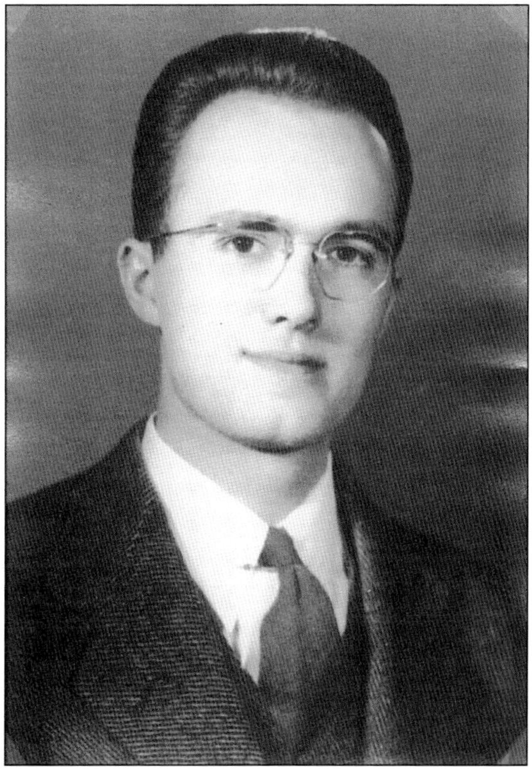

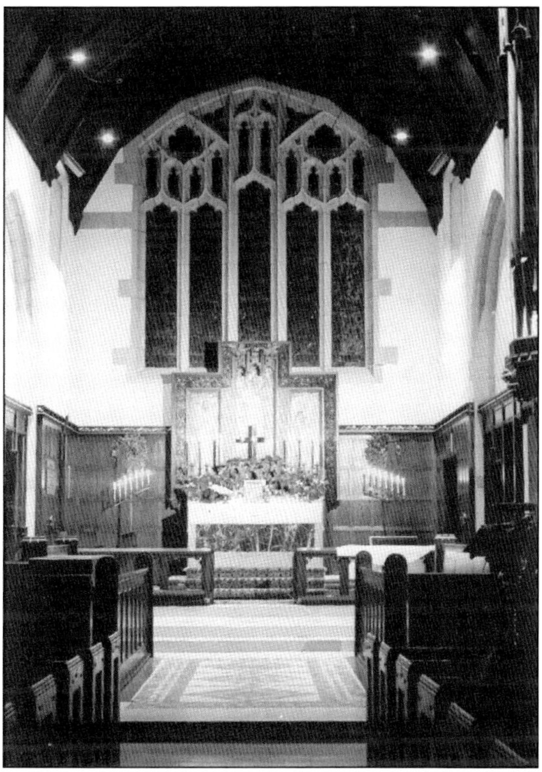

Martin was very popular with the parishioners of Christ Church, the second-oldest Episcopal church in the northeast, and was eventually recognized for his work by the church hierarchy. When Christ Church recently merged with St. John's By-The-Sea, it was renamed the Church of the Holy Spirit.

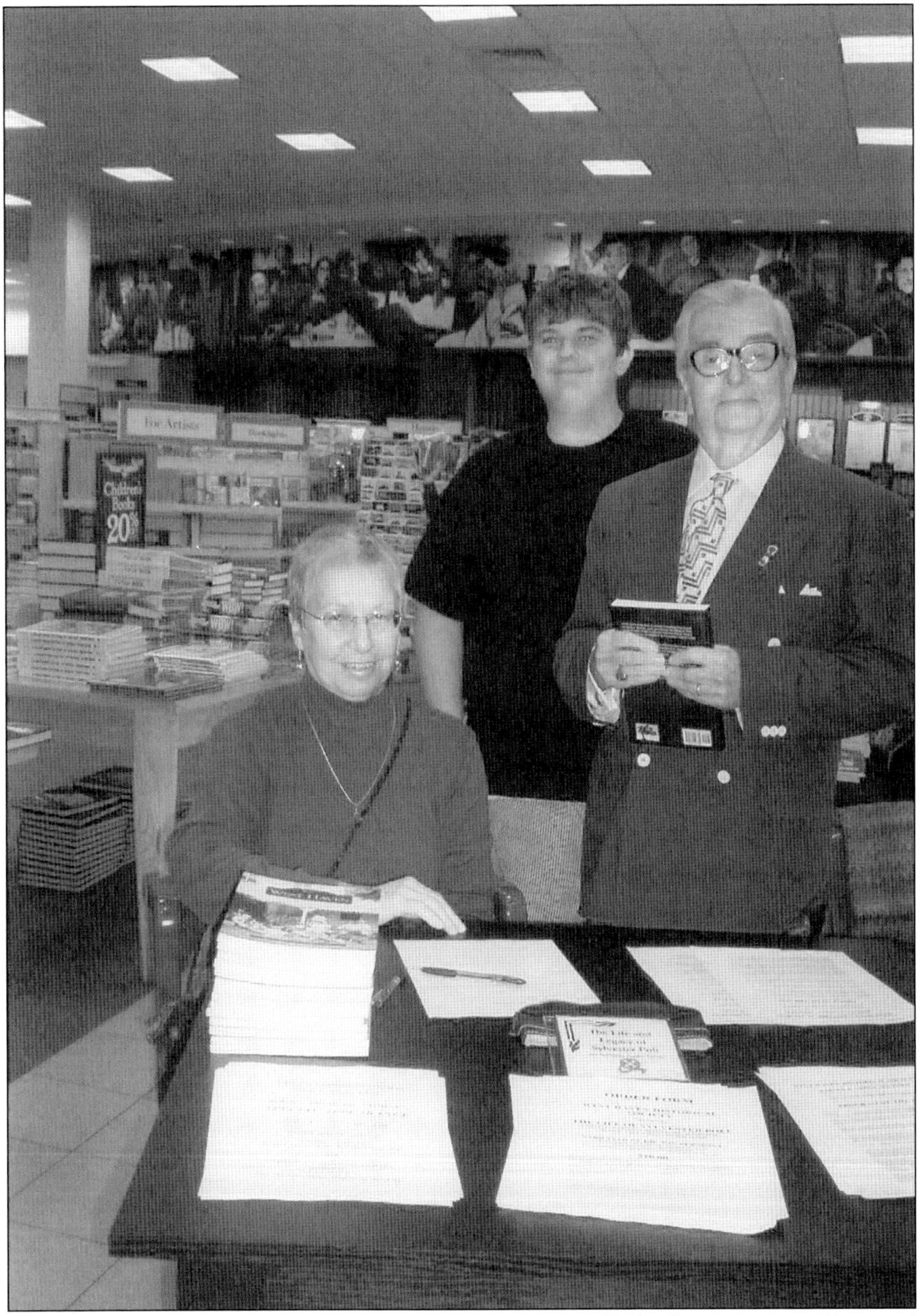

Edward "Ted" Wolfe now lectures on "The Ghosts of Maxey Hall" for the West Haven Historical Society. Wolfe appeared with fellow society member Maureen Coughlin and his grandson Teddy at a Barnes and Noble event promoting the society's first West Haven book (from Arcadia) and lecture series.

Six

From Cows to Keys, Filling Every Need

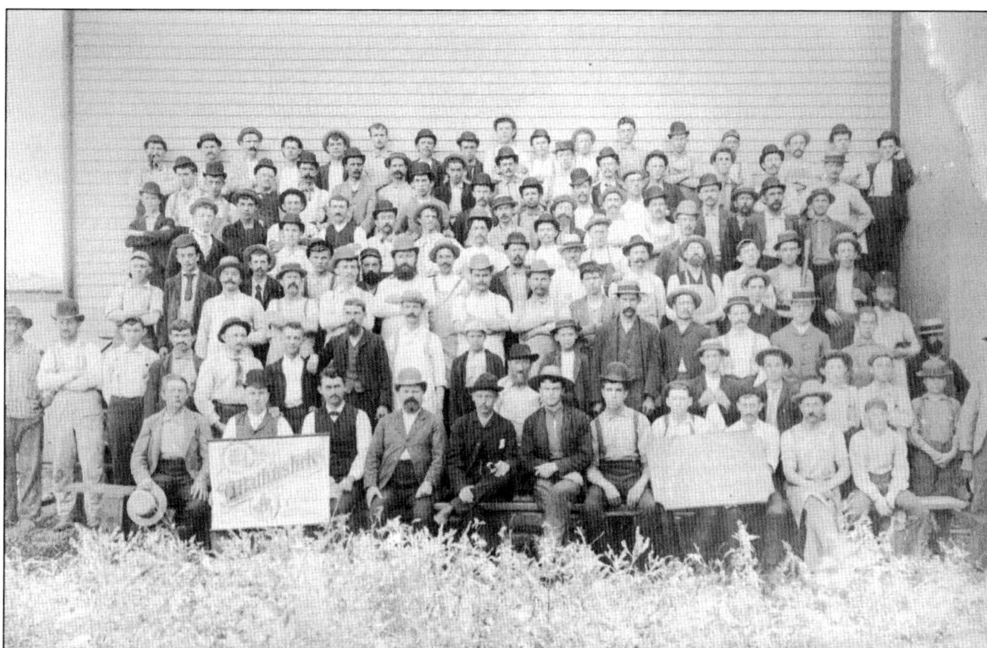

The award-winning, innovative Mathushek Piano Company was located on Brown Street between Washington and Campbell Avenues in 1897, moving to 88 Elm Street in 1906. The large local company boasted having sold more than 30,000 grand, upright, and specialty pianos.

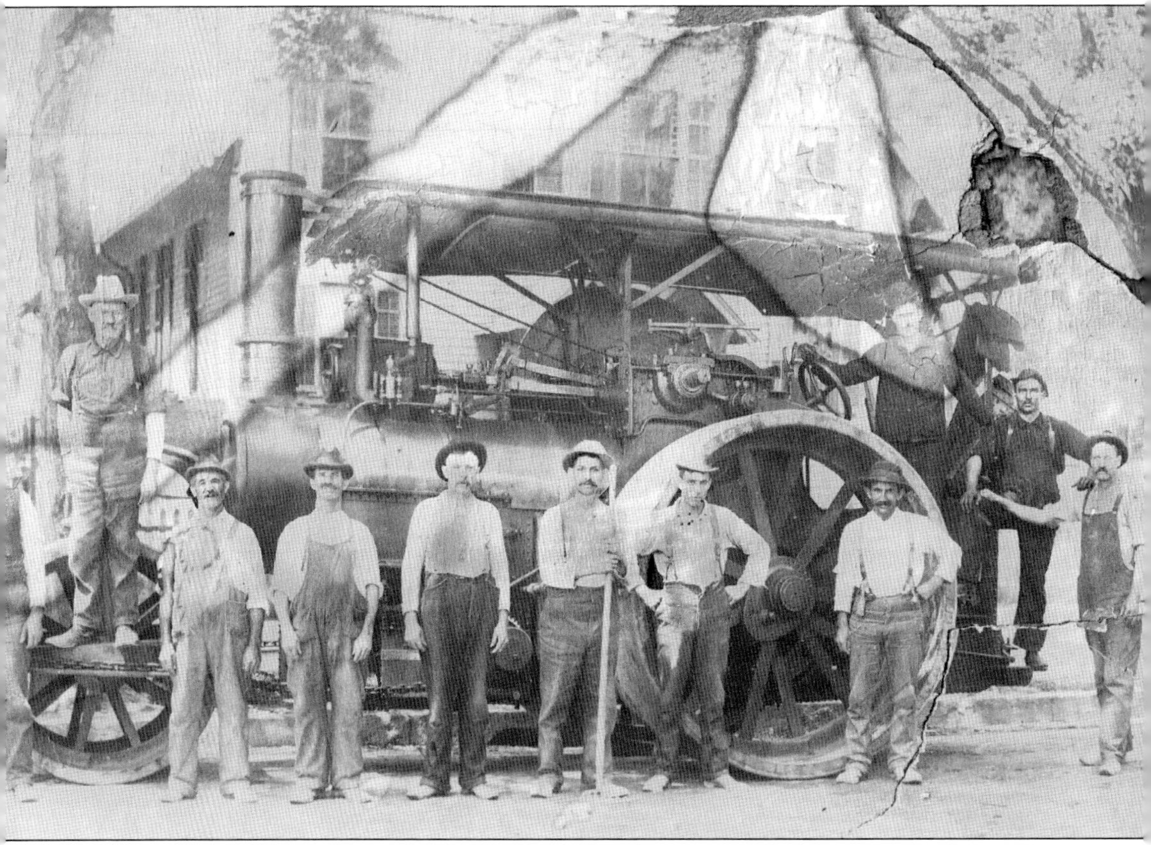

At approximately the same time, road building became a major industry requiring skilled mechanics to maintain and repair the huge equipment. Shown at the steering wheel (third from right) is young engineer Michael Richards. Richards owned a machine shop at the intersection of Lambert and Boston Post Roads until West Haven became an independent town in 1921. He then moved his business and family to Court Street in West Haven. (Author's collection.)

Engineers had to be licensed each year, and Richards was no exception. (Author's collection.)

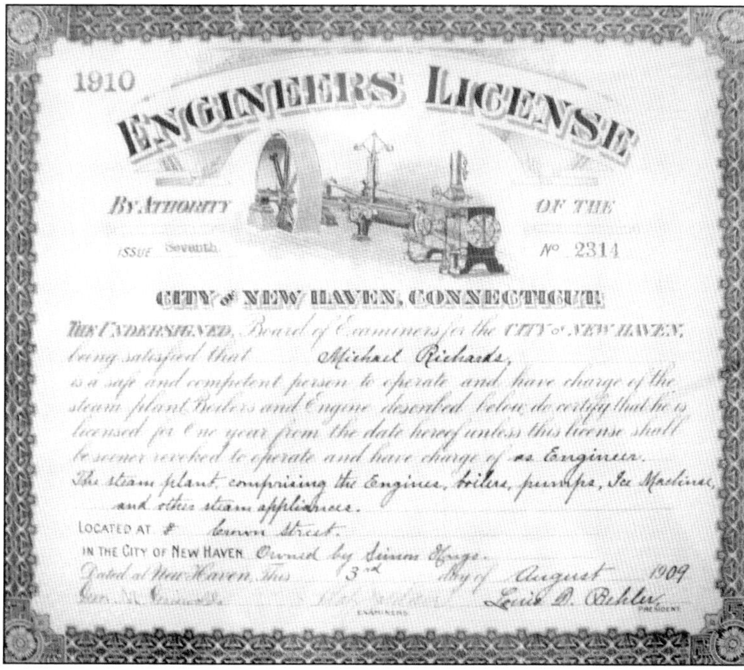

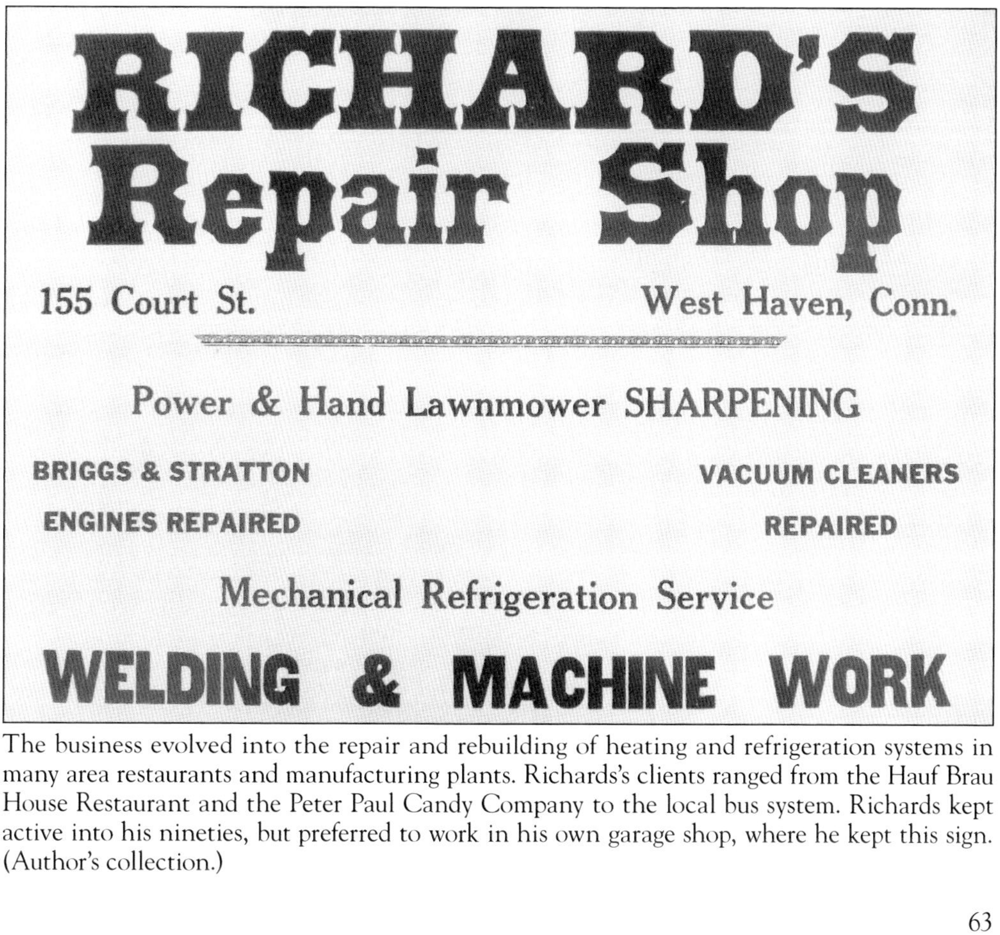

The business evolved into the repair and rebuilding of heating and refrigeration systems in many area restaurants and manufacturing plants. Richards's clients ranged from the Hauf Brau House Restaurant and the Peter Paul Candy Company to the local bus system. Richards kept active into his nineties, but preferred to work in his own garage shop, where he kept this sign. (Author's collection.)

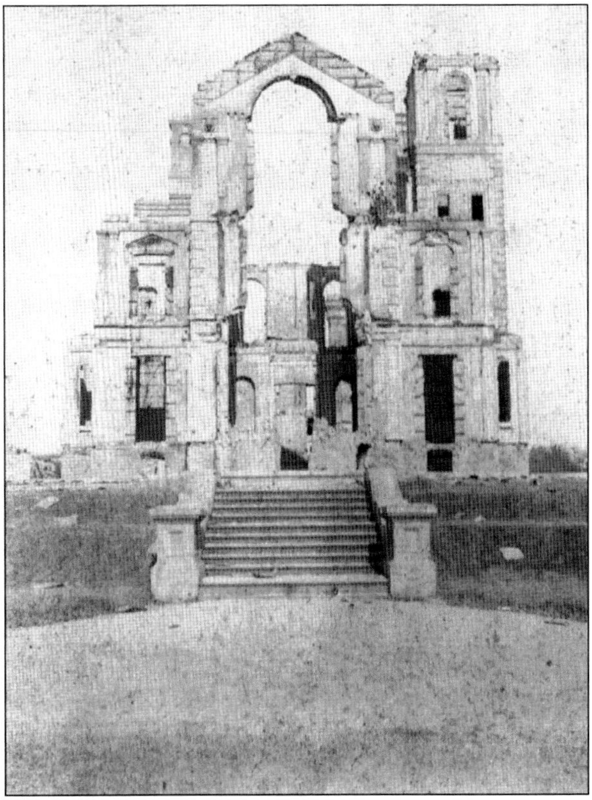

Perhaps the wealthiest resident of West Haven was Canadian Wilson Waddingham, who made his fortune as a cattle baron, railroad tycoon, and owner of productive gold mines. He built the largest, most elegant mansion in the northeast on the acreage bordered by Elm and Wood Streets and First and Third Avenues, but had little time to spend there. A disastrous fire destroyed the mansion in 1903, leaving only a ghostlike shell standing.

Fighting a fire of such enormous proportions was impossible. Most often if the blaze had advanced, bystanders could only watch through the smoke as the building disintegrated into a pile of ash, as seen with this small house.

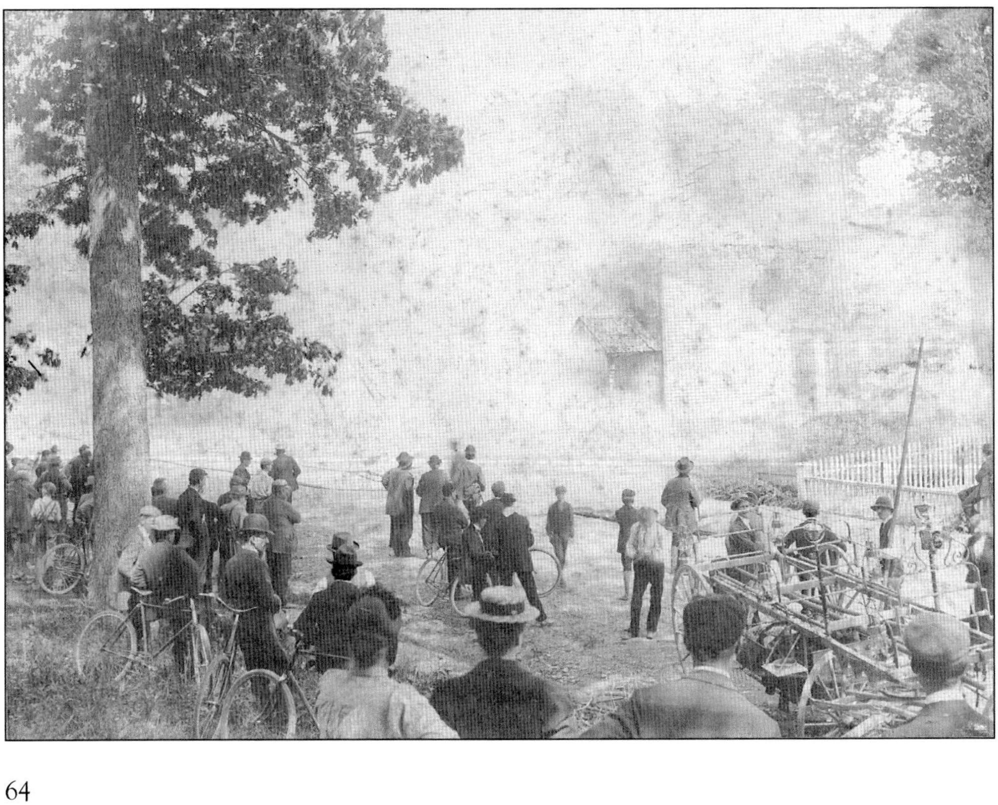

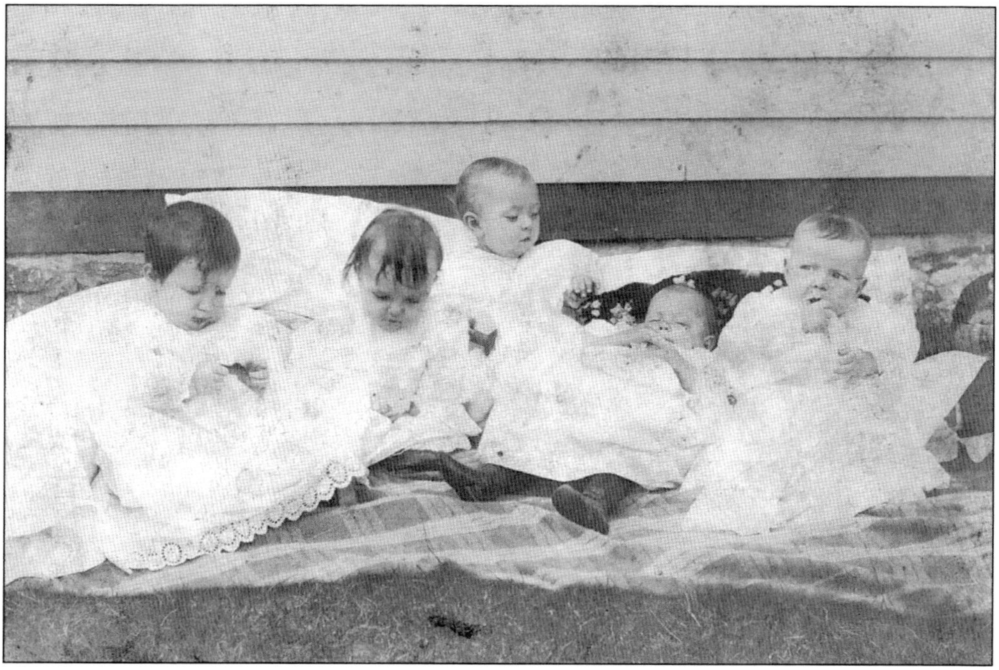

Families and friends reunited each summer at the Elm Terrace Inn, catching up on the news of the past year and introducing the newest generation. These five babies wear their finest for their own day in the sun.

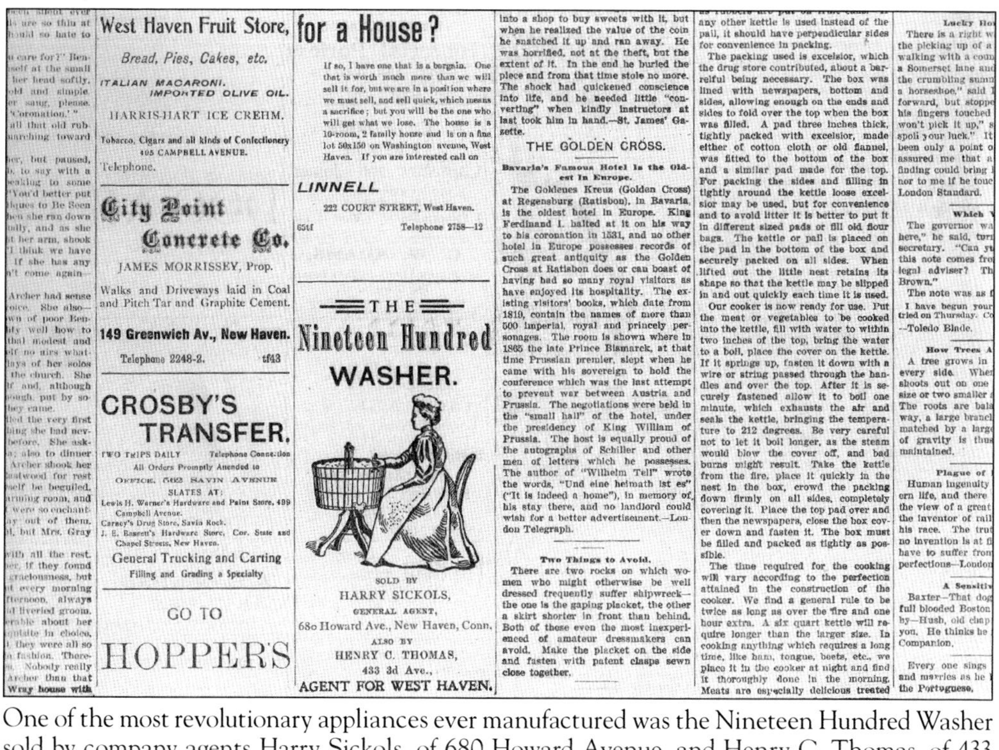

into a shop to buy sweets with it, but when he realized the value of the coin he snatched it up and ran away. He was horrified, not at the theft, but the extent of it. In the end he buried the piece and from that time stole no more. The shock had quickened conscience into life, and he needed little "converting" when kindly instructors at last took him in hand.—St. James' Gazette.

THE GOLDEN CROSS.

Bavaria's Famous Hotel Is the Oldest In Europe.

The Goldenes Kreuz (Golden Cross) at Regensburg (Ratisbon), in Bavaria, is the oldest hotel in Europe. King Ferdinand I. halted at it on his way to his coronation in 1531, and no other hotel in Europe possesses records of such great antiquity as the Golden Cross at Ratisbon does or can boast of having had so many royal visitors as have enjoyed its hospitality. The existing visitors' books, which date from 1819, contain the names of more than 500 imperial, royal and princely personages. The room is shown where in 1865 the late Prince Bismarck, at that time Prussian premier, slept when he came with his sovereign to hold the conference which was the last attempt to prevent war between Austria and Prussia. The negotiations were held in the "small hall" of the hotel, under the presidency of King William of Prussia. The host is equally proud of the autographs of Schiller and other men of letters which he possesses. The author of "Wilhelm Tell" wrote the words, "Und eine heimath ist es" ("It is indeed a home"), in memory of his stay there, and no landlord could wish for a better advertisement.—London Telegraph.

Two Things to Avoid.

There are two rocks on which women who might otherwise be well dressed frequently suffer shipwreck—the one is the gaping placket, the other a skirt shorter in front than behind. Both of these even the most inexperienced of amateur dressmakers can avoid. Make the placket on the side and fasten with patent clasps sewn close together.

any other kettle is used instead of the pail, it should have perpendicular sides for convenience in packing.

The packing used is excelsior, which the drug store contributed, about a barrelful being necessary. The box was lined with newspapers, bottom and sides, allowing enough on the ends and sides to fold over the top when the box was filled. A pad three inches thick, tightly packed with excelsior, made either of cotton cloth or old flannel, was fitted to the bottom of the box and a similar pad made for the top. For packing the sides and filling in tightly around the kettle loose excelsior may be used, but for convenience and to avoid litter it is better to put it in different sized pads or fill old flour bags. The kettle or pail is placed on the pad in the bottom of the box and securely packed on all sides. When lifted out the little nest retains its shape so that the kettle may be slipped in and out quickly each time it is used.

Our cooker is now ready for use. Put the meat or vegetables to be cooked into the kettle, fill with water to within two inches of the top, bring the water to a boil, place the cover on the kettle. If it springs up, fasten it down with a wire or string passed through the handles and over the top. After it is securely fastened allow it to boil one minute, which exhausts the air and seals the kettle, bringing the temperature to 212 degrees. Be very careful not to let it boil longer, as the steam would blow the cover off, and bad burns might result. Take the kettle from the fire, place it quickly in the nest in the box, crowd the packing down firmly on all sides, completely covering it. Place the top pad over and then the newspapers, close the box cover down and fasten it. The box must be filled and packed as tightly as possible.

The time required for the cooking will vary according to the perfection attained in the construction of the cooker. We find a general rule to be twice as long as over the fire and one hour extra. A six quart kettle will require longer than the larger size. In cooking anything which requires a long time, like ham, tongue, beets, etc., we place it in the cooker at night and find it thoroughly done in the morning. Meats are especially delicious treated

One of the most revolutionary appliances ever manufactured was the Nineteen Hundred Washer sold by company agents Harry Sickols, of 680 Howard Avenue, and Henry C. Thomas, of 433 Third Avenue.

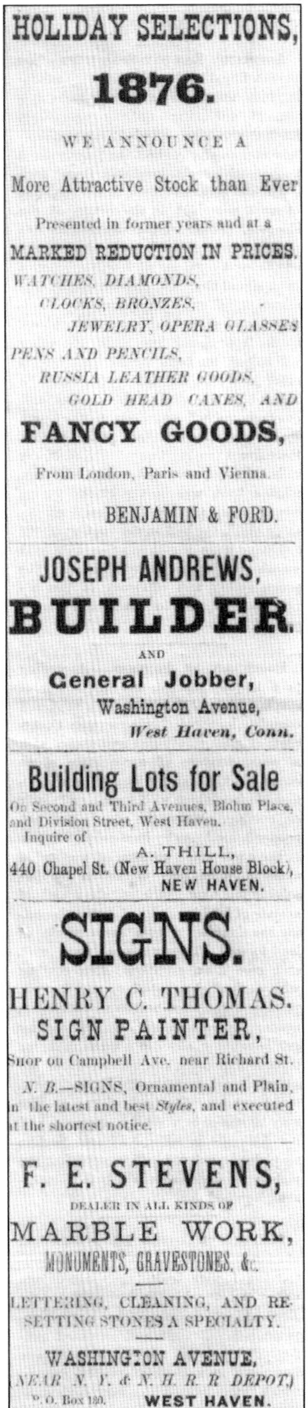

HOLIDAY SELECTIONS,

1876.

WE ANNOUNCE A

More Attractive Stock than Ever

Presented in former years and at a

MARKED REDUCTION IN PRICES.

WATCHES, DIAMONDS,
CLOCKS, BRONZES,
JEWELRY, OPERA GLASSES
PENS AND PENCILS,
RUSSIA LEATHER GOODS,
GOLD HEAD CANES, AND

FANCY GOODS,

From London, Paris and Vienna.

BENJAMIN & FORD.

JOSEPH ANDREWS,

BUILDER

AND

General Jobber,

Washington Avenue,

West Haven, Conn.

Building Lots for Sale

On Second and Third Avenues, Blohm Place, and Division Street, West Haven.
Inquire of

A. THILL,

440 Chapel St. (New Haven House Block),

NEW HAVEN.

SIGNS.

HENRY C. THOMAS.

SIGN PAINTER,

Shop on Campbell Ave. near Richard St.

N. B.—SIGNS, Ornamental and Plain, in the latest and best *Styles*, and executed at the shortest notice.

F. E. STEVENS,

DEALER IN ALL KINDS OF

MARBLE WORK,

MONUMENTS, GRAVESTONES, &c.

LETTERING, CLEANING, AND RE-SETTING STONES A SPECIALTY.

WASHINGTON AVENUE,

(NEAR N. Y. & N. H. R. R. DEPOT.)

P. O. Box 180. WEST HAVEN.

Local companies advertised extensively in the various West Haven newspapers.

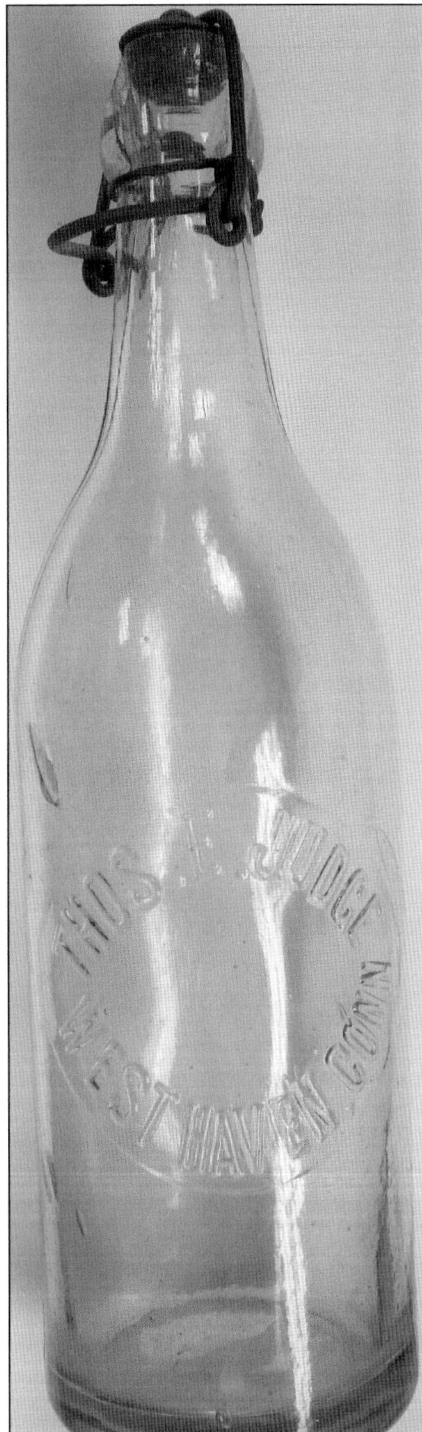

Over the years, West Haven had many breweries and bottling companies. This green bottle bears the name of Thomas E. Judge, West Haven.

Not all businesses were conducted on a grand scale. Summer businesses thrived along the shore, and green grocer Joseph Conte Sr. was considered one of the best fruit and vegetable vendors.

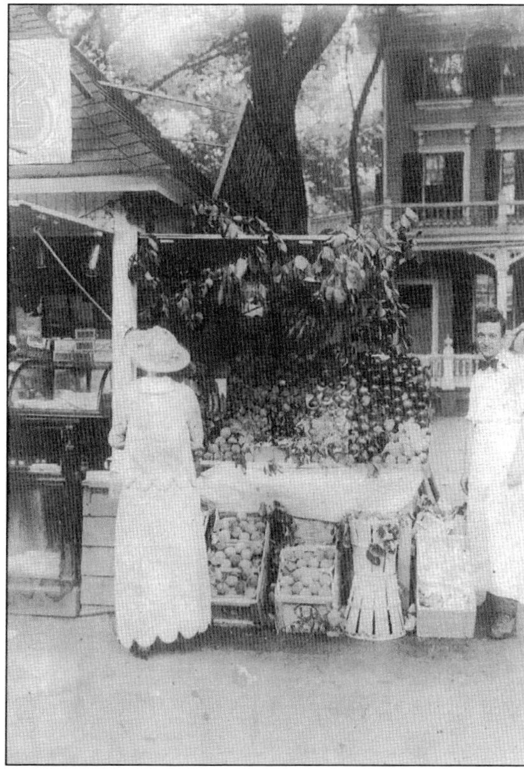

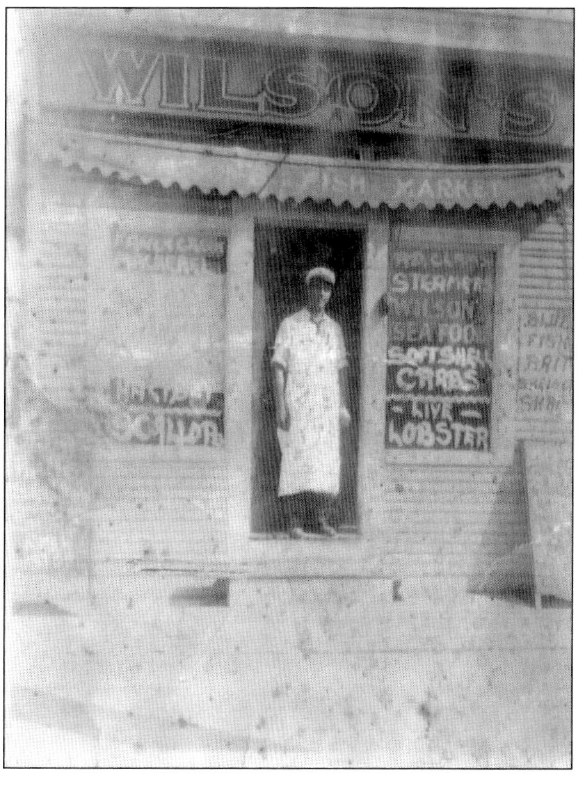

Cedric "George" Stowe left his job at Wilson's Seafood Company of New Haven to open his own business at the end of Campbell Avenue around 1929. Great-grandfather Harvard Stowe had an oyster boat that was under sail from 1870 to 1890. Great-great-grandfather Chanty Stowe owned a sturgeon boat and took fishing parties to the Connecticut River for three days at a time.

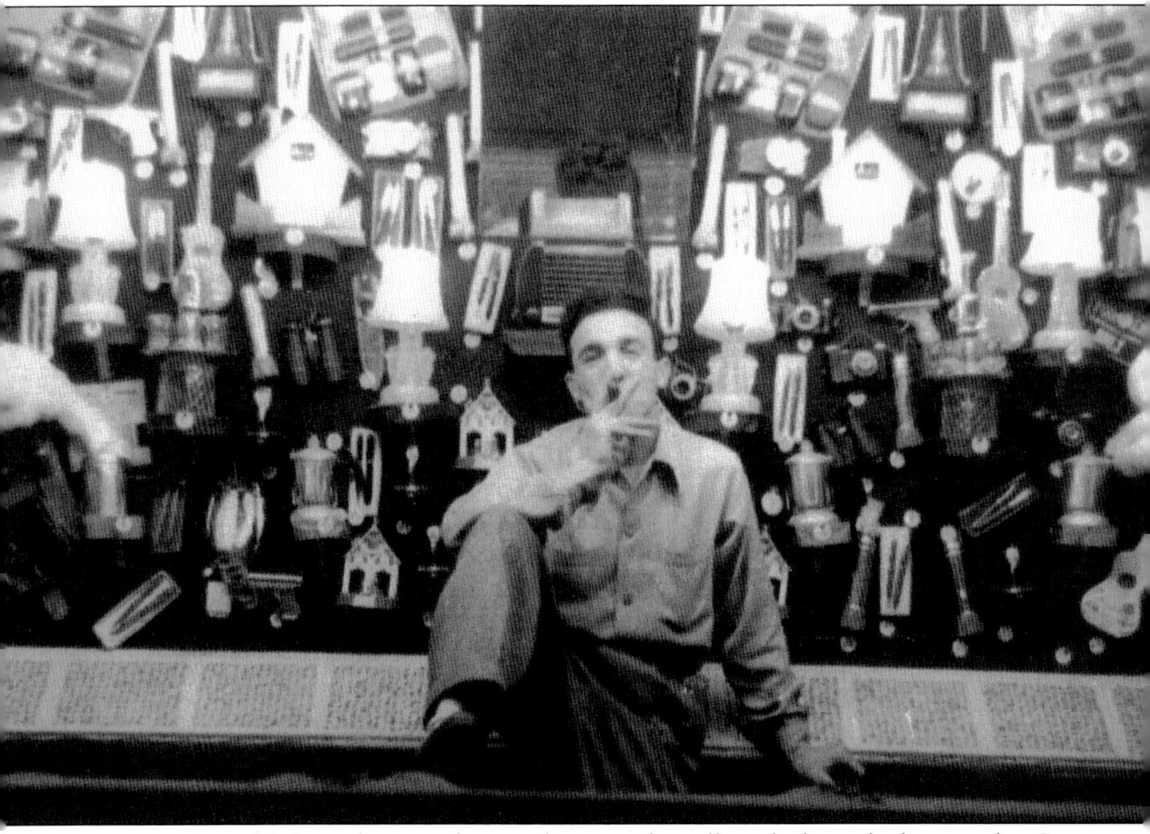

Ernest "Stretch" Conte became the proud owner of a well-stocked arcade dart stand at Savin Rock Amusement Park when a friend went into the service in World War II. The rides, beaches, restaurants, and stands drew huge crowds, and it was not beneath some stand owners to involve shills to promote their business.

It was not long before Savin Rock was projected as a source of tax revenue for the town, thus all of the amusements were categorized and assigned a fee.

The following fees shall be charged and paid for licenses and permits required by the Borough ordinances:

1. Billiard and pool tables and bowling alleys for hire, each	.50
2. Circus, feats of horsemanship in tent or other temporary structure, for the first day-	75.00
for each succeeding day-	50.00
3. Menagerie, caravan, exhibition of living animals in tent or other temporary structure for the first day-	75.00
for each succeeding day-	50.00
4. Theatrical performance, opera or concert by professional performers in any building usually occupied by professional performers, for each day-	1.00
but if the owners or lessees of any theater shall pay $15.00 on the first day of any month in advance for license to play during the month, said payment shall be in lieu of the nightly license fee.	
5. For scenic railway, "Chute the Chute," figure eight- each	50.00
Miniature Wild West Show-	15.00
Miniature railways-	5.00
Exhibition of curiosities and freaks	10.00
Mazes-	10.00
Exhibition of fireworks, limited to set pieces-	25.00
Scenic theaters-	10.00
Penny in the slot photograph machines, each	50 ~~1.00~~
Dancing halls and pavilions, each	20.00
Laughing gallery-	20.00
Ocean Waves	10.00 ?
Old Mill-	25.00
Flying Horses-	25.00
Circle Swings,	25.00 50.00
Small Swings-	5.00
Shooting galleries, each	5.00
Ping Pong games-	15.00
Cane boards- knife boards- each-	5.00
Fish ponds, each-	5.00
Automatic Vaudeville-	40.00
Weighing machines-each	1.00
Gate license, "White City" (so called)	25.00
~~Gate license, Baseball Gronds-~~	30.00
Exhibitions of palmistry and sleight of hand for each place where the same is carried on-	25.00
For game known as African dodger-	5.00
For game known as ball game-	5.00
6. Stands, booths or vehicles, including push carts for the sale of temperance drinks, candy, pop corn, peanuts, fruits or any other wares or merchandise upon the streets or sidewalks, or in any other public place in the borough-	5.00

Visitors to the Barnacle Coffee and Gift Shop at Bradley Point had an unobstructed view of Long Island Sound, a pleasant sea breeze, and a bit of quiet away from the busier Savin Rock area.

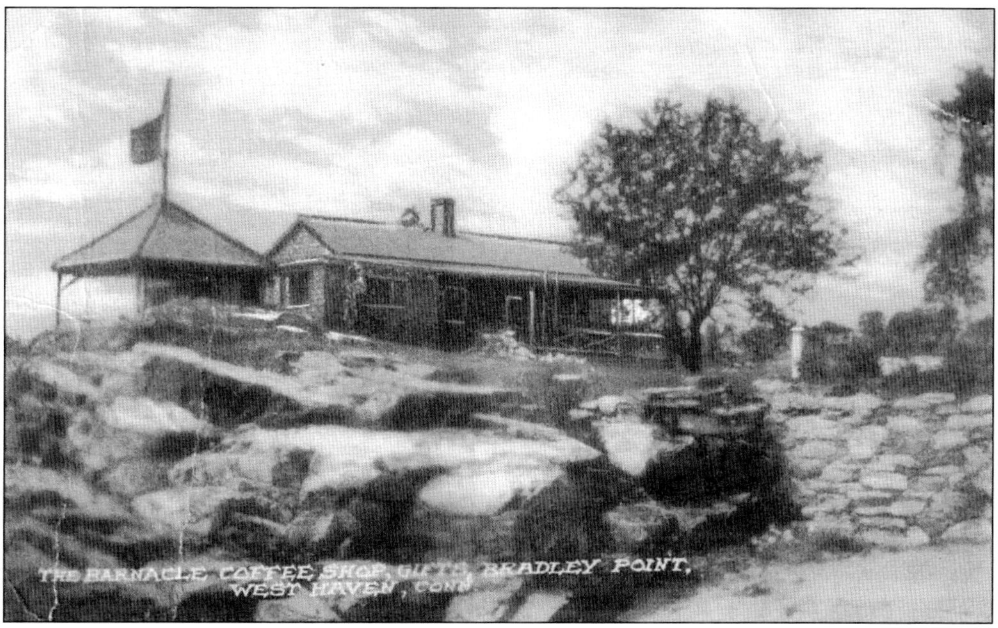

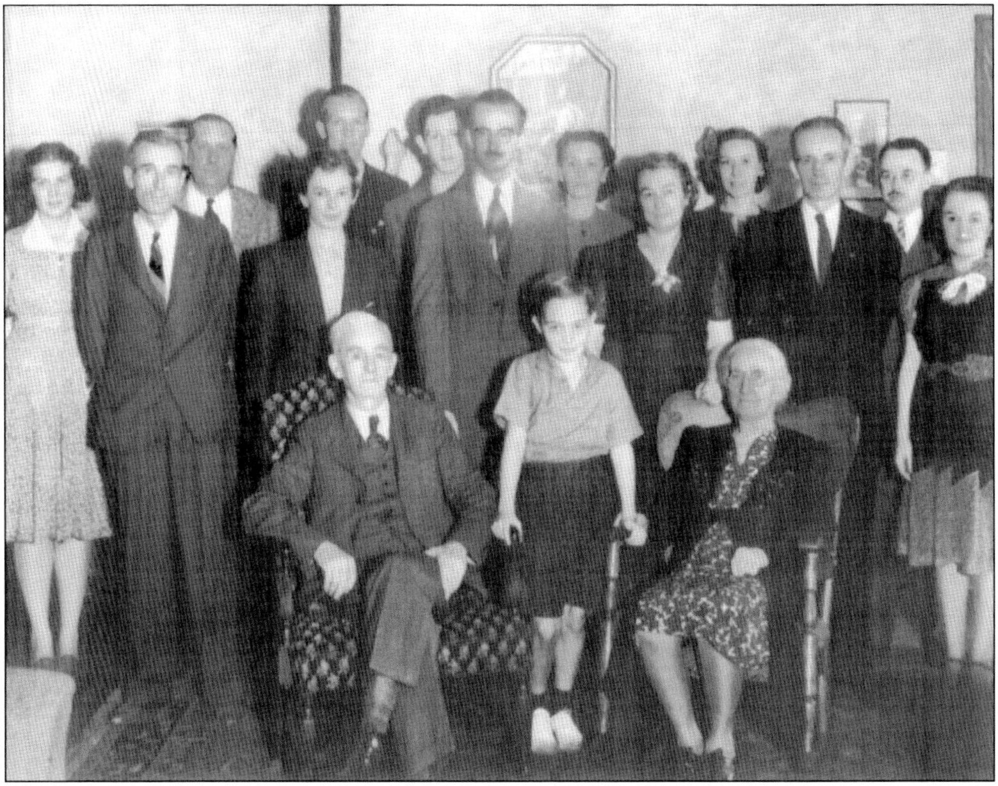

The town would not have survived without Warner's Hardware Store. Lewis Warner took time from his hectic schedule to celebrate the golden wedding anniversary with his wife, Etta Kettle Warner, and their children and grandchildren.

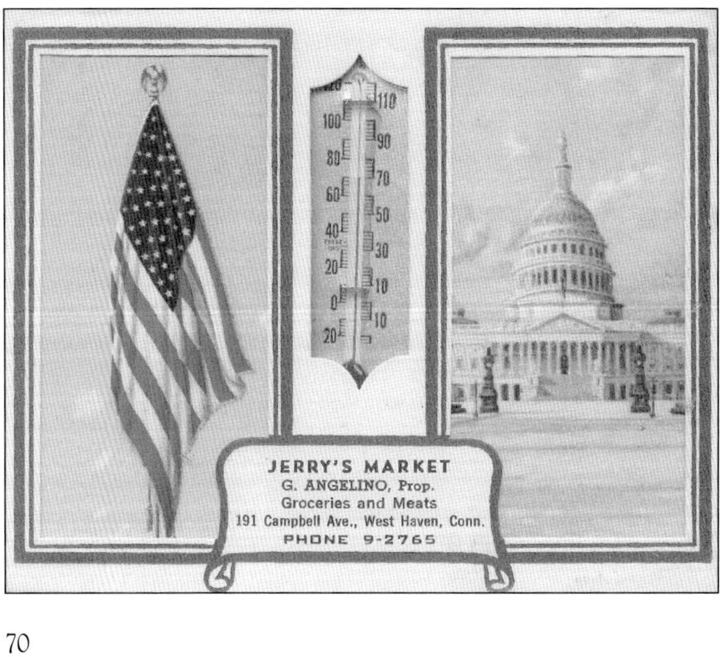

Business advertisements came in many forms, as the customers of Jerry's Market on Campbell Avenue learned when its patriotic proprietor Gennaro Angelino presented them with this thermometer.

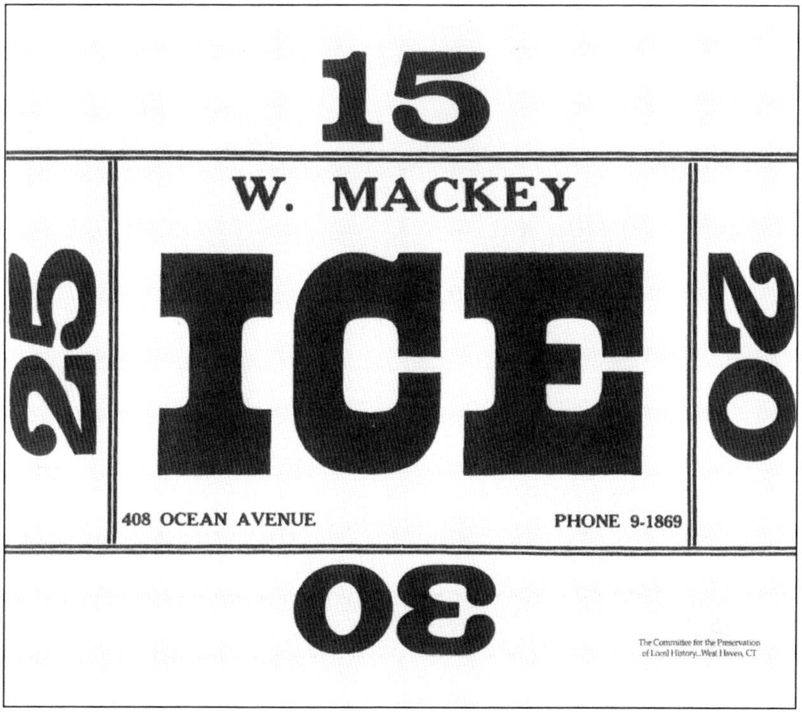

Customers of the Mackey Ice Company knew they could rely on timely delivery of a properly sized block of ice for their iceboxes. One only had to place the card in the window with the selected price at the top. The iceman would don a black rubber sheet over his shoulder, hoist the ice with a pair of tongs, and deliver the block.

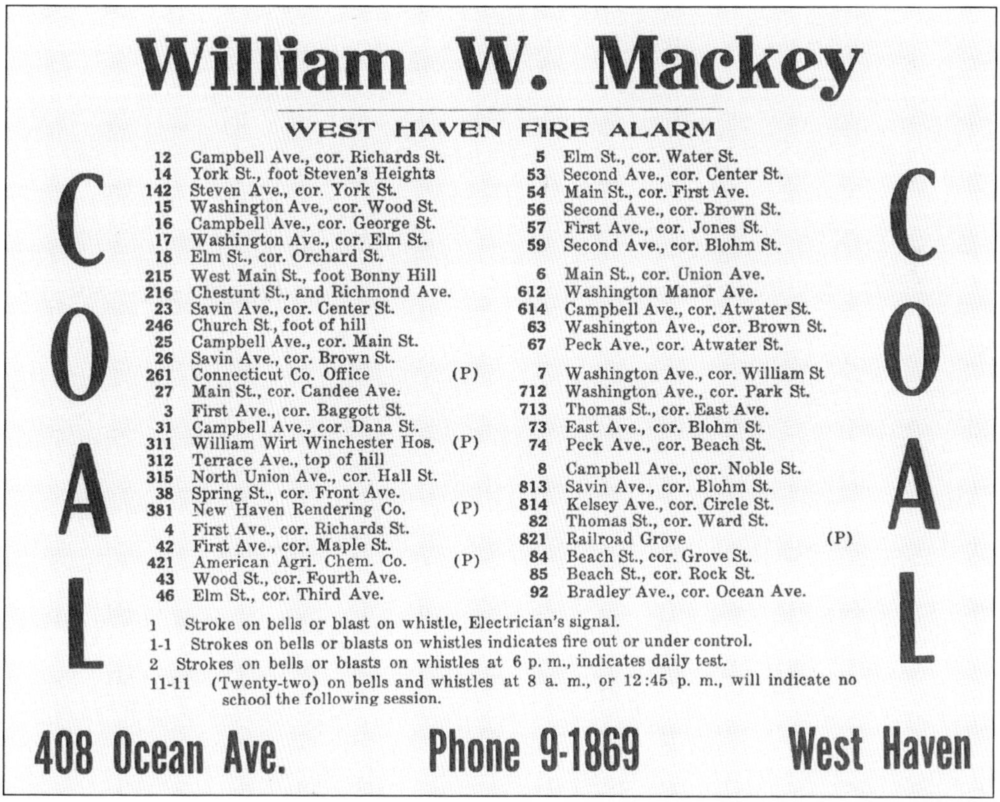

William W. Mackey

WEST HAVEN FIRE ALARM

COAL

12	Campbell Ave., cor. Richards St.	5	Elm St., cor. Water St.
14	York St., foot Steven's Heights	53	Second Ave., cor. Center St.
142	Steven Ave., cor. York St.	54	Main St., cor. First Ave.
15	Washington Ave., cor. Wood St.	56	Second Ave., cor. Brown St.
16	Campbell Ave., cor. George St.	57	First Ave., cor. Jones St.
17	Washington Ave., cor. Elm St.	59	Second Ave., cor. Blohm St.
18	Elm St., cor. Orchard St.		
215	West Main St., foot Bonny Hill	6	Main St., cor. Union Ave.
216	Chestunt St., and Richmond Ave.	612	Washington Manor Ave.
23	Savin Ave., cor. Center St.	614	Campbell Ave., cor. Atwater St.
246	Church St., foot of hill	63	Washington Ave., cor. Brown St.
25	Campbell Ave., cor. Main St.	67	Peck Ave., cor. Atwater St.
26	Savin Ave., cor. Brown St.		
261	Connecticut Co. Office (P)	7	Washington Ave., cor. William St
27	Main St., cor. Candee Ave.	712	Washington Ave., cor. Park St.
3	First Ave., cor. Baggott St.	713	Thomas St., cor. East Ave.
31	Campbell Ave., cor. Dana St.	73	East Ave., cor. Blohm St.
311	William Wirt Winchester Hos. (P)	74	Peck Ave., cor. Beach St.
312	Terrace Ave., top of hill		
315	North Union Ave., cor. Hall St.	8	Campbell Ave., cor. Noble St.
38	Spring St., cor. Front Ave.	813	Savin Ave., cor. Blohm St.
381	New Haven Rendering Co. (P)	814	Kelsey Ave., cor. Circle St.
4	First Ave., cor. Richards St.	82	Thomas St., cor. Ward St.
42	First Ave., cor. Maple St.	821	Railroad Grove (P)
421	American Agri. Chem. Co. (P)	84	Beach St., cor. Grove St.
43	Wood St., cor. Fourth Ave.	85	Beach St., cor. Rock St.
46	Elm St., cor. Third Ave.	92	Bradley Ave., cor. Ocean Ave.

1 Stroke on bells or blast on whistle, Electrician's signal.
1-1 Strokes on bells or blasts on whistles indicates fire out or under control.
2 Strokes on bells or blasts on whistles at 6 p. m., indicates daily test.
11-11 (Twenty-two) on bells and whistles at 8 a. m., or 12:45 p. m., will indicate no school the following session.

COAL

408 Ocean Ave. Phone 9-1869 West Haven

Mackey's window card did double duty, as it listed the alerts for various fires and firefighters.

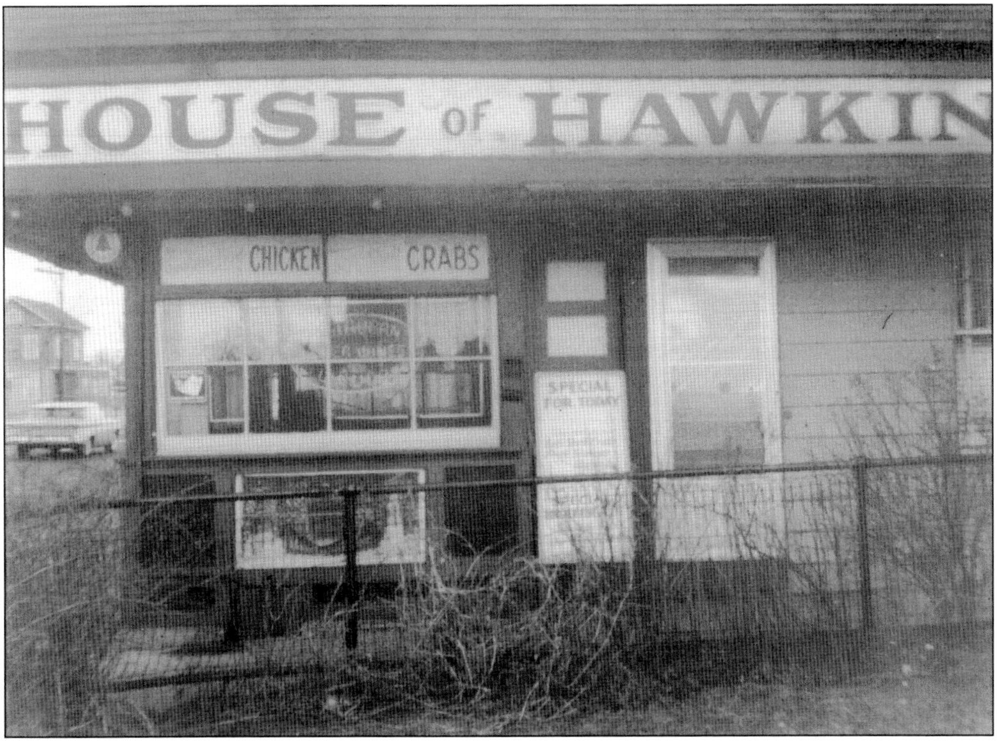

The House of Hawkins, located at 372 Beach Street, was one of the busiest hotels and restaurants in Savin Rock.

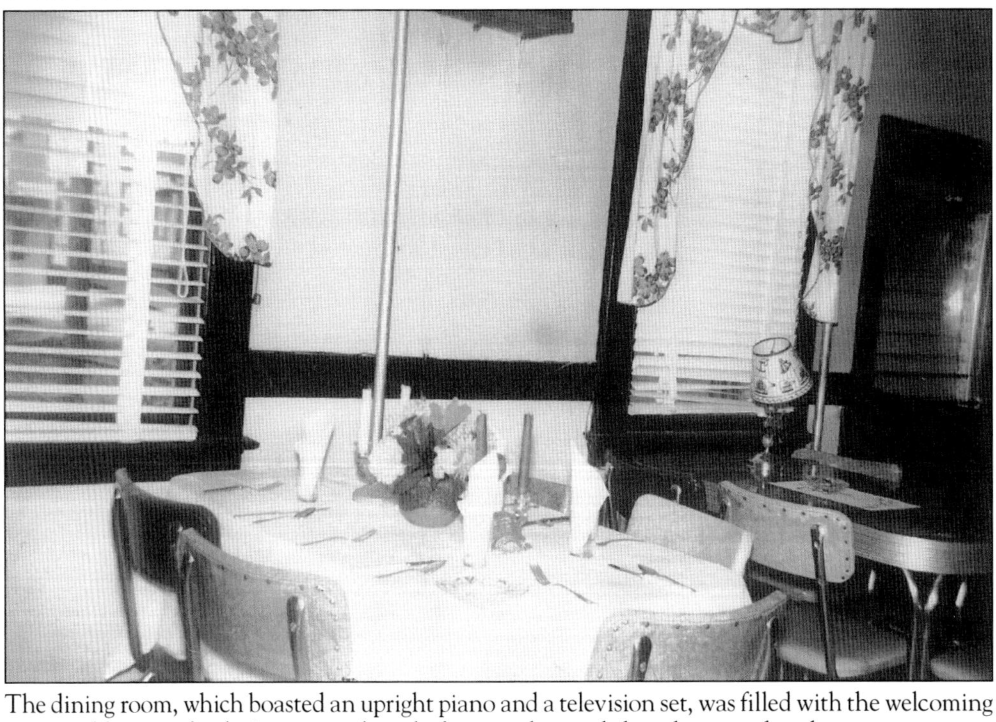

The dining room, which boasted an upright piano and a television set, was filled with the welcoming aroma of favorite foods. It was not long before word spread that this was the place to visit.

Taking a moment to sit at the side entrance to the hotel and restaurant bearing their name are proud proprietors Mary and James Hawkins. The lodging and dining room are still remembered today.

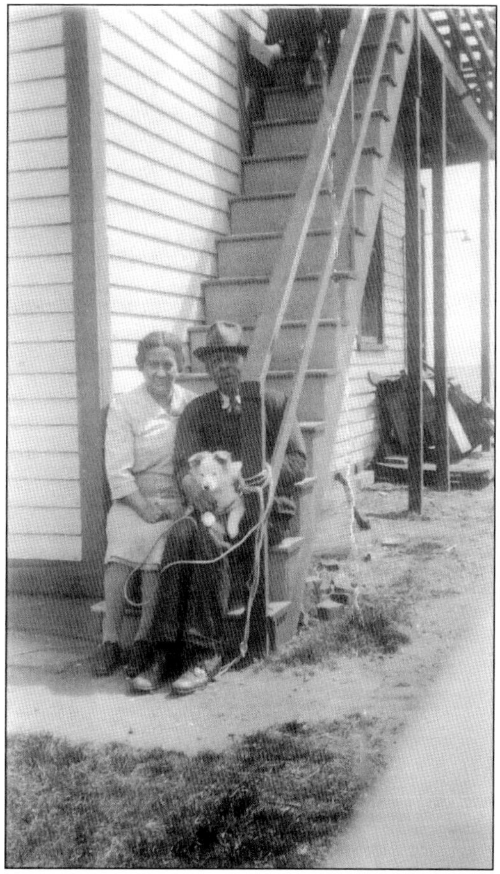

James and Mary Hawkins (far left) joined the Duarte family for a special celebration in the dining room of their establishment, the House of Hawkins.

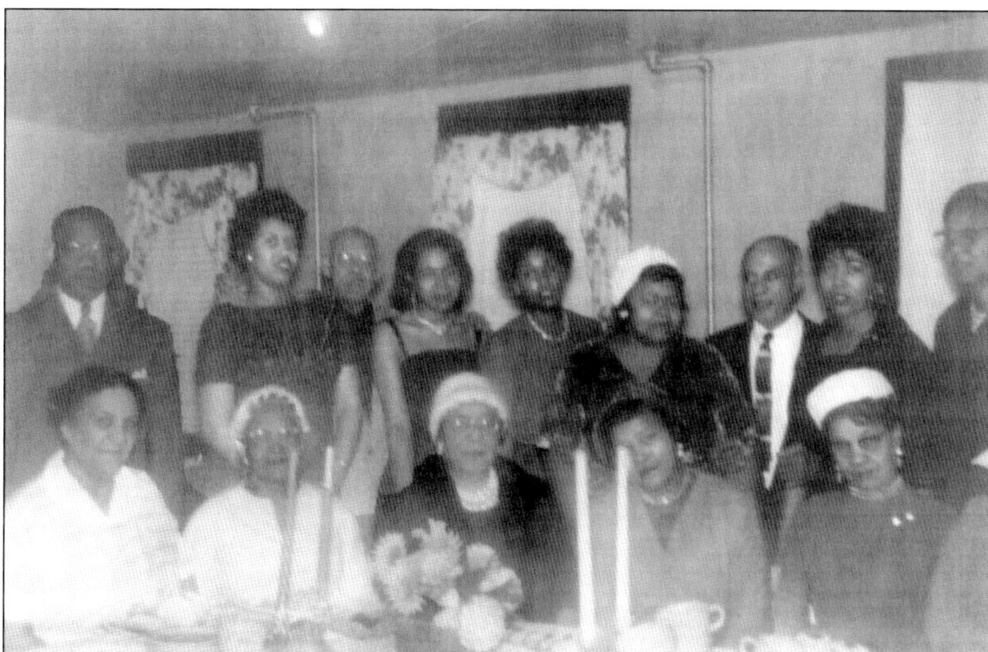

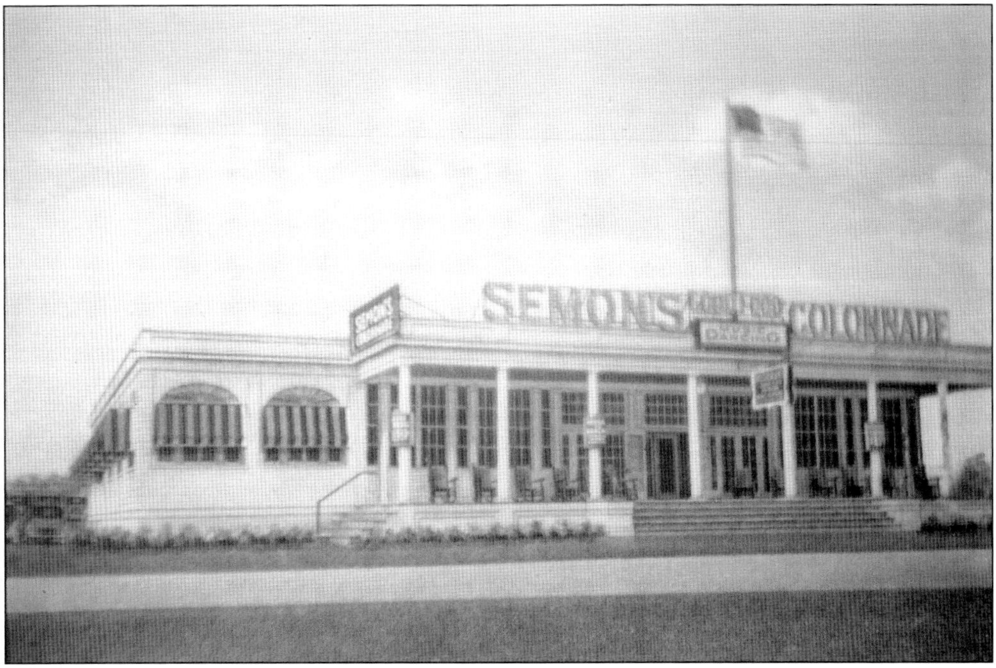

Semon's Colonnade offered food and entertainment. Large, and sometimes rowdy, crowds of university students were known to be a bit disruptive, as was noted when Victor Borge appeared there for an evening. Borge expected the respect of the dinner crowd, but found a more nightclub-like atmosphere. It is said that he soon left the area for Hollywood, appearing not long after in a Frank Sinatra movie.

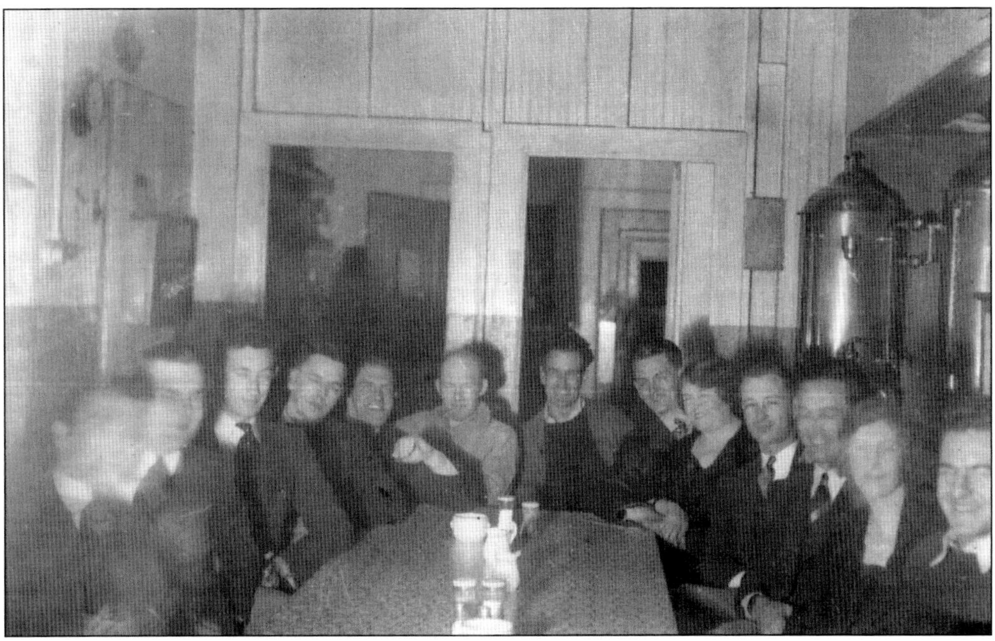

Yale students and their dates enjoyed motoring or taking the open trolley to Savin Rock.

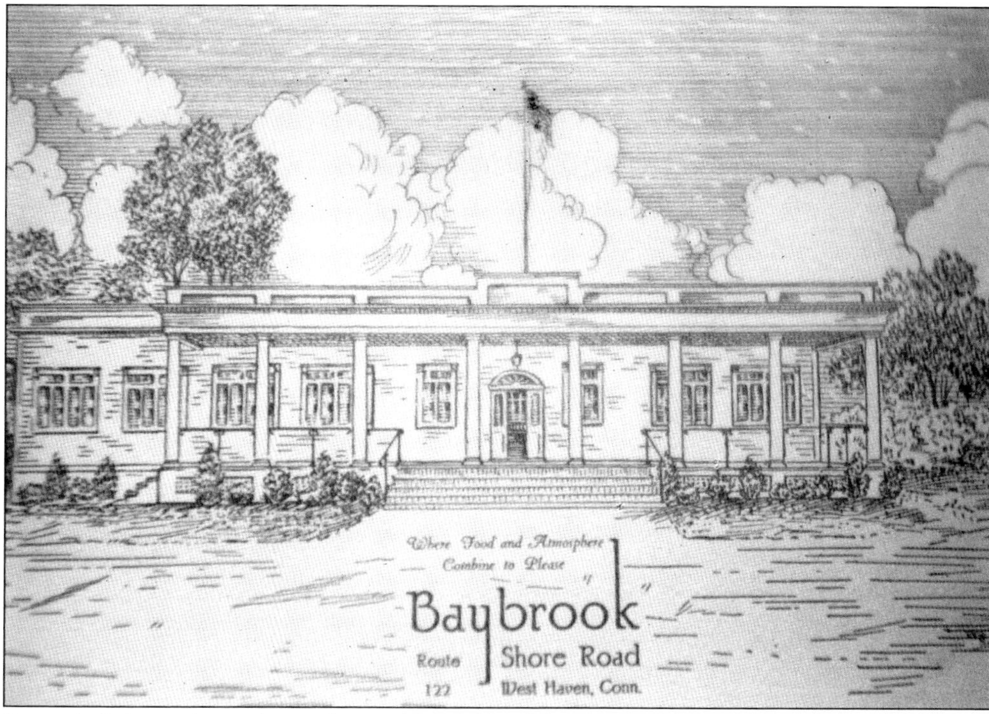

Semon's Colonnade was located near the mouth of the Oyster River and was renamed Baybrook Colonnade when the building came under new ownership.

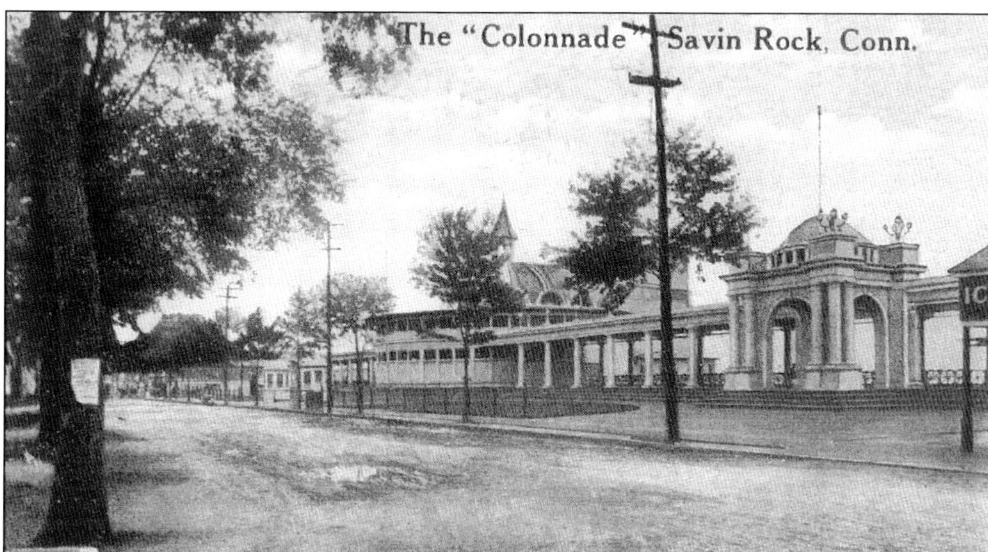

The charm and beauty of the original Colonnade at Savin Rock was timeless.

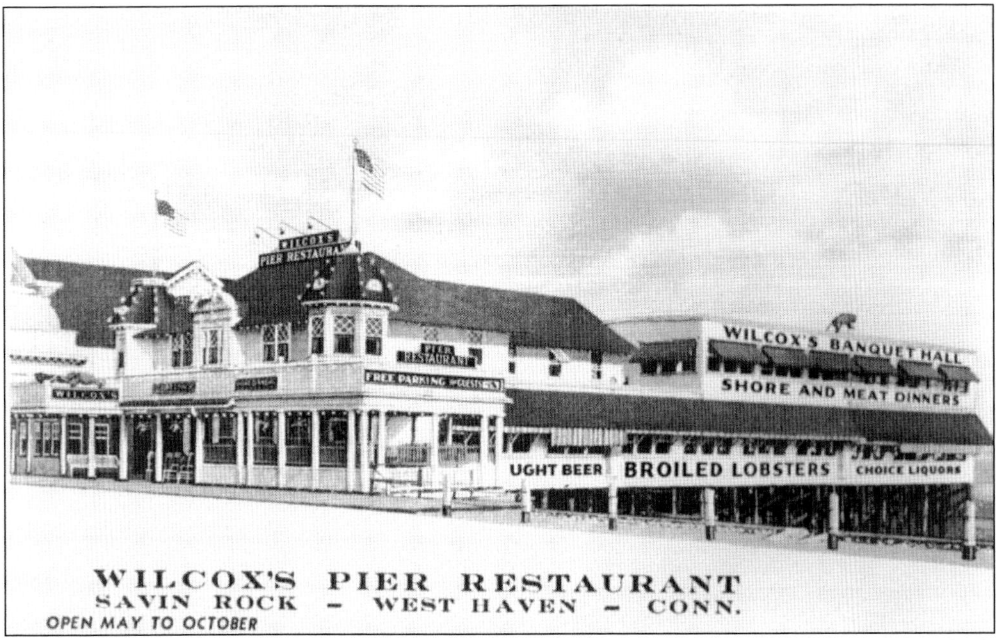

One of the longest-lasting, best-remembered dining rooms was in Wilcox's Pier Restaurant, which served fine food to the public and to private groups.

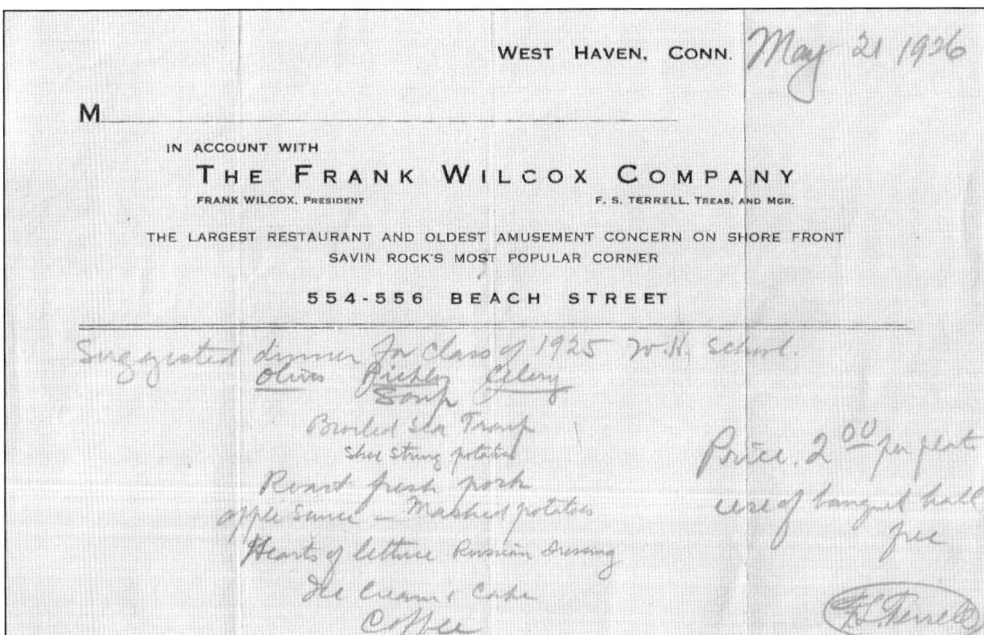

WEST HAVEN, CONN. May 21 1926

M

IN ACCOUNT WITH

THE FRANK WILCOX COMPANY

FRANK WILCOX, PRESIDENT F. S. TERRELL, TREAS. AND MGR.

THE LARGEST RESTAURANT AND OLDEST AMUSEMENT CONCERN ON SHORE FRONT

SAVIN ROCK'S MOST POPULAR CORNER

554-556 BEACH STREET

Suggested dinner for class of 1925 W.H. School.

Olives Pickles Celery

Soup

Broiled Sea Trout

Shoe string potatoes

Roast fresh pork

apple sauce — Mashed potatoes

Hearts of lettuce Russian dressing

Ice Cream & Cake

Coffee

Price, 2.00 per plate

use of banquet hall free

F. S. Terrell

Wilcox's Pier was the gathering place for the West Haven High School class of 1925. The suggested dinner menu included crudités, soup, a choice of broiled sea trout with shoestring potatoes or roast fresh pork with mashed potatoes and applesauce, hearts of lettuce with Russian dressing, ice cream and cake, and coffee. The banquet hall was free, and the cost was $2 per plate (per person).

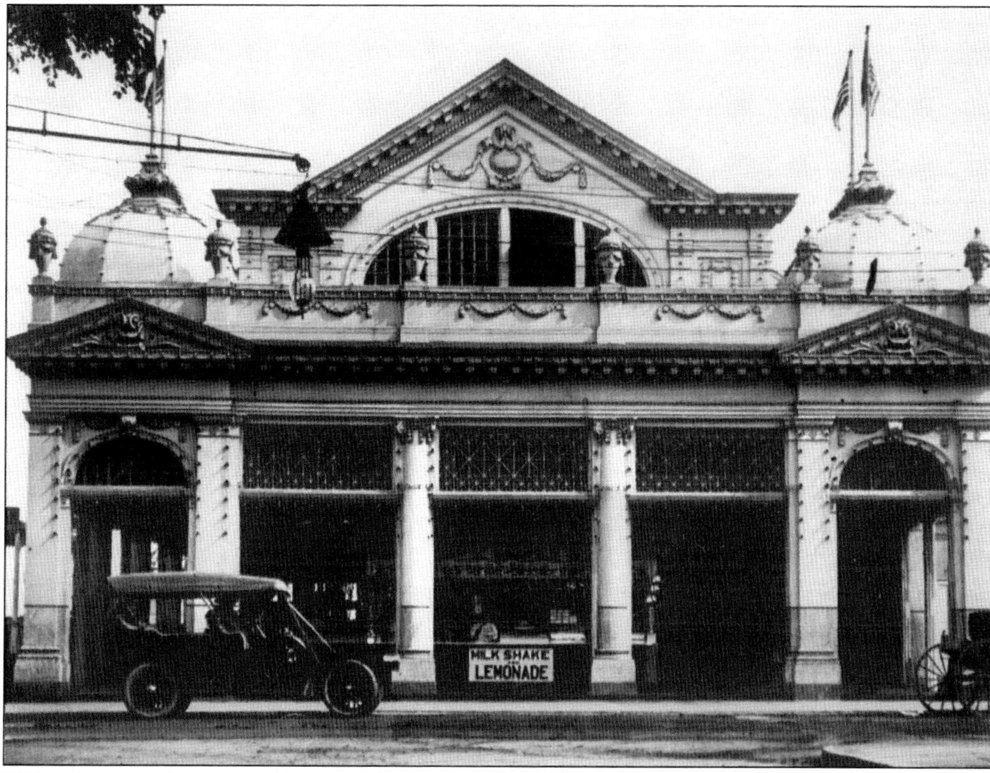

Wilcox's magnificence and size can be seen in this older image.

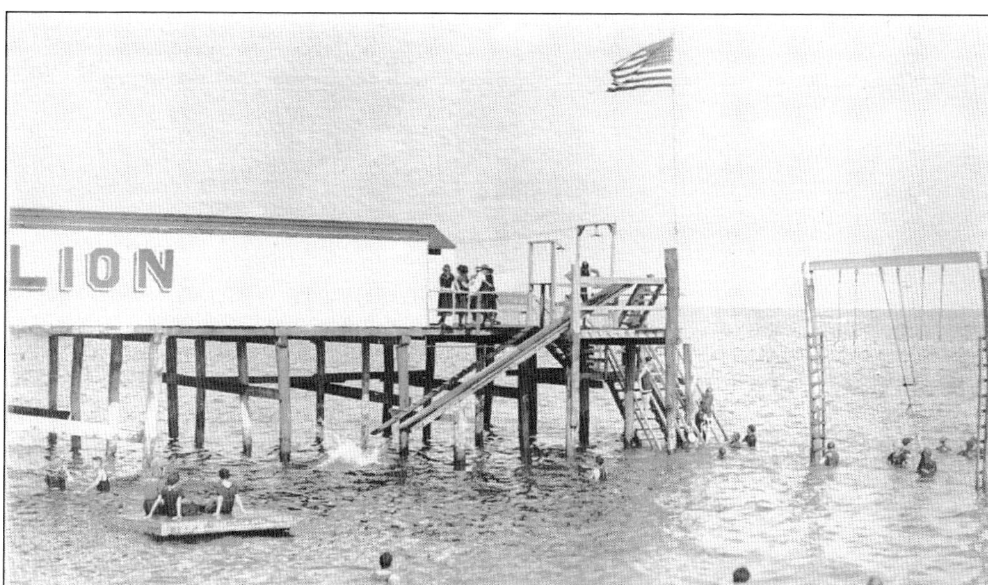

Bathers enjoyed the beach and cabanas adjacent to Wilcox's Pier.

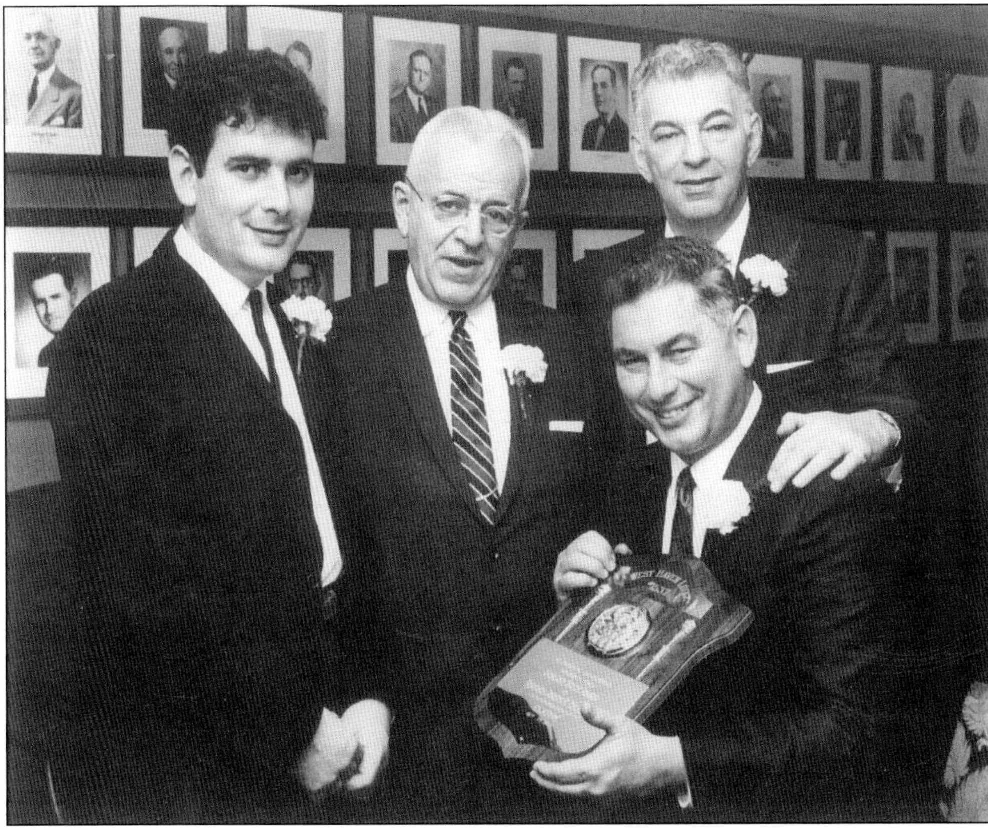

The 1950s were good to young men going into their own or their families' businesses. Entrepreneur Joseph "Chick" Celentano (holding plaque) was recognized by a local lodge for his efforts. Chick's uncle, Dr. Luca Celentano (second from left), looks on admiringly.

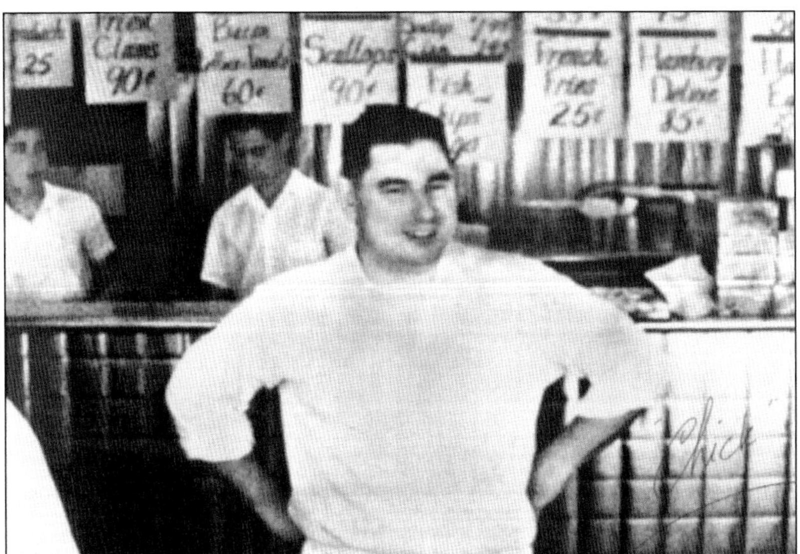

Chick owned his own hot dog emporium at an early age. The days were long and the lines longer as bathers, park goers, and racetrack fans waited for their tasty hot dogs, onion rings, and fries—all probably about $1 with a drink.

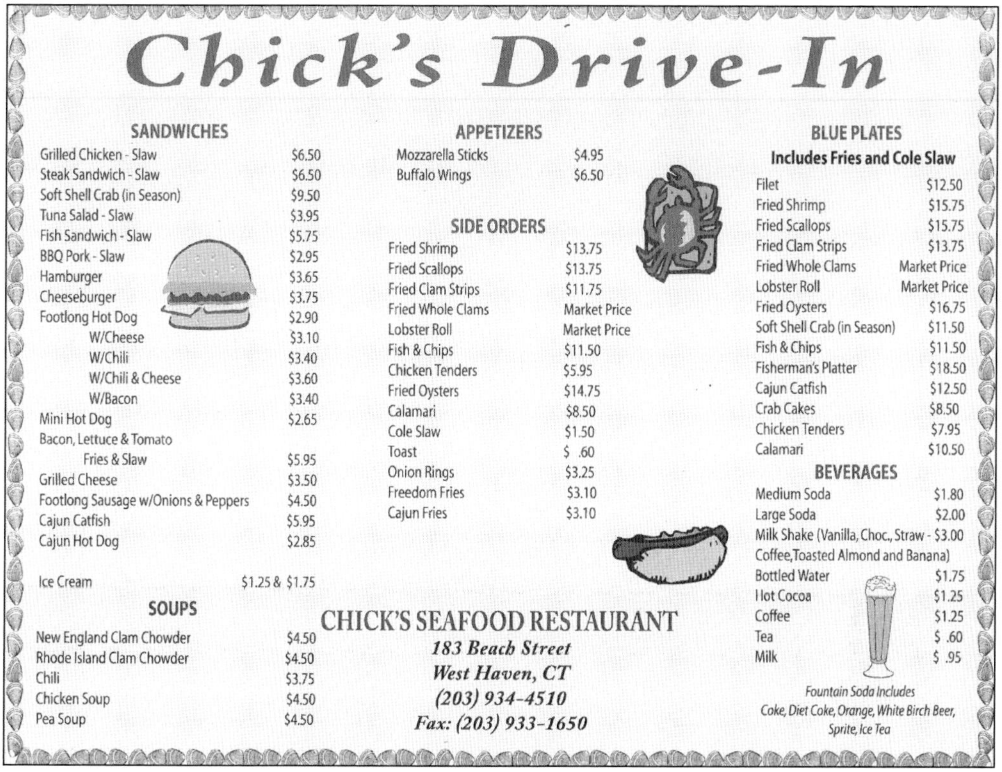

Chick's Drive-In

SANDWICHES

Grilled Chicken - Slaw	$6.50
Steak Sandwich - Slaw	$6.50
Soft Shell Crab (in Season)	$9.50
Tuna Salad - Slaw	$3.95
Fish Sandwich - Slaw	$5.75
BBQ Pork - Slaw	$2.95
Hamburger	$3.65
Cheeseburger	$3.75
Footlong Hot Dog	$2.90
W/Cheese	$3.10
W/Chili	$3.40
W/Chili & Cheese	$3.60
W/Bacon	$3.40
Mini Hot Dog	$2.65
Bacon, Lettuce & Tomato Fries & Slaw	$5.95
Grilled Cheese	$3.50
Footlong Sausage w/Onions & Peppers	$4.50
Cajun Catfish	$5.95
Cajun Hot Dog	$2.85
Ice Cream	$1.25 & $1.75

SOUPS

New England Clam Chowder	$4.50
Rhode Island Clam Chowder	$4.50
Chili	$3.75
Chicken Soup	$4.50
Pea Soup	$4.50

APPETIZERS

Mozzarella Sticks	$4.95
Buffalo Wings	$6.50

SIDE ORDERS

Fried Shrimp	$13.75
Fried Scallops	$13.75
Fried Clam Strips	$11.75
Fried Whole Clams	Market Price
Lobster Roll	Market Price
Fish & Chips	$11.50
Chicken Tenders	$5.95
Fried Oysters	$14.75
Calamari	$8.50
Cole Slaw	$1.50
Toast	$ .60
Onion Rings	$3.25
Freedom Fries	$3.10
Cajun Fries	$3.10

CHICK'S SEAFOOD RESTAURANT
183 Beach Street
West Haven, CT
(203) 934-4510
Fax: (203) 933-1650

BLUE PLATES
Includes Fries and Cole Slaw

Filet	$12.50
Fried Shrimp	$15.75
Fried Scallops	$15.75
Fried Clam Strips	$13.75
Fried Whole Clams	Market Price
Lobster Roll	Market Price
Fried Oysters	$16.75
Soft Shell Crab (in Season)	$11.50
Fish & Chips	$11.50
Fisherman's Platter	$18.50
Cajun Catfish	$12.50
Crab Cakes	$8.50
Chicken Tenders	$7.95
Calamari	$10.50

BEVERAGES

Medium Soda	$1.80
Large Soda	$2.00
Milk Shake (Vanilla, Choc., Straw - Coffee, Toasted Almond and Banana)	$3.00
Bottled Water	$1.75
Hot Cocoa	$1.25
Coffee	$1.25
Tea	$ .60
Milk	$ .95

Fountain Soda Includes Coke, Diet Coke, Orange, White Birch Beer, Sprite, Ice Tea

Just over 55 years ago, a generous serving of scallops or fried clams cost 90¢, and a hamburger deluxe was just 85¢—making Chick's Drive-In a very busy place. This place mat reflects today's prices.

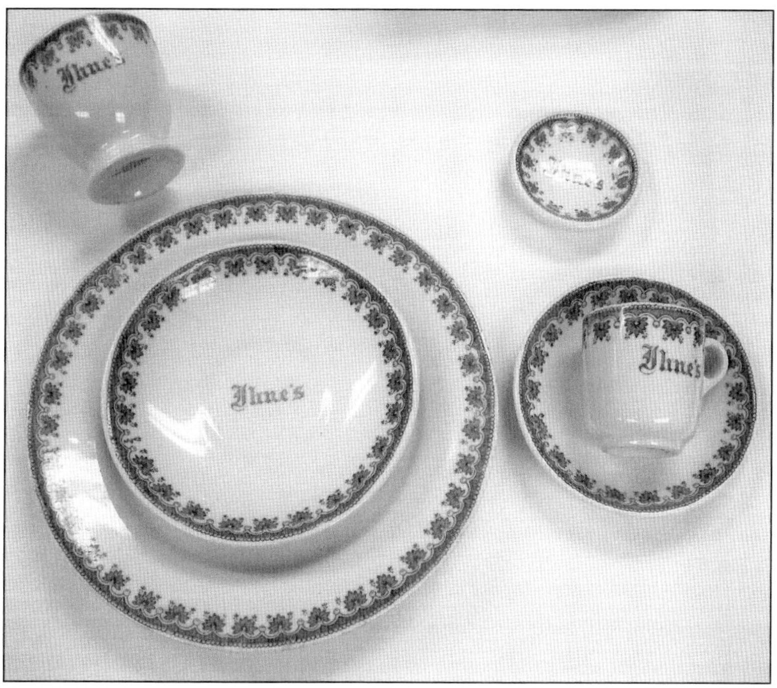

Of all the hotels at Savin Rock, the most recognized was the Victorian Ihne Hotel, with its own china, huge Bavarian bar in the Rathskellar, and wraparound porch.

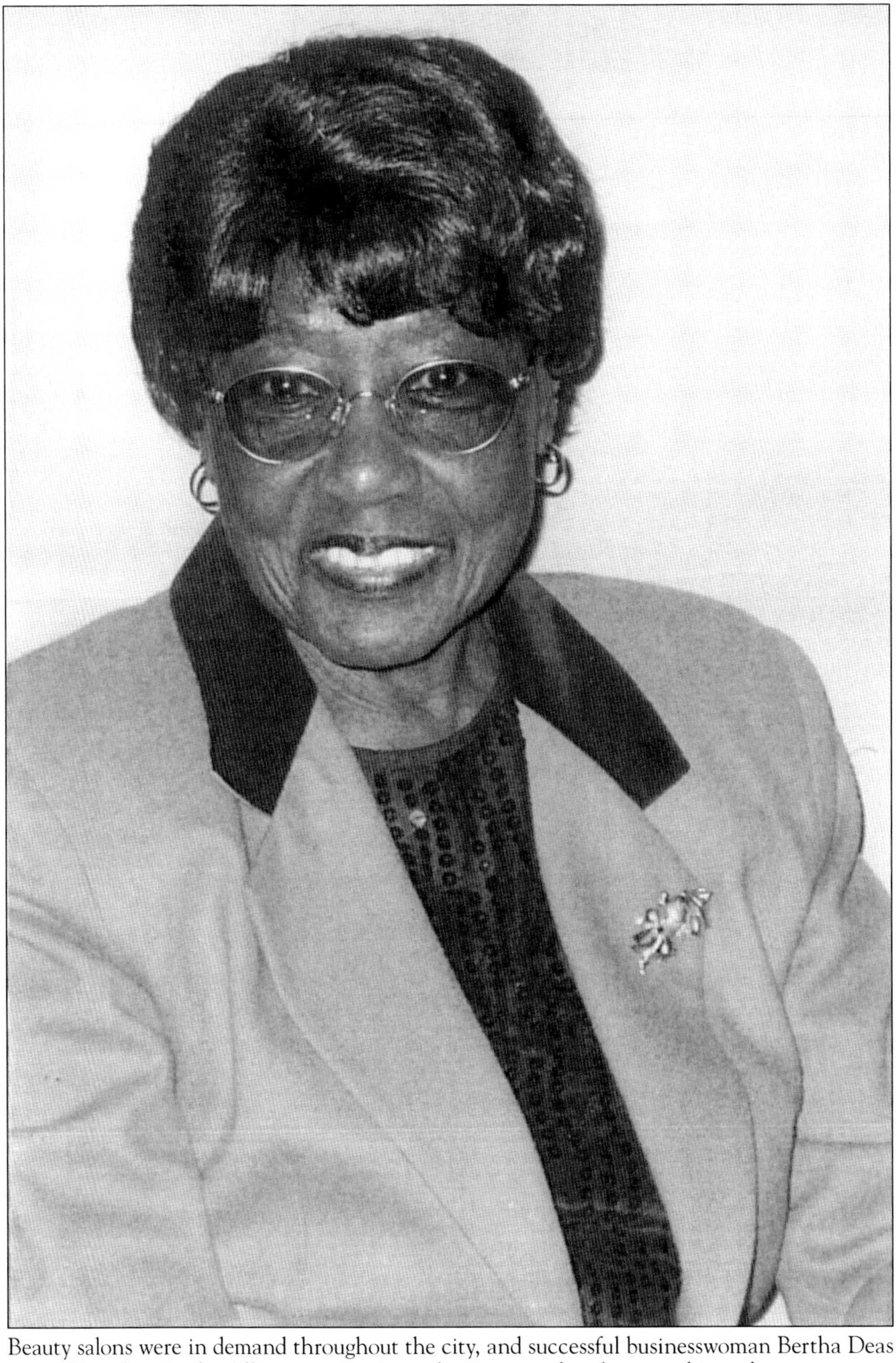

Beauty salons were in demand throughout the city, and successful businesswoman Bertha Deas opened her shop in the Allingtown section only one year after she moved into the area.

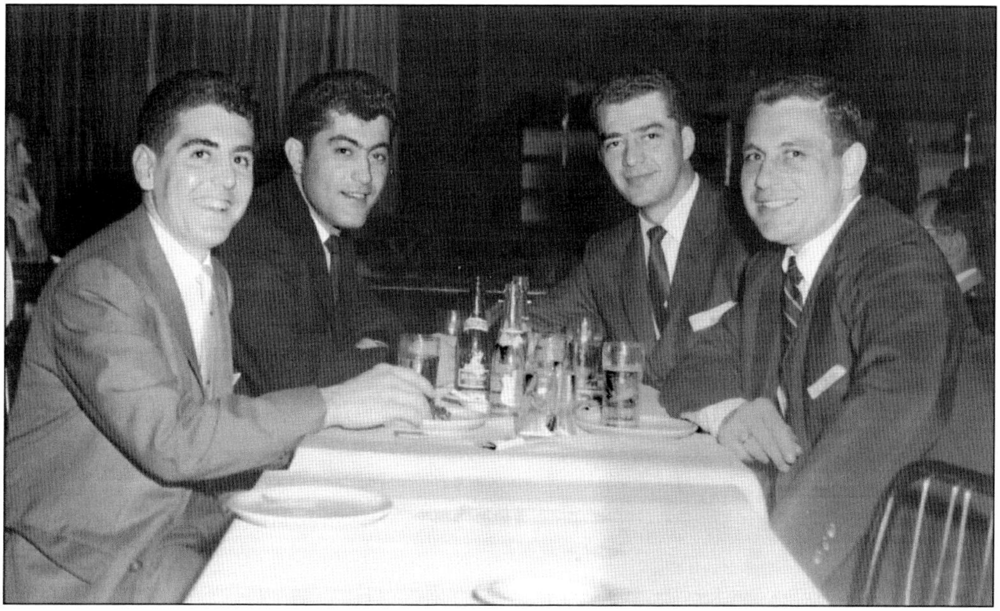

Enjoying a night out at the Hotel Americana in New York in the 19050s are, from left to right, Harold Peschell, Bernie Muro, Frank Consorte, and Larry Rully. Peschell still operates a bakery on Campbell Avenue, and Consorte ran the West End Market at the intersection of Elm Street and Wagner Place until a few years ago.

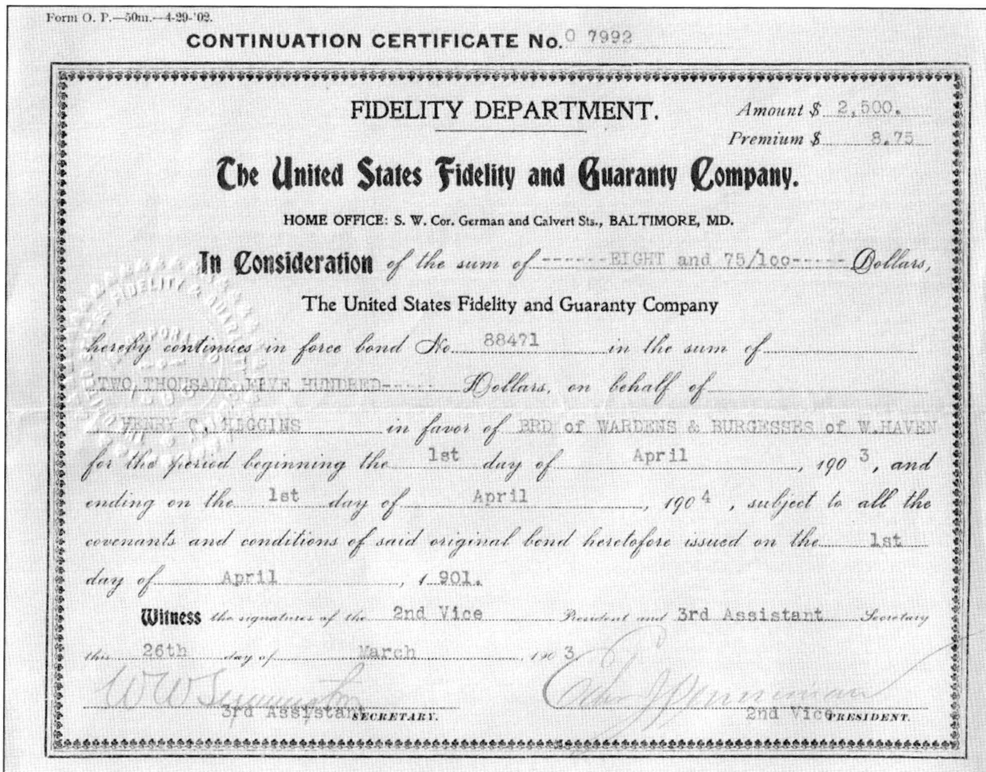

Form O. P.—50m.—4-29-'02.

CONTINUATION CERTIFICATE No. 0 7992

FIDELITY DEPARTMENT.

Amount $ 2,500.
Premium $ 8.75

The United States Fidelity and Guaranty Company.

HOME OFFICE: S. W. Cor. German and Calvert Sts., BALTIMORE, MD.

In Consideration of the sum of ------EIGHT and 75/100----- Dollars, The United States Fidelity and Guaranty Company hereby continues in force bond No. 88471 in the sum of TWO THOUSAND FIVE HUNDRED----- Dollars, on behalf of HENRY C. HIGGINS in favor of BRD of WARDENS & BURGESSES of W.HAVEN for the period beginning the 1st day of April, 1903, and ending on the 1st day of April, 1904, subject to all the covenants and conditions of said original bond heretofore issued on the 1st day of April, 1901.

Witness the signatures of the 2nd Vice President and 3rd Assistant Secretary this 26th day of March, 1903.

3rd Assistant SECRETARY.

2nd Vice PRESIDENT.

These surety bonds were kept with essential deeds and town records.

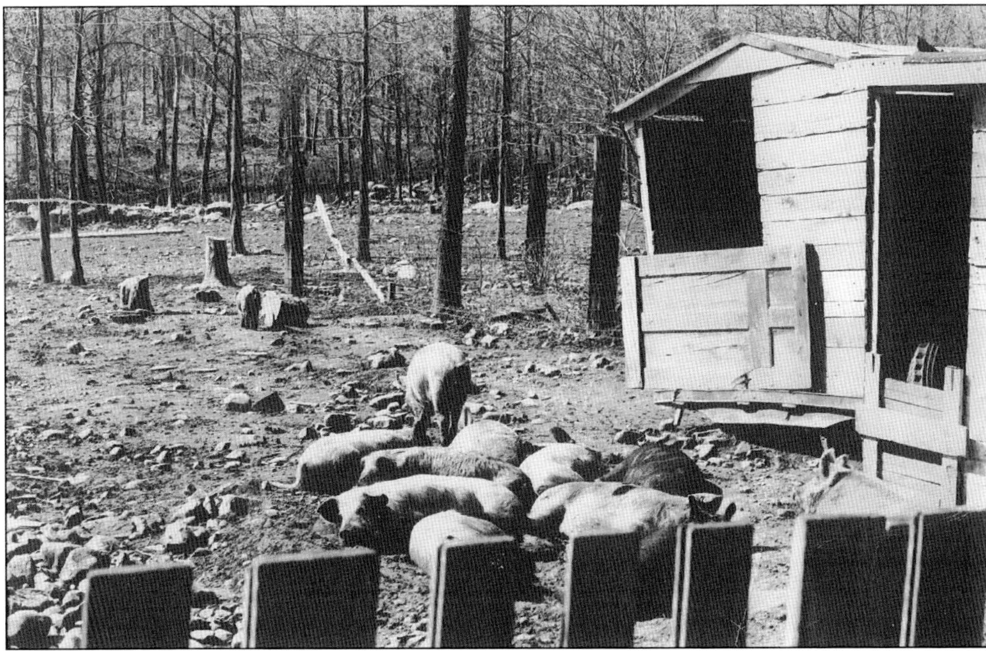

Before the days of trash pickup and garbage disposals, pig farmers collected kitchen scraps to feed their animals. The Rully pig farm on Morgan Lane was sold to Miles Laboratories (later Bayer).

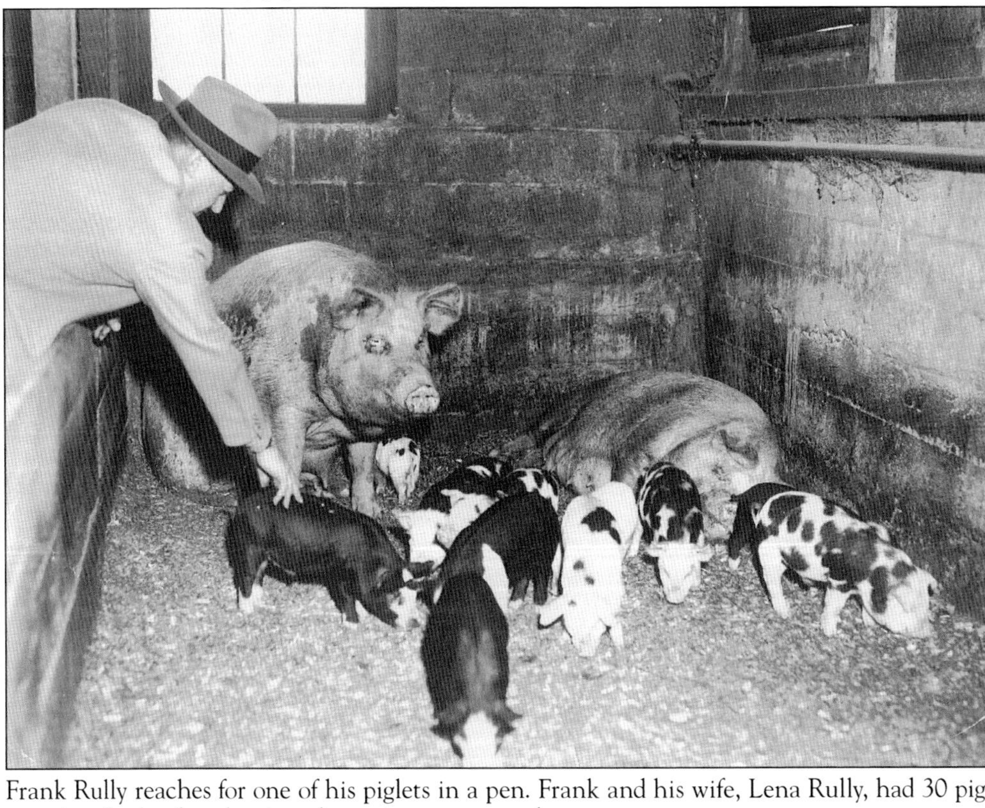

Frank Rully reaches for one of his piglets in a pen. Frank and his wife, Lena Rully, had 30 pigs roaming the land at the time these pictures were taken.

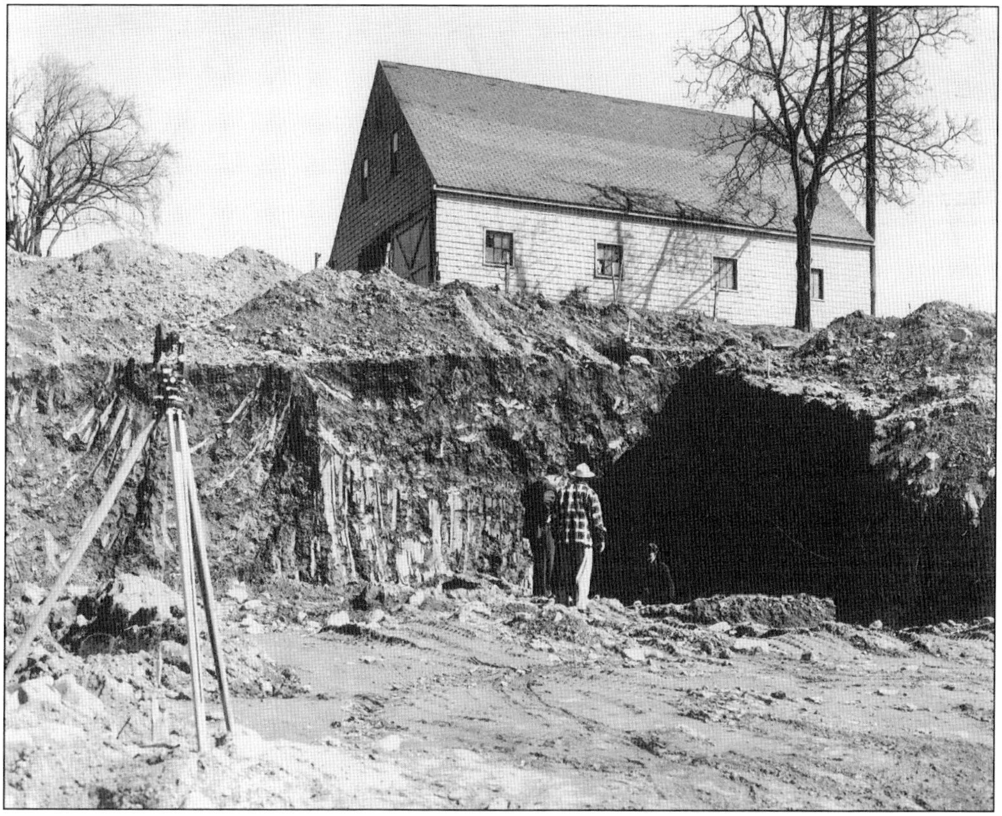

Here Rully oversees an excavation project on his farm.

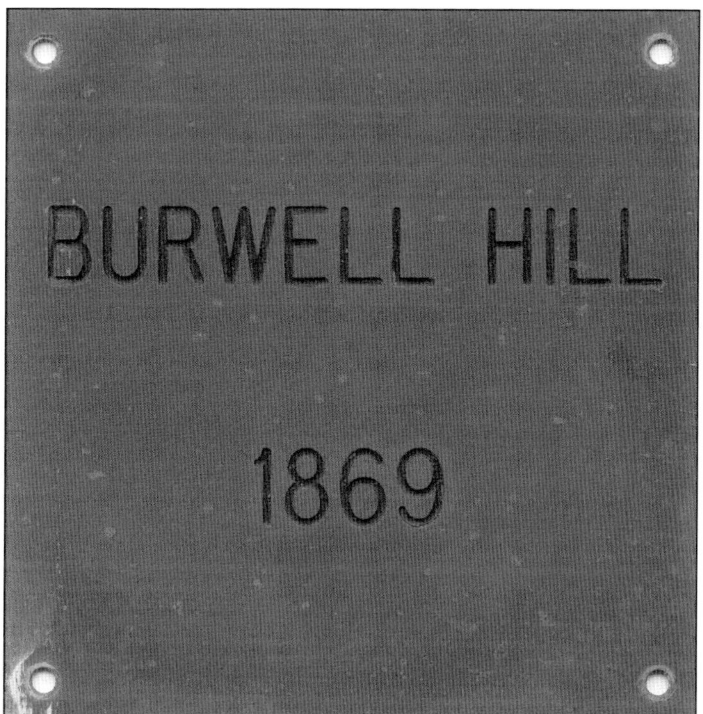

Generations of the Burwell family originally owned up to 120 acres at the highest site in the city. The panoramic view of New Haven and its harbor was unmatched. The family manufactured bar soap around the time of the Civil War.

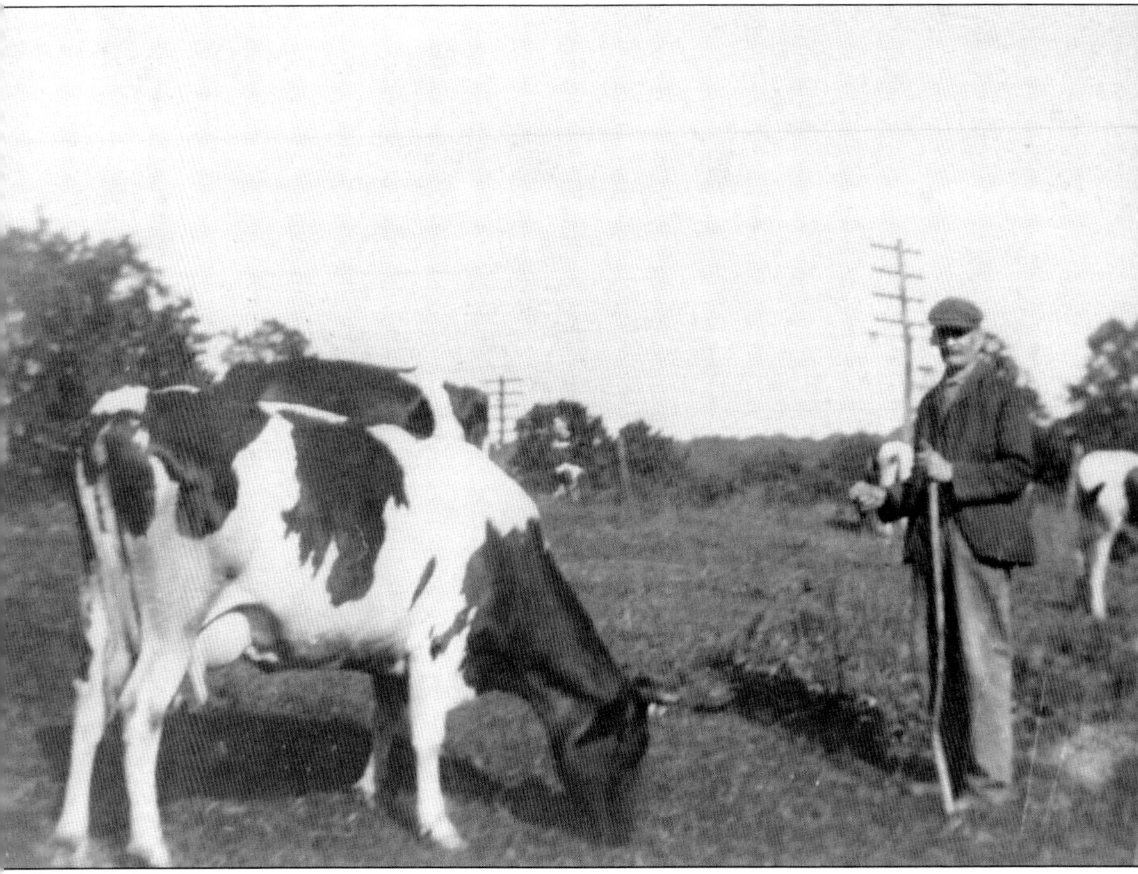

Oak Hill Dairy was located on Church Street within a block of the town green. It was not unusual to see Mr. Johnson herding his cattle down Savin Avenue to the fields near Benham Hill. Johnson had a large dairy and several horses, which were well cared for.

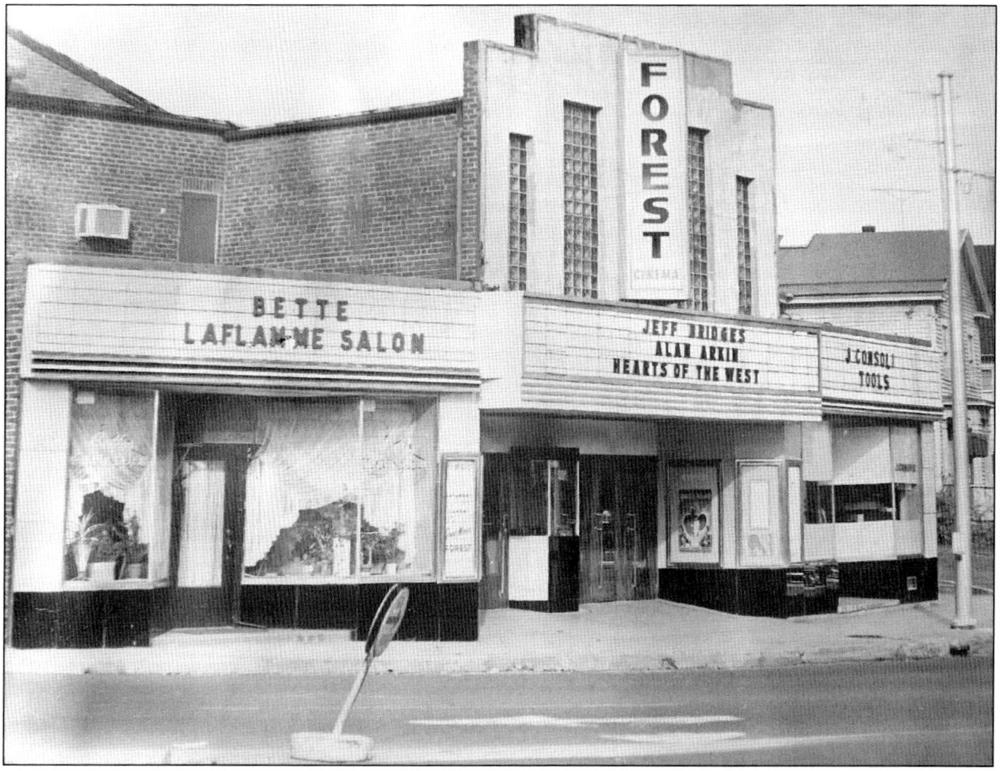

While people tend to romanticize movie theaters, they must realize that these were businesses. Large movie houses could accommodate 1,000 to 2,500 people for two or three performances in the days before television. West Haven boasted two theaters downtown and two in Allingtown, plus those at Savin Rock Amusement Park. The Forest Theatre was among the most popular and was family owned and operated until it closed almost 10 years ago.

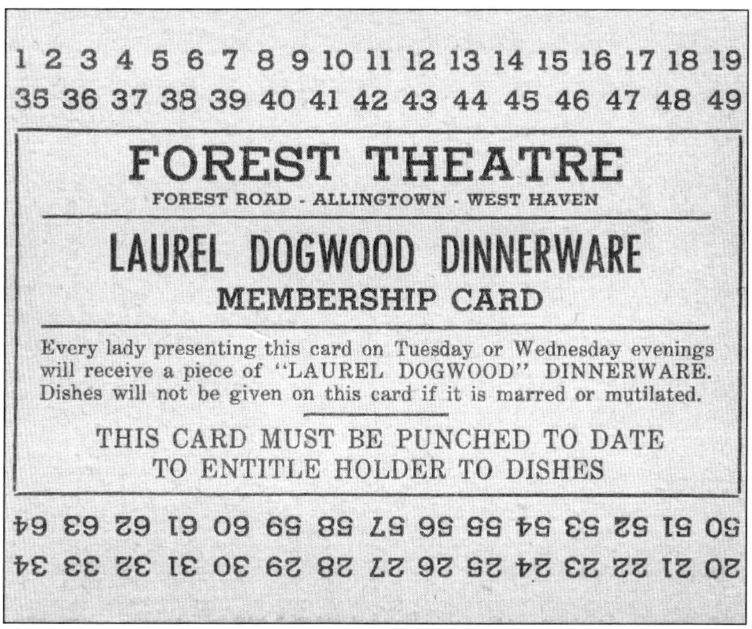
1 2 3 4 5 6 7 8 9 10 11 12 13 14 15 16 17 18 19
35 36 37 38 39 40 41 42 43 44 45 46 47 48 49

FOREST THEATRE

FOREST ROAD - ALLINGTOWN - WEST HAVEN

LAUREL DOGWOOD DINNERWARE

MEMBERSHIP CARD

Every lady presenting this card on Tuesday or Wednesday evenings will receive a piece of "LAUREL DOGWOOD" DINNERWARE. Dishes will not be given on this card if it is marred or mutilated.

THIS CARD MUST BE PUNCHED TO DATE
TO ENTITLE HOLDER TO DISHES

50 51 52 53 54 55 56 57 58 59 60 61 62 63 64
20 21 22 23 24 25 26 27 28 29 30 31 32 33 34

Tuesdays and Wednesdays were "dish days" at the Forest Theatre. For 25¢, moviegoers could see a double feature, a newsreel, previews, and a cartoon, plus receive the week's feature piece of Homer Laughlin china. Cards would be punched each week, and it could take anywhere from six months to a year to collect eight 5-piece place settings.

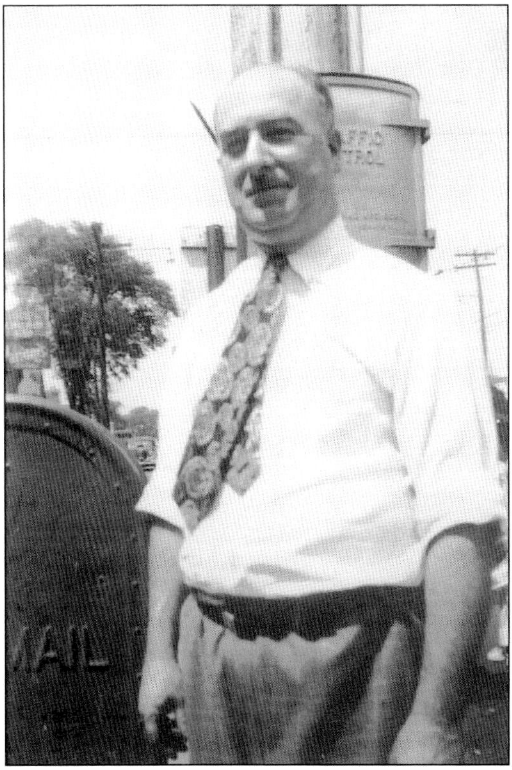

Pharmacists were well respected and well educated members of the community, knowing their customers and their medical histories, dispensing drugs and advice, and sometimes just providing a shoulder to lean on. Eugene "Gene" Anquillare was a familiar figure at Liggett's Pharmacy on Campbell Avenue, within a block of Silver's and three short blocks from Mayer's. (Author's collection.)

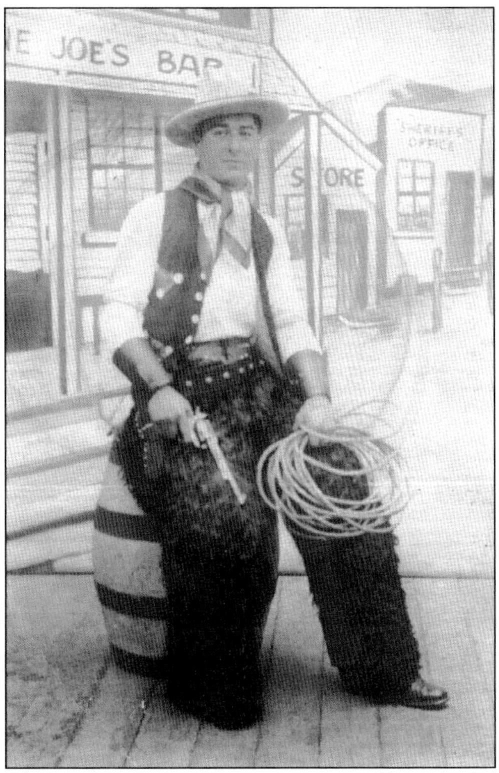

Anquillare and his college friends often went to Savin Rock in the 1920s, enjoying rides, the beach, and, in this case, the chance to don a costume to have postcards made. (Author's collection.)

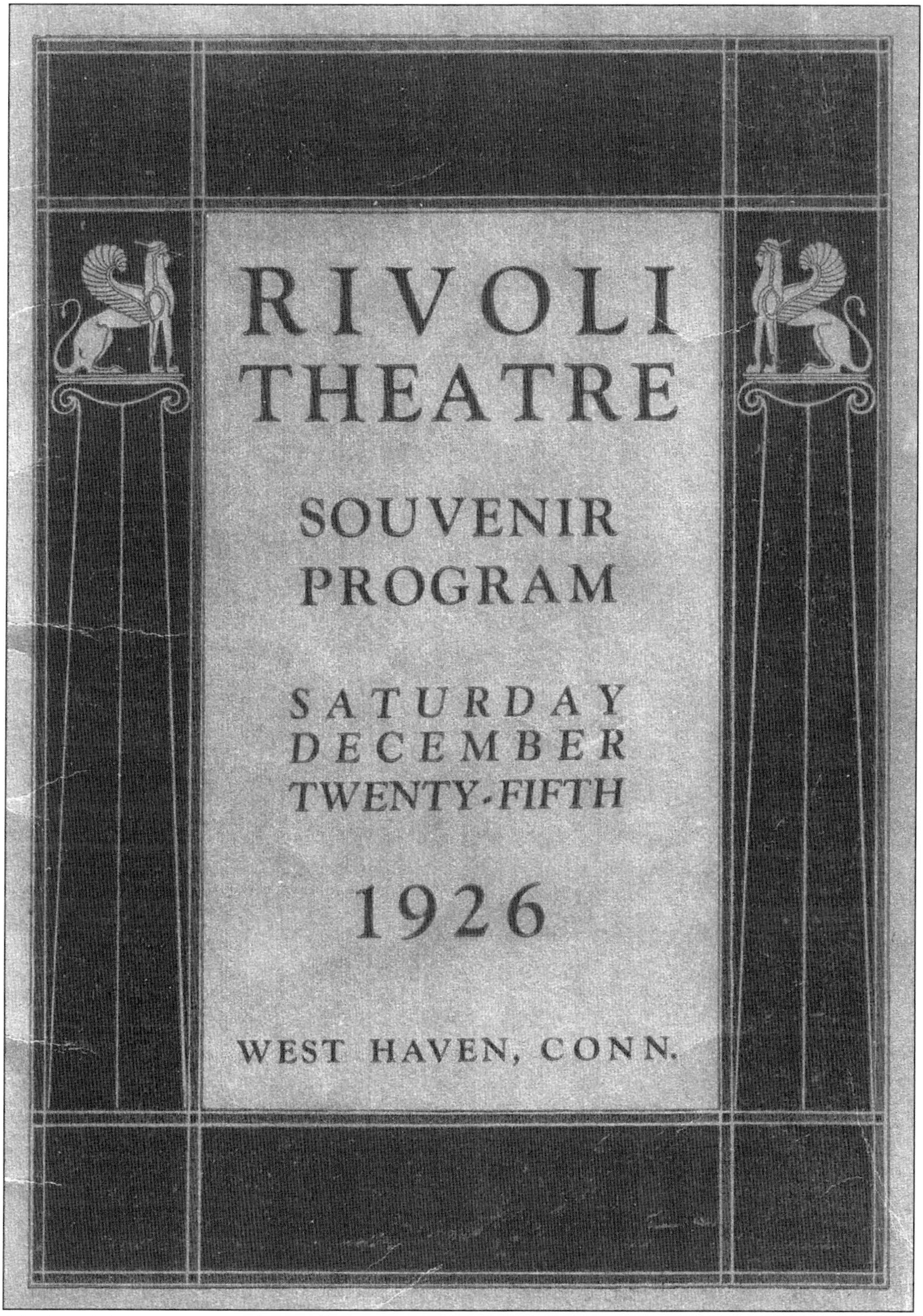

The Rivoli Theatre opened on Christmas Day 1926, the beginning of a week of different double features and top films each day. The elegant gold and navy souvenir program had an art deco motif and featured photographs of the stars. Management promised the best movies they could buy, the best features, and special attractions to help "ease these strenuous days."

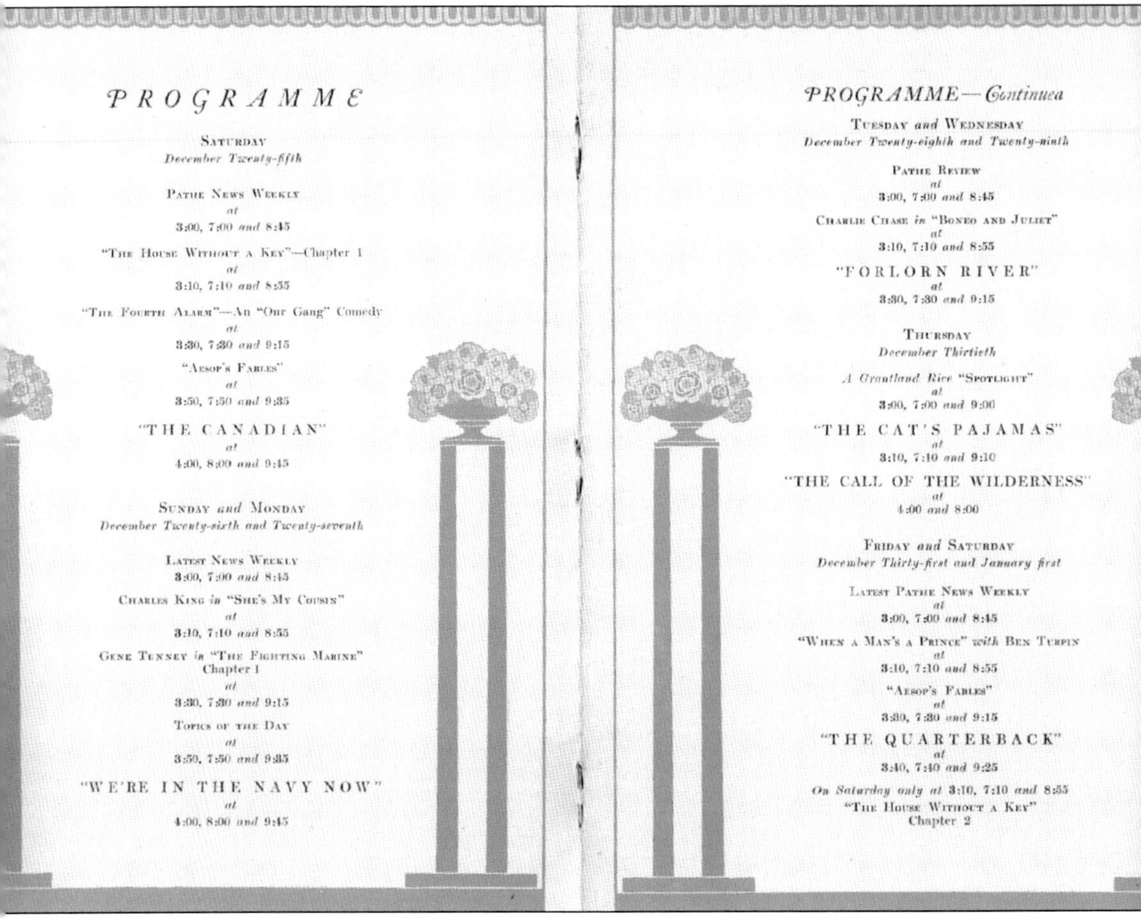

PROGRAMME

SATURDAY
December Twenty-fifth

PATHE NEWS WEEKLY
at
3:00, 7:00 *and* 8:45

"THE HOUSE WITHOUT A KEY"—Chapter 1
at
3:10, 7:10 *and* 8:55

"THE FOURTH ALARM"—An "Our Gang" Comedy
at
3:30, 7:30 *and* 9:15

"AESOP'S FABLES"
at
3:50, 7:50 *and* 9:35

"THE CANADIAN"
at
4:00, 8:00 *and* 9:45

SUNDAY *and* MONDAY
December Twenty-sixth and Twenty-seventh

LATEST NEWS WEEKLY
3:00, 7:00 *and* 8:45

CHARLES KING *in* "SHE'S MY COUSIN"
at
3:10, 7:10 *and* 8:55

GENE TENNEY *in* "THE FIGHTING MARINE"
Chapter 1
at
3:30, 7:30 *and* 9:15

TOPICS OF THE DAY
at
3:50, 7:50 *and* 9:35

"WE'RE IN THE NAVY NOW"
at
4:00, 8:00 *and* 9:45

PROGRAMME—Continued

TUESDAY *and* WEDNESDAY
December Twenty-eighth and Twenty-ninth

PATHE REVIEW
at
3:00, 7:00 *and* 8:45

CHARLIE CHASE *in* "BONEO AND JULIET"
at
3:10, 7:10 *and* 8:55

"FORLORN RIVER"
at
3:30, 7:30 *and* 9:15

THURSDAY
December Thirtieth

A Grantland Rice "SPOTLIGHT"
at
3:00, 7:00 *and* 9:00

"THE CAT'S PAJAMAS"
at
3:10, 7:10 *and* 9:10

"THE CALL OF THE WILDERNESS"
at
4:00 *and* 8:00

FRIDAY *and* SATURDAY
December Thirty-first and January first

LATEST PATHE NEWS WEEKLY
at
3:00, 7:00 *and* 8:45

"WHEN A MAN'S A PRINCE" *with* BEN TURPIN
at
3:10, 7:10 *and* 8:55

"AESOP'S FABLES"
at
3:30, 7:30 *and* 9:15

"THE QUARTERBACK"
at
3:40, 7:40 *and* 9:25

On Saturday only at 3:10, 7:10 *and* 8:55
"THE HOUSE WITHOUT A KEY"
Chapter 2

The Rivoli Theatre opened with great pomp and circumstance. It was the beginning of the days of the Vaudeville Association, and theaters brought a completely different form of entertainment—one in which film became the focus.

Showing

FRIDAY AND SATURDAY

December Thirty-first and January First

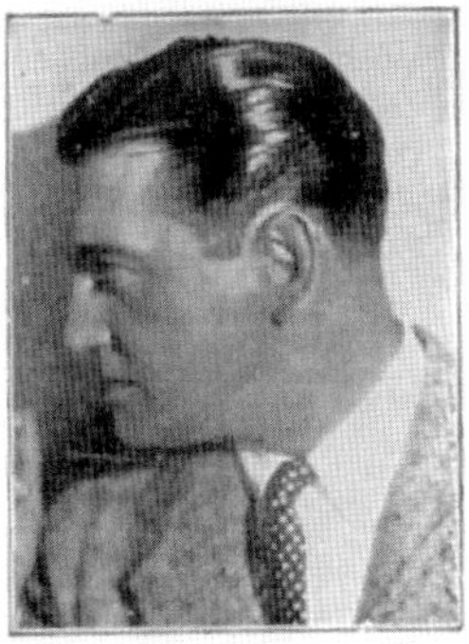

RICHARD DIX

— *in* —

"THE QUARTERBACK"

'ow! Just look at that baby go! He's the fastest-steppin ar on the screen today. And as the smashing, crishing, dash g quarterback, Dix sure does come through gloriously!

THE PLAYERS

Jack Stone	Richard Dix
Louise aMson	Esther Ralston
Elmer Stone	Harry Beresford
'Lumpy' Goggins	David Butler
Denny Walters	Robert W Craig
Nellie Webster	Mona Palma

Showing

SUNDAY AND MONDAY

January Second and Third

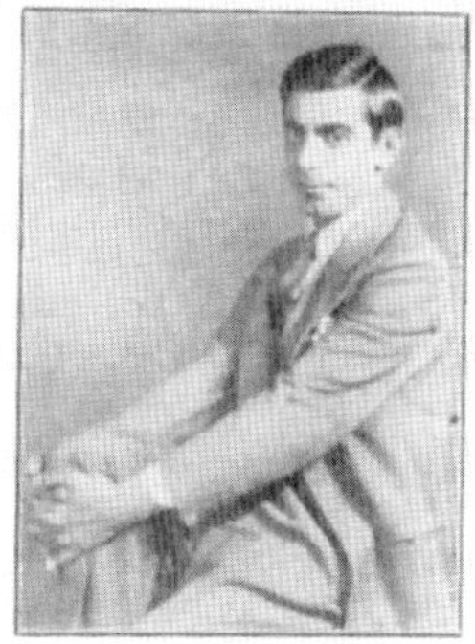

EDDIE CANTOR

— in —

"KID BOOTS"

Ziegfeld girls! Ziegfeld magnificence of gowns and settings! A Ziegfeld personally supervised de luxe picturization of his greatest musical comedy success! The extravaganza that convulsed and dazzled Broadway for over a year.

THE PLAYERS

Kid Boots	Eddie Cantor
Jane Martin	Clara Bow
Polly Pendleton	Billie Dove
Tom Sterling	Lawrence Gray
Carmen Mendoza	Natalie Kingston
George Fitch	Malcolm Waite
Polly's Father	William J. Worthington
Carmen's Lawyer	Harry Von Meter
Tom's Lawyer	Fred Esmelton

Management emphasized the family aspect of its new theater. The newest and best films were introduced, along with groundbreaking newsreels and early Mickey Mouse cartoons.

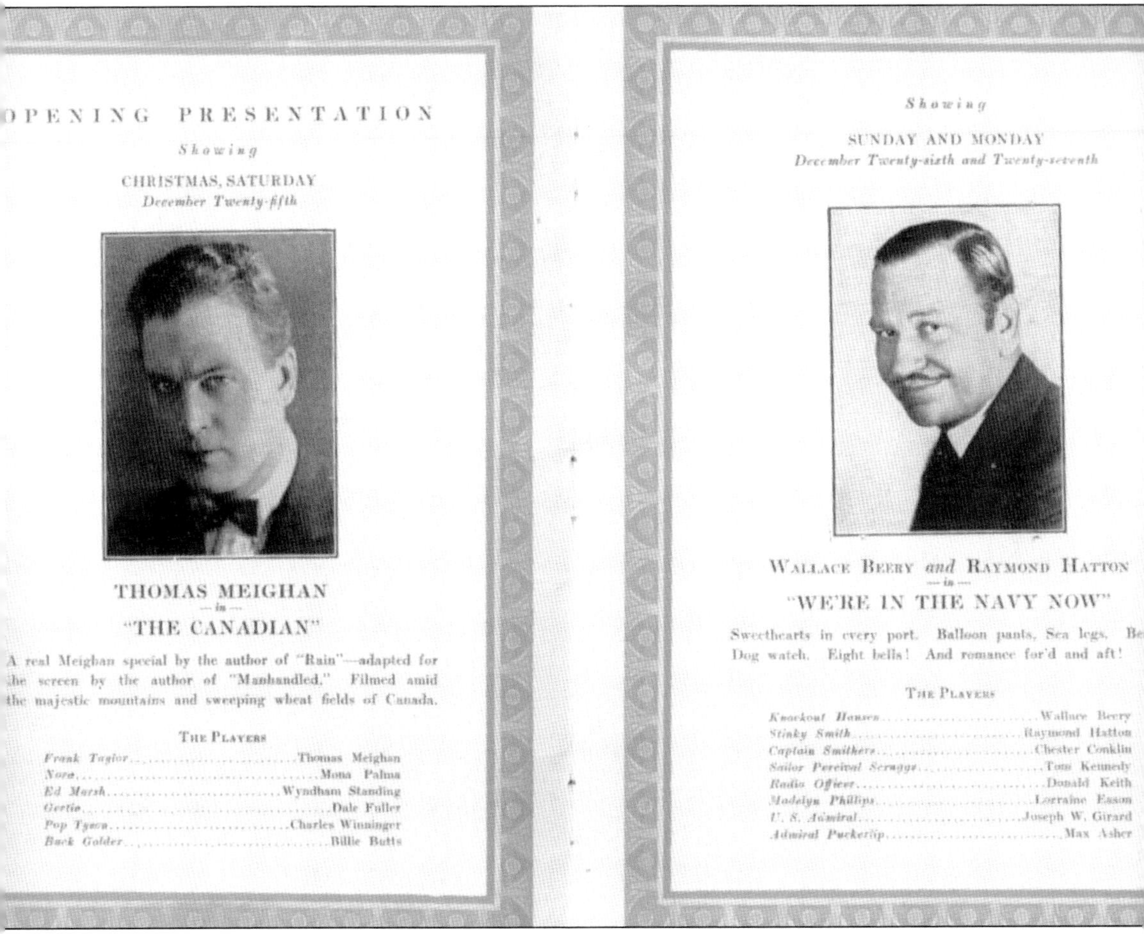
OPENING PRESENTATION

Showing

CHRISTMAS, SATURDAY

December Twenty-fifth

THOMAS MEIGHAN

— in —

"THE CANADIAN"

A real Meighan special by the author of "Rain"—adapted for the screen by the author of "Manhandled." Filmed amid the majestic mountains and sweeping wheat fields of Canada.

THE PLAYERS

Frank Taylor.......Thomas Meighan
Nora.......Mona Palma
Ed Marsh.......Wyndham Standing
Gertie.......Dale Fuller
Pop Tyson.......Charles Winninger
Buck Golder.......Billie Butts

Showing

SUNDAY AND MONDAY

December Twenty-sixth and Twenty-seventh

WALLACE BEERY *and* RAYMOND HATTON

— in —

"WE'RE IN THE NAVY NOW"

Sweethearts in every port. Balloon pants. Sea legs. Be
Dog watch. Eight bells! And romance for'd and aft!

THE PLAYERS

Knockout Hansen.......Wallace Beery
Stinky Smith.......Raymond Hatton
Captain Smithers.......Chester Conklin
Sailor Percival Scruggs.......Tom Kennedy
Radio Officer.......Donald Keith
Madelyn Phillips.......Lorraine Eason
U. S. Admiral.......Joseph W. Girard
Admiral Puckerlip.......Max Asher

The gala opening celebration spanned seven days, and there were three separate programs per day. These offered double features, which meant it was not unusual to have an all-day and a late-night event.

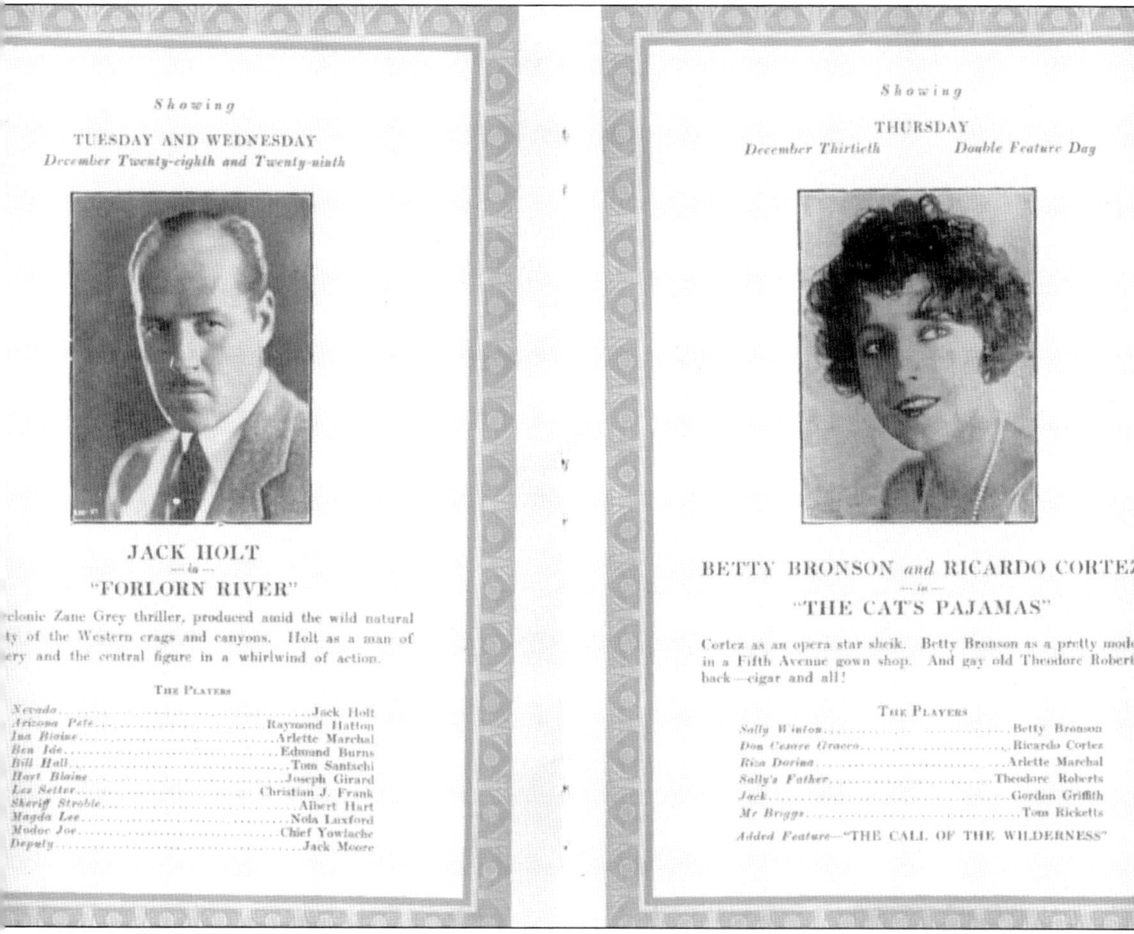

Showing

TUESDAY AND WEDNESDAY

December Twenty-eighth and Twenty-ninth

JACK HOLT

— in —

"FORLORN RIVER"

clonic Zane Grey thriller, produced amid the wild natural ty of the Western crags and canyons. Holt as a man of ery and the central figure in a whirlwind of action.

THE PLAYERS

Nevada........Jack Holt
Arizona Pete........Raymond Hatton
Ina Blaine........Arlette Marchal
Ben Ide........Edmund Burns
Bill Hall........Tom Santschi
Hart Blaine........Joseph Girard
Lee Setter........Christian J. Frank
Sheriff Strobie........Albert Hart
Magda Lee........Nola Luxford
Modoc Joe........Chief Yowlache
Deputy........Jack Moore

Showing

THURSDAY

December Thirtieth *Double Feature Day*

BETTY BRONSON *and* RICARDO CORTEZ

— in —

"THE CAT'S PAJAMAS"

Cortez as an opera star sheik. Betty Bronson as a pretty model in a Fifth Avenue gown shop. And gay old Theodore Roberts back—cigar and all!

THE PLAYERS

Sally Winton........Betty Bronson
Don Cesare Gracco........Ricardo Cortez
Riza Dorina........Arlette Marchal
Sally's Father........Theodore Roberts
Jack........Gordon Griffith
Mr Briggs........Tom Ricketts

Added Feature—"THE CALL OF THE WILDERNESS"

Glamour, mystery, murder, and mayhem were the order of the day. It must have been difficult to determine how and when a person would spend his or her 20¢ or 30¢ admission during the week.

Showing

FRIDAY AND SATURDAY
January Seventh and Eighth

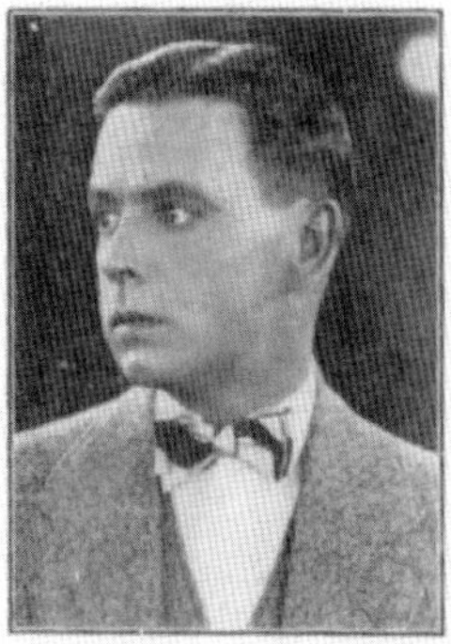

DOUGLAS MacLEAN
— in —
"HOLD THAT LION"

See "Hold That Lion" and laugh till you're cryin'! The laughingest, side-splittingest film ever. Good clean fun—and plenty of it. Young and old alike will love it!

THE PLAYERS

Daniel Hastings....................Douglas MacLean
Dick Warren....................Walter Hiers
Marjorie Brand....................Constance Howard
H. Horace Smythe....................Cyril Chadwick
Andrew MacTavish....................Wade Boteler
Professor Brand....................George C. Pearce

COMING to the RIVOLI
Watch for Dates

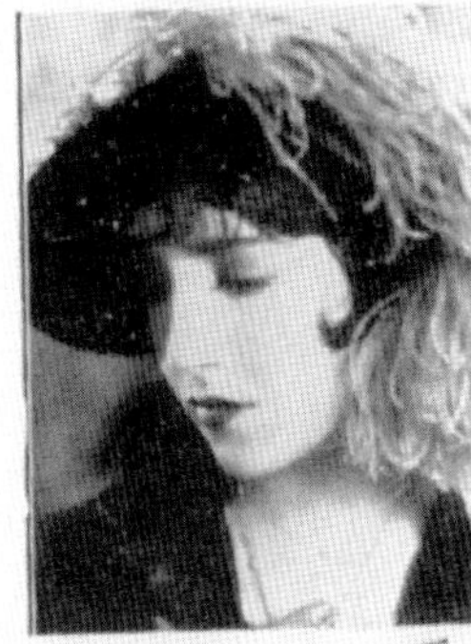

BEBE DANIELS
— in —
"STRANDED IN PARIS"

Count that day lost when you pass up the chance to see Be
her finest love and laughter special to date. Come and see
"do" gay Paree with a vengeance!

THE PLAYERS

Julie McFadden....................Bebe Daniels
Robert Van Wye....................James Hall
Count Pasada....................Ford Sterling
Theresa Halstead....................Iris Stuart
Countess Pasada....................Mabel Julienne Scott
Herr Rederson....................Tom Ricketts
Mrs. Van Wye....................Helen Dunbar
Mrs. Halstead....................Ida Darling
Pettipan....................George Grandee
Schwab....................Andre Lanoy

Most of these old films are no longer available, having deteriorated or been lost. Others are not available for circulation. The names of many of the stars, however, are still familiar to some audiences today.

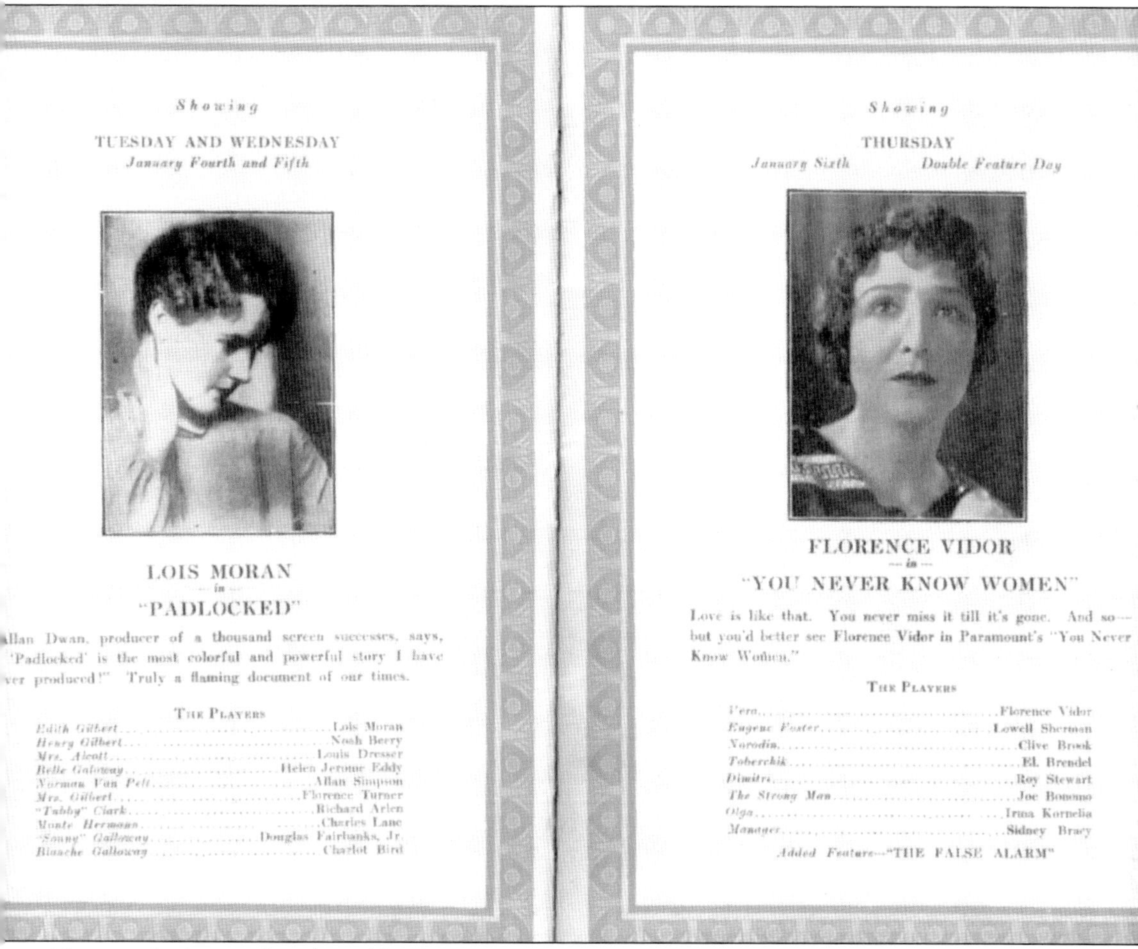

Showing

TUESDAY AND WEDNESDAY

January Fourth and Fifth

LOIS MORAN

— in —

"PADLOCKED"

llan Dwan, producer of a thousand screen successes, says, 'Padlocked' is the most colorful and powerful story I have ver produced!" Truly a flaming document of our times.

THE PLAYERS

Edith Gilbert......Lois Moran
Henry Gilbert......Noah Berry
Mrs. Alcott......Louis Dresser
Belle Galoway......Helen Jerome Eddy
Norman Van Pelt......Allan Simpson
Mrs. Gilbert......Florence Turner
"Tubby" Clark......Richard Arlen
Monte Hermann......Charles Lane
"Sonny" Galloway......Douglas Fairbanks, Jr.
Blanche Galloway......Charlot Bird

Showing

THURSDAY

January Sixth *Double Feature Day*

FLORENCE VIDOR

— in —

"YOU NEVER KNOW WOMEN"

Love is like that. You never miss it till it's gone. And so— but you'd better see **Florence Vidor in Paramount's** "You Never Know Women."

THE PLAYERS

Vera......Florence Vidor
Eugene Foster......Lowell Sherman
Norodin......Clive Brook
Toberchik......El. Brendel
Dimitri......Roy Stewart
The Strong Man......Joe Bonomo
Olga......Irma Kornelia
Manager......Sidney Bracy

Added Feature—"THE FALSE ALARM"

Heroines had marcel curls and bright smiles. Villains sneered and sported mustaches and hair that was slicked back and glossy. Eyes told the whole story, regardless of the story line.

Rivoli Theatre

Telephone, West 3593
576 CAMPBELL AVENUE,
WEST HAVEN, CONN.

F. G. WILSON,
President

COURTENAY SAVAGE,
Managing Director

A. G. HURLBURT,
Resident Manager

For Time of Performances
See Center Program Pages

Program Subject to Change at
Discretion of Management

PERFORMANCES:
Daily
3:00, 7:00 and 8:45
Sunday
7:00 and 8:45

PRICES:
Matinees—20c. *Evenings*—30c.

The Rivoli Theatre was one of several cinemas in West Haven—others included the Cameo, Park, and Forest Theatres and the Orpheum at Savin Rock. The price was right, and they were within walking distance from home and offered entertainment and the opportunity to socialize with friends and neighbors.

Early movie theaters would not have been complete without an organist, often one whose platform rose dramatically from a lower level at performance time. The Hall Organ Company handcrafted instruments for personal and professional use. During World War II, there was a shortage of metal, and the company was forced to expand its woodcraft division. As a result, the company created a custom line of handcrafted humidors and other personal-sized boxes for high-end jewelers. One of the humidors sold at auction from the Kennedy estate was identified as a Hall Company product.

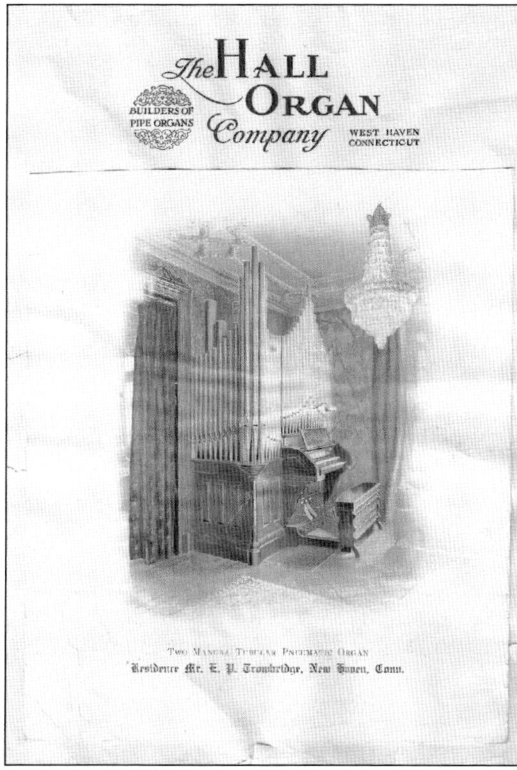

Representatives Of The Hall Organ Company

throughout the United States

ARIZONA

Roger A. Lyon,
Box 443, Route 7,
Phoenix, Ariz.

CALIFORNIA

Wm. R. Dorr,
4348 West 3rd St.,
Los Angeles, Calif.

Kohler & Chase,
San Francisco, Calif.

COLORADO

Knight-Campbell Co.,
Denver, Colorado.

DISTRICT OF COLUMBIA

E. F. Droop & Son,
1300 G. St., N. W.,
Washington, D. C.

ILLINOIS

Kenneth Butler,
805 S. Humphrey Ave.,
Oak Park, Ill.

IOWA

Jackson Organ & Piano Co.,
Burlington, Iowa.

IOWA (Continued)

F. M. Lilyard,
503 E. 4th St.,
Fairmont, Minn.

MAINE

H. C. Harrison,
34 Pitt St.,
Portland, Maine.

MASSACHUSETTS

Chas. F. Chadwick,
28 Dorchester St.,
Springfield, Mass.

MINNESOTA

Holstead Music Co.,
109 South Ninth St.,
Minneapolis, Minn.

NEW JERSEY

Riggins Piano Co.,
Broadway & Benson Sts.,
Camden, N. J.

PENNSYLVANIA

The Estey Co.,
17th and Walnut Sts.
Philadelphia, Penna.

PENN. (Continued)

G. Logan McElvany,
1205 Morningside Ave.,
Pittsburg, Penna.

A. H. Rosewig,
133 So. 11th St.,
Philadelphia, Penna.

Owen J. W. Burness,
5905 Greene St.,
Germantown, Phila., Penna

Kirk-Johnson Co.,
16-18 West King St.,
Lancaster, Penna.

TENNESSEE

Henry S. Wesson,
Ward-Belmont School,
Nashville, Tenn.

VIRGINIA

John T. Kernodle,
1536 E. Broad St.,
Richmond, Va.

WISCONSIN

Edmund Gram,
414 Milwaukee Ave.,
Milwaukee, Wis.

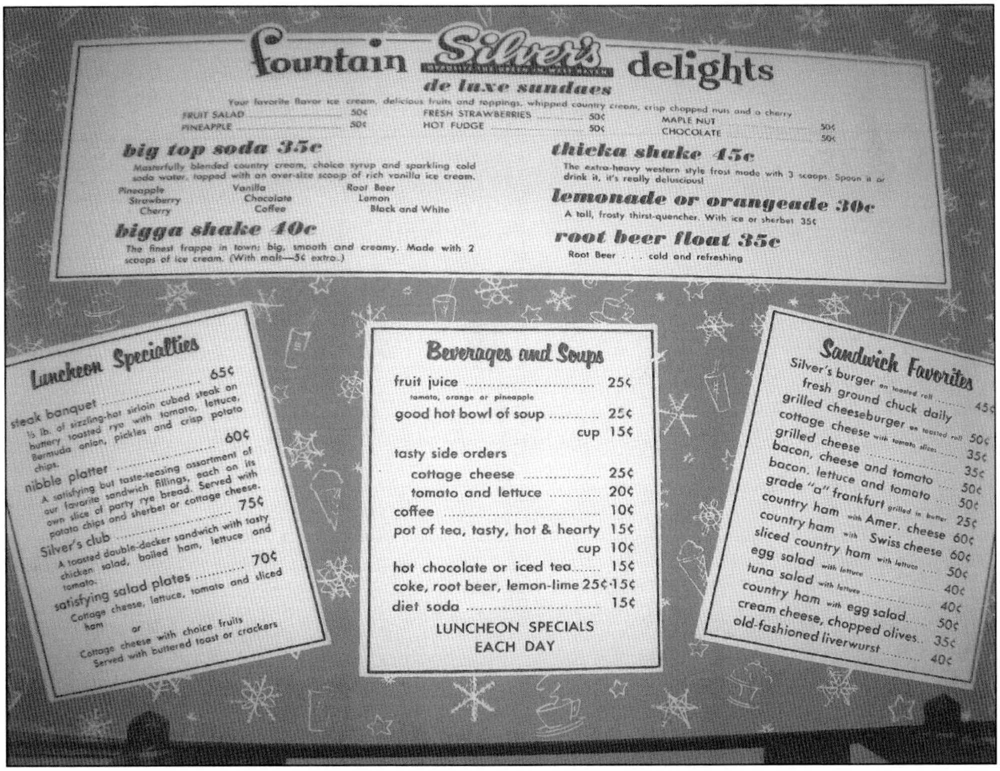

A special treat was always available at the lunch counter of Silver's on the Green, which was a step beyond the ice cream fountain of other pharmacies.

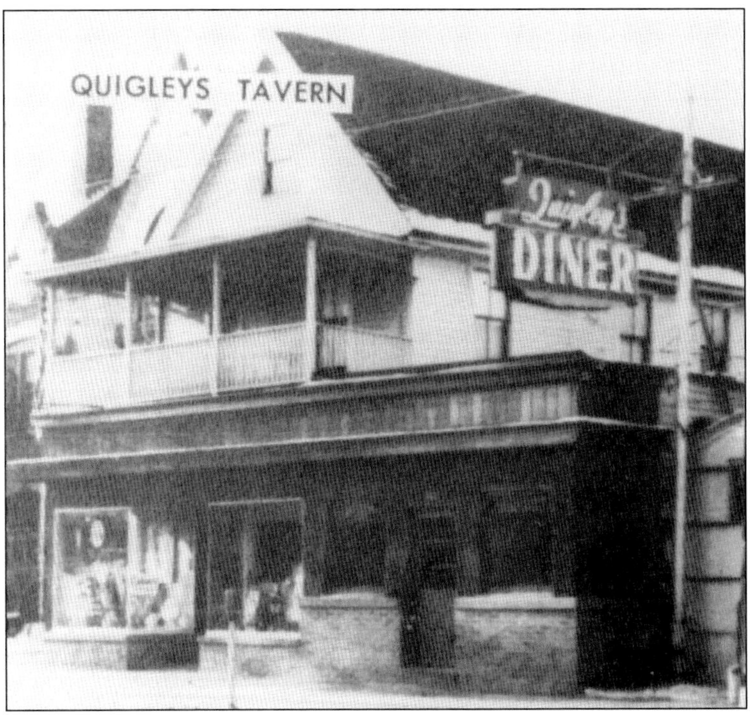

Across the street from Silver's, behind the town hall, was Quigley's, a gathering spot for all ages where everyone knew each other's name. Teens, professional workers, housewives, and shoppers all stopped by for a bite to eat or to catch up on the latest news in town.

The label on Watch Tower Brand Pure California Port stated that the wine was "withdrawn and bottled from tax paid containers" of the Old Elm Wine and Liquor bottling company of West Haven.

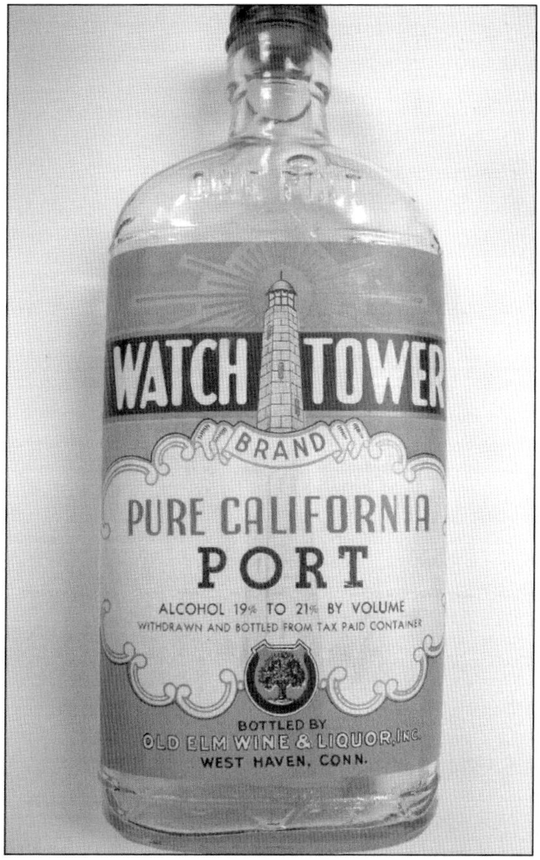

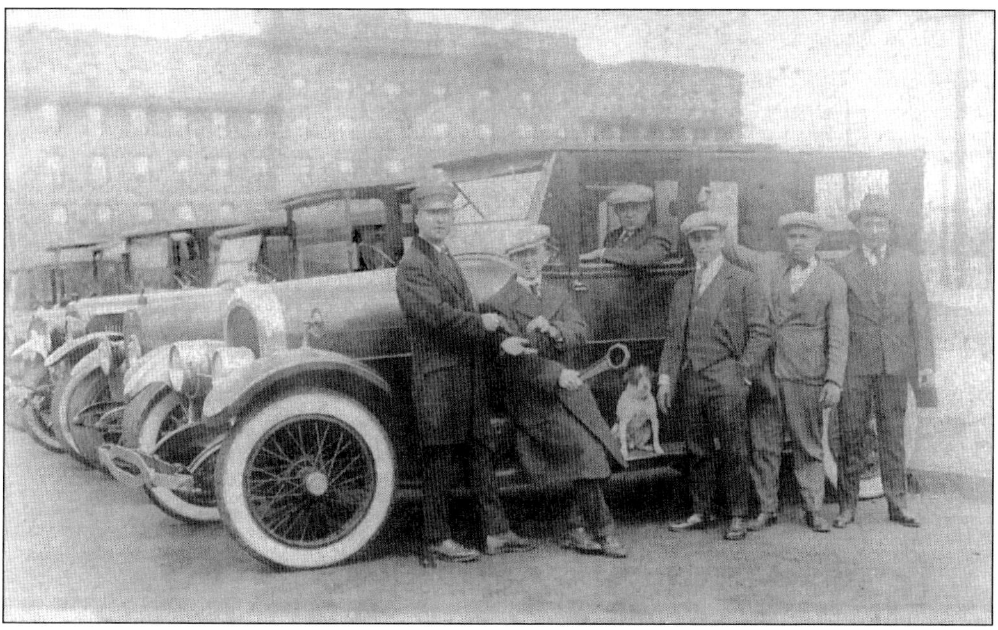

The introduction of the automobile created new careers. Chauffeurs, cab drivers, and livery men were seen everywhere.

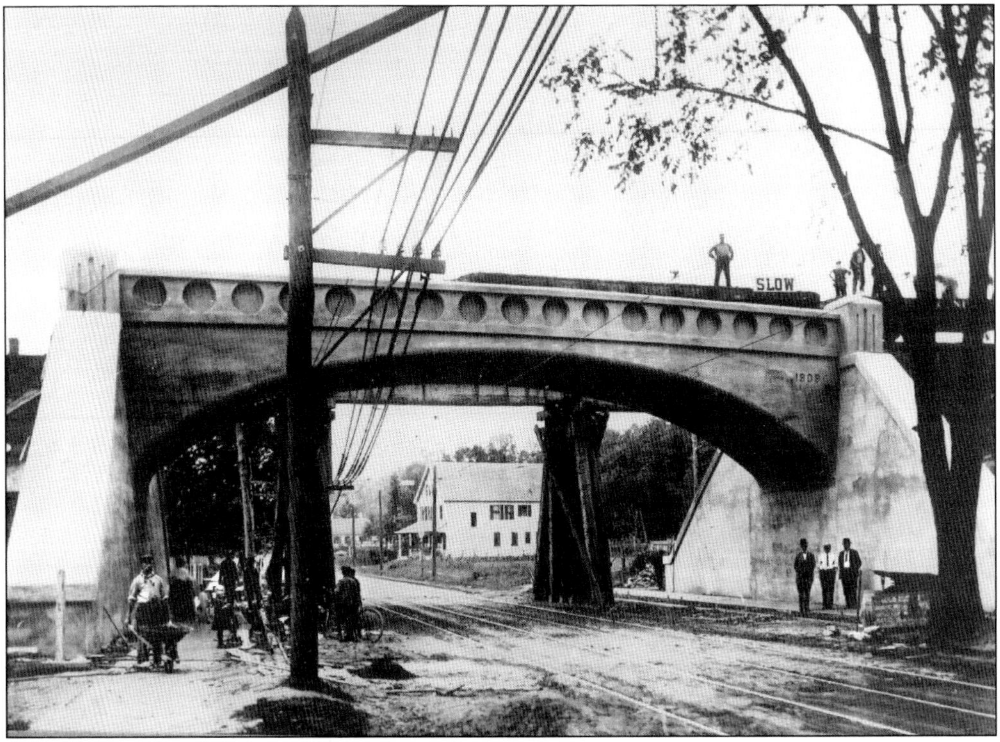

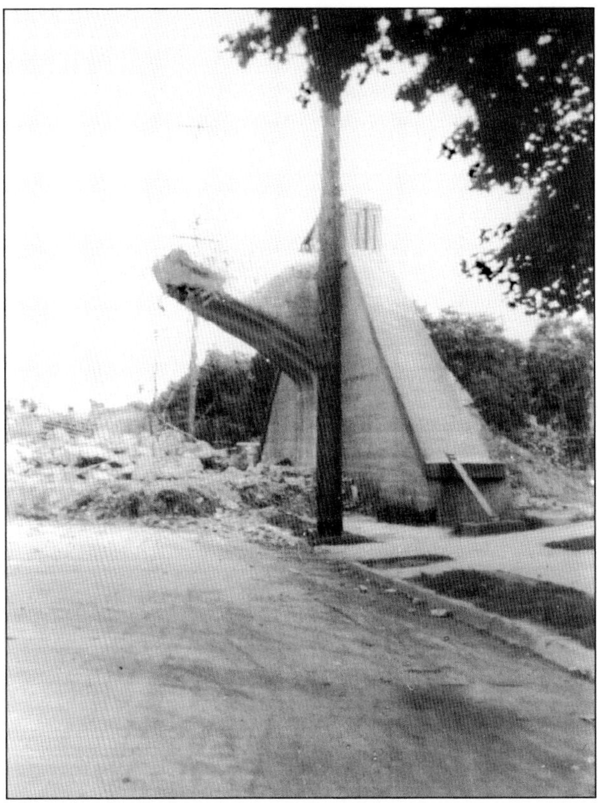

In 1909, a railroad bridge was constructed over Campbell Avenue, near the Veterans Administration Hospital. The line carried passengers to the valley town of Derby.

By 1940, the rail line was defunct and the bridge demolished.

Seven

The Poli Mystique

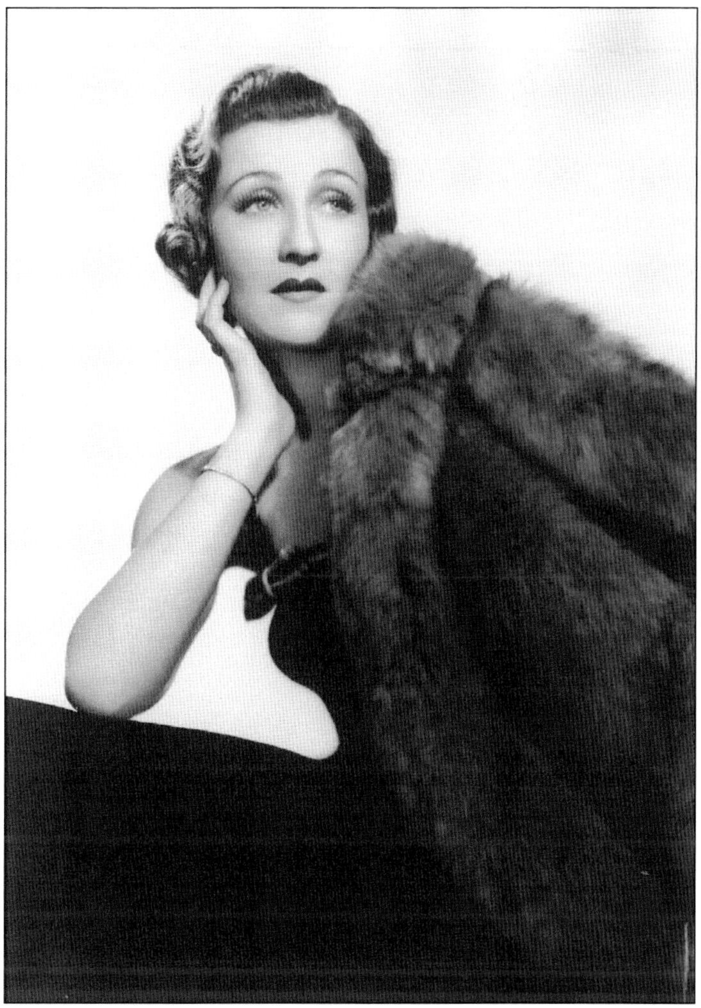

Actress Jeanne Poli was a combination of the mystery of Greta Garbo and the beauty of Carol Lombard. In later years, her desire for privacy generated a curious public.

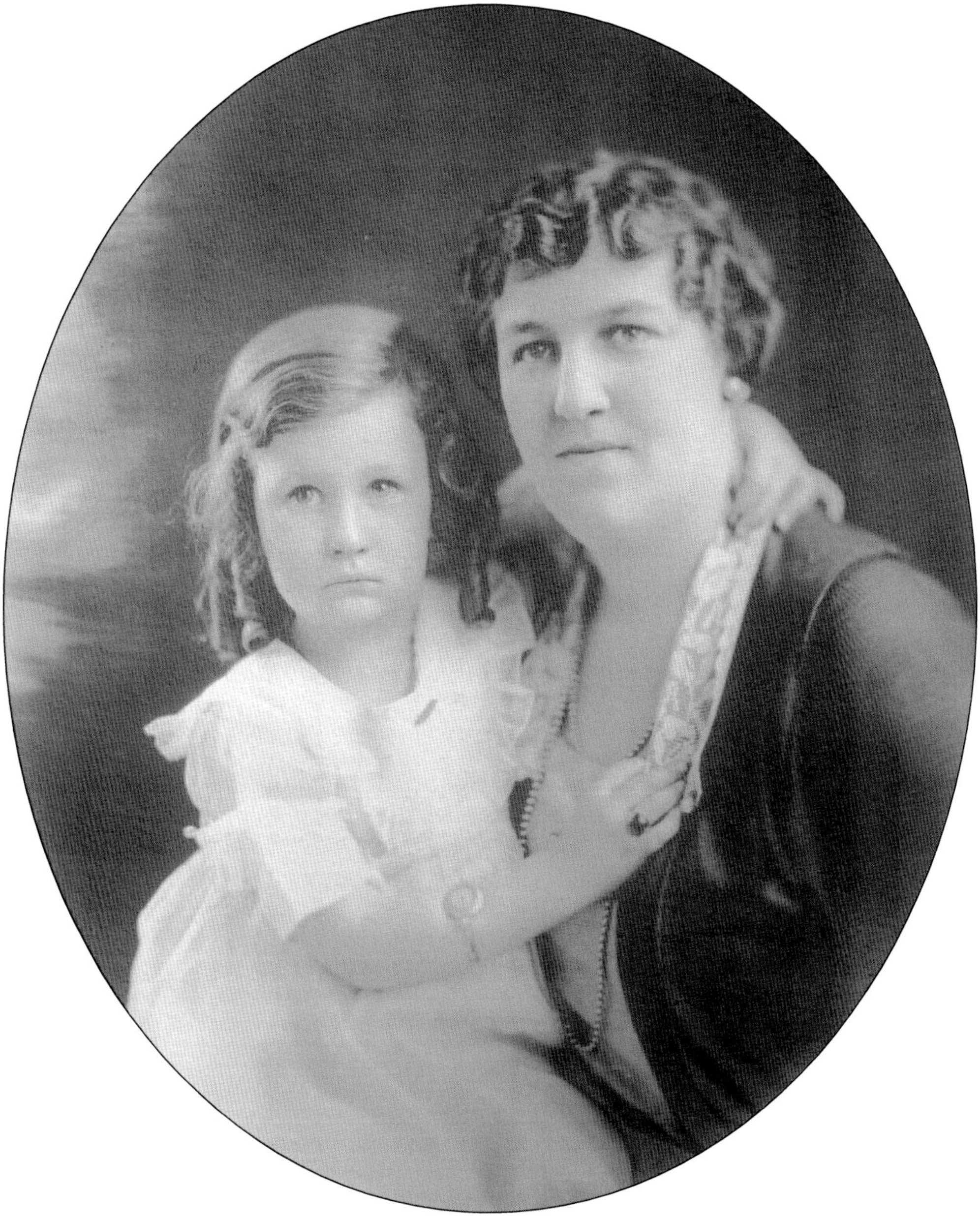

Grandmother Rosa Poli had her own Shirley Temple in young Jeanne, with her corkscrew curls and dimpled smile. The pair seemed to have a special bond.

Jeanne and her mother, Adelaina Poli, were "best friends," and Adelaina made certain that Jeanne had all of the privileges and opportunities available at the time.

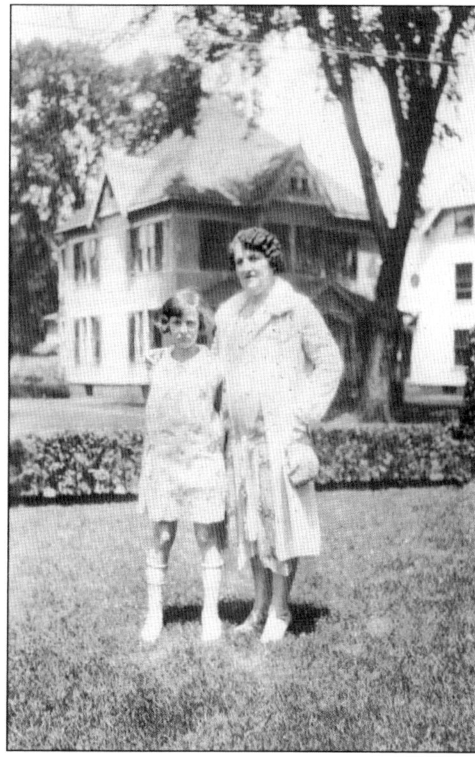

In 1917, Sylvester Z. Poli gifted his daughter Adelaina with a Dutch Colonial home at the intersection of Savin Avenue and Main Street, a prime spot for exquisite real estate in that day.

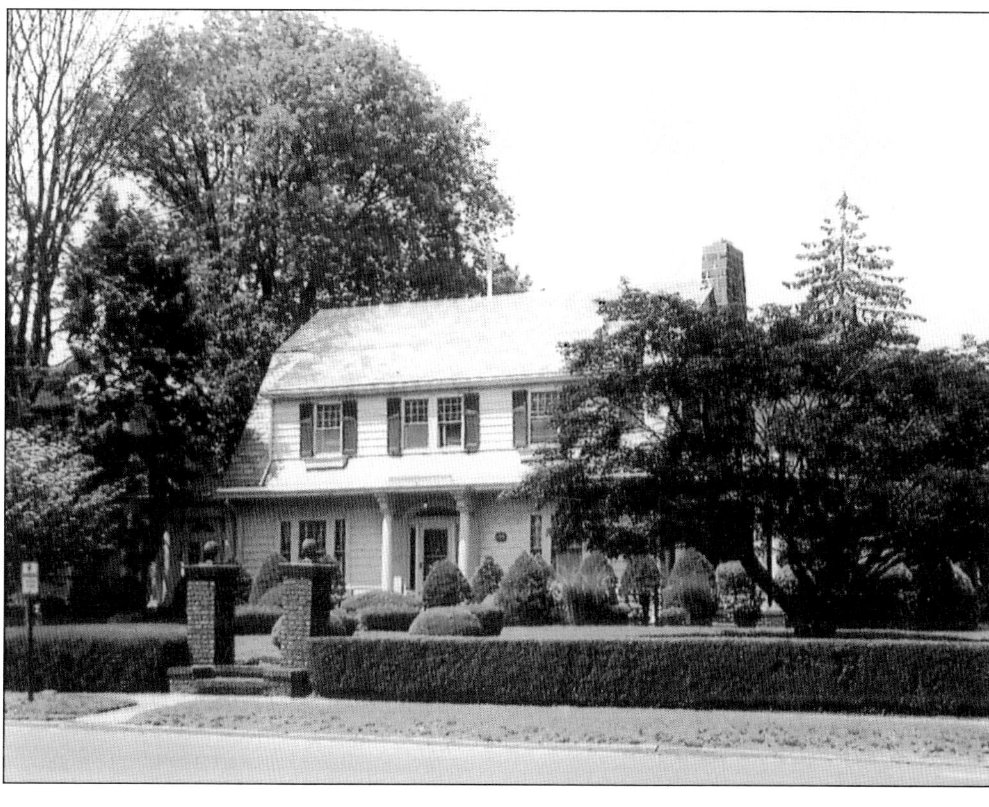

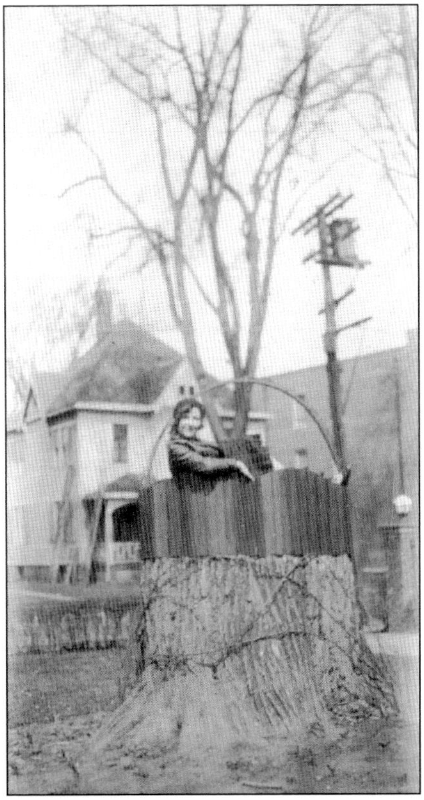

There was an enormous tree on the front lawn, and eventually it had to be removed. Jeanne Poli used the moment to create a humorous shot.

Even with statuary and garden benches, there was enough room for Jeanne's dog, Sarge, to romp around the formal gardens in the rear of the house.

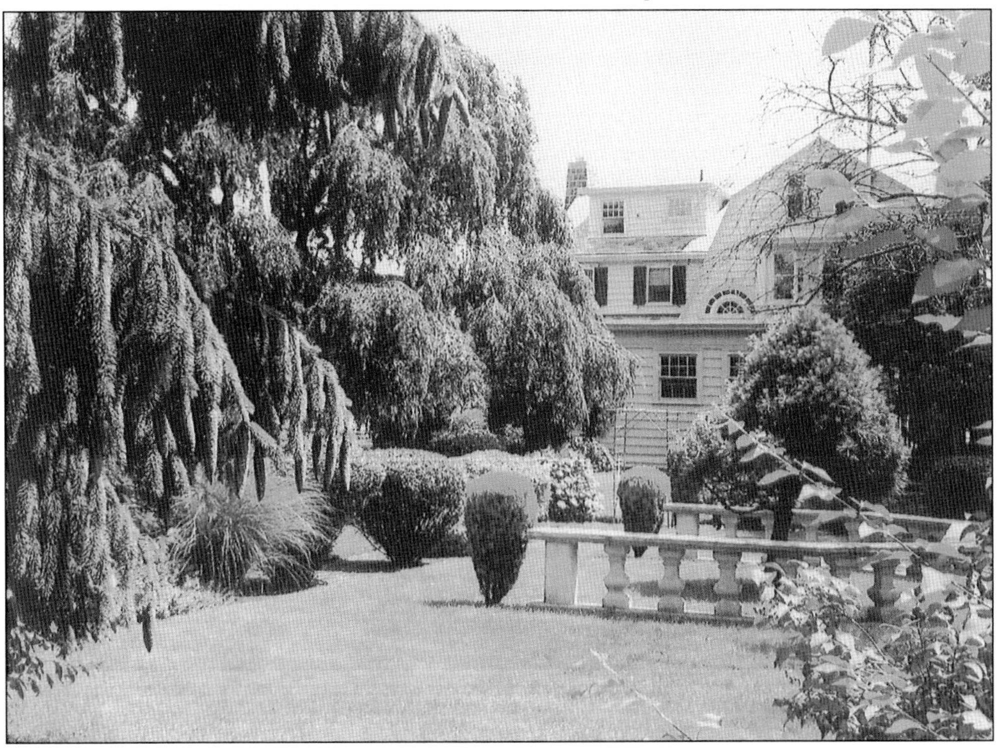

Education was very important to the Poli family, and Jeanne (left) was soon to be wearing the conservative uniform of St. Elizabeth's, a proper school for a proper girl.

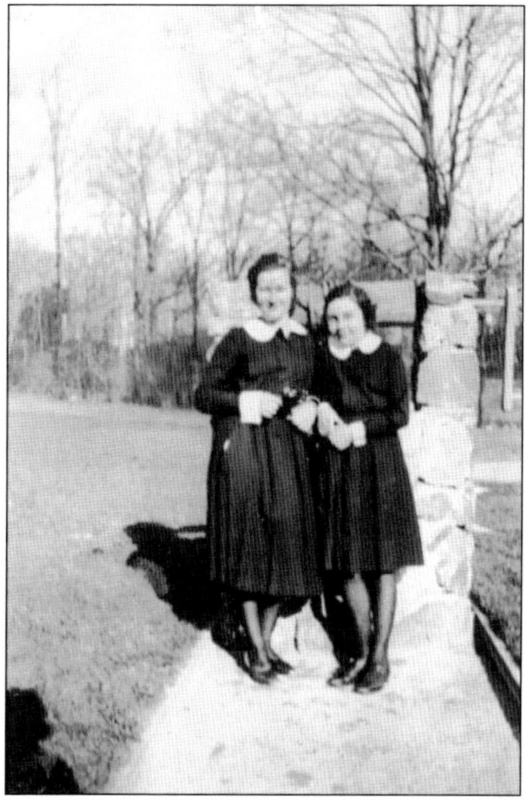

Whether young Jeanne had aspirations to become an actress by the time she graduated from St. Elizabeth's is questionable, but she did have a picture of Carole Lombard in her scrapbook.

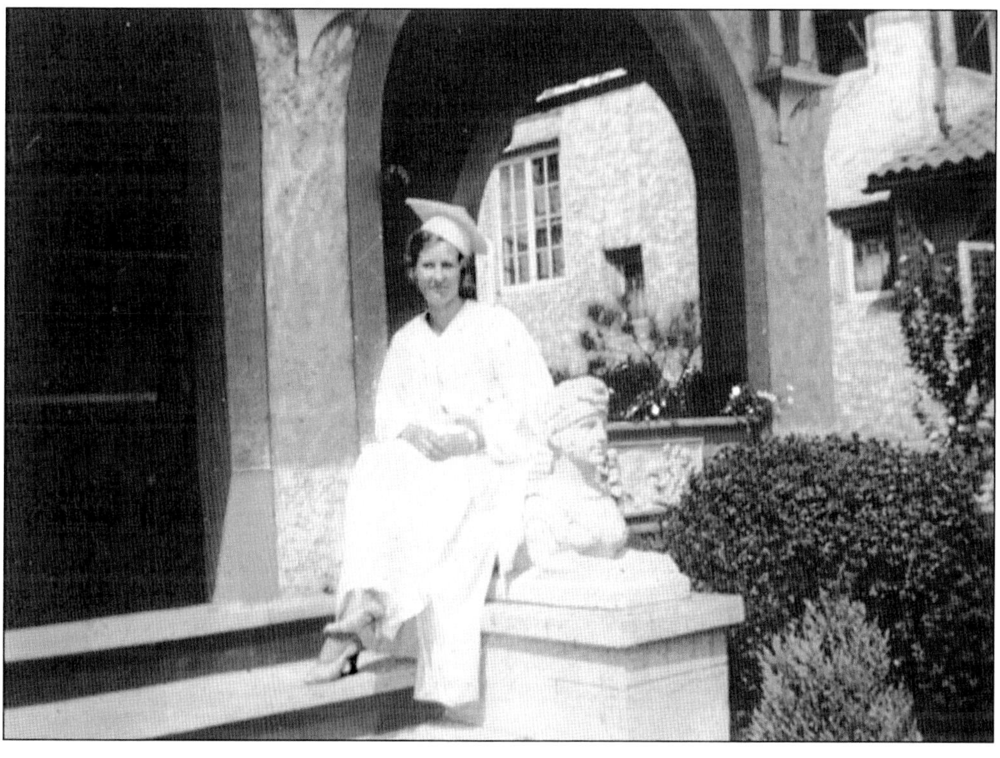

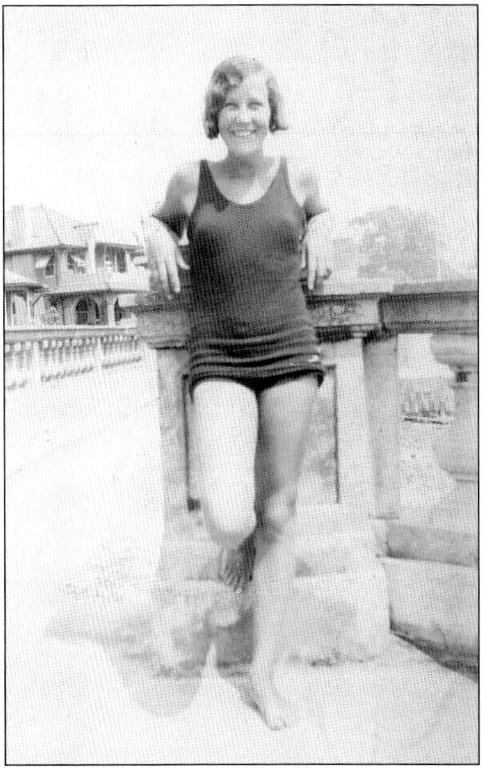

Family time was important, and vacations at "The Camp" in New Hampshire or at the Chateau Frontenac in Quebec were times to remember.

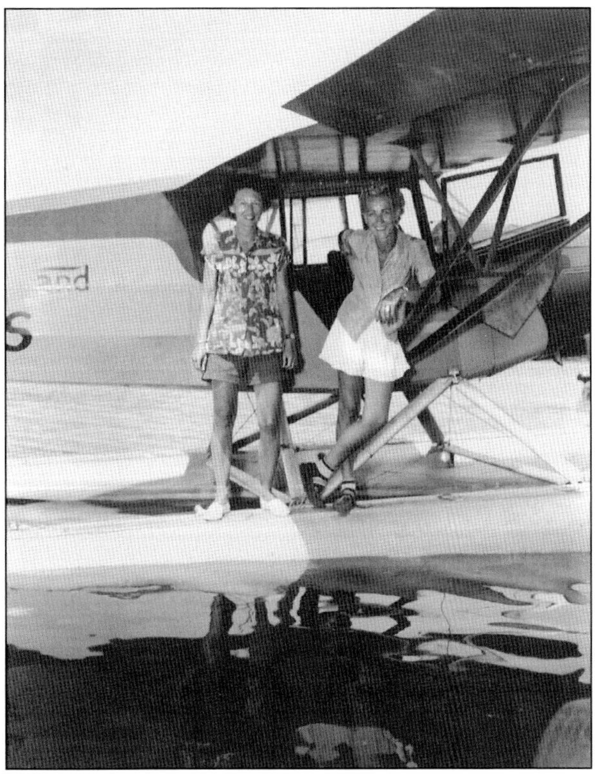

Independent and adventurous and encouraged by her accomplished grandparents and adoring mother, Jeanne Poli stepped out into her own world. Jeanne (right) reinforced her independence by getting her pilot's license, as so many women were doing with the influence of Amelia Earhart.

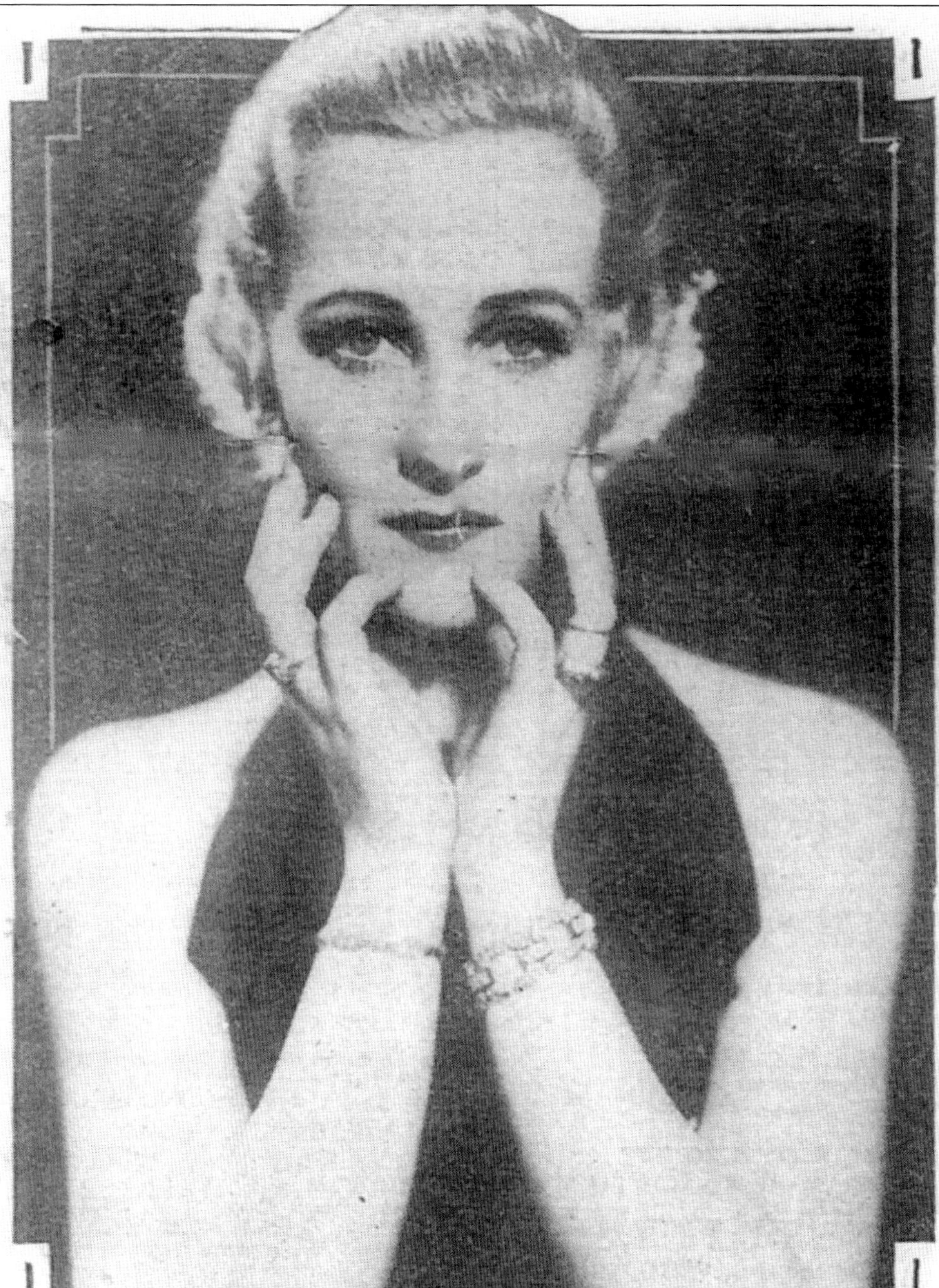

JEAN POLI, *grand-daughter of the theatrical magnate, bright star of the WELI Players.*

Fame and recognition finally came to Jeanne Poli as an actress and radio personality, first in Boston and then in the New Haven area. She was featured in newspapers and professional journals, both as an individual and as a member of a studio performance group.

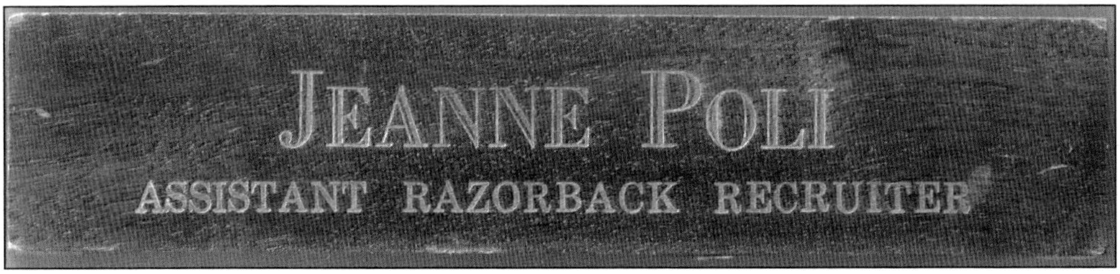

When Jeanne Poli left the theater world behind, she became very involved with the University of Arkansas Lady Razorbacks marketing and recruiting program, as her desk plate indicates. Jeanne owned a residence in Arkansas, and when the opportunity for a recruitment position at the University of Arkansas became available, she applied and got the job.

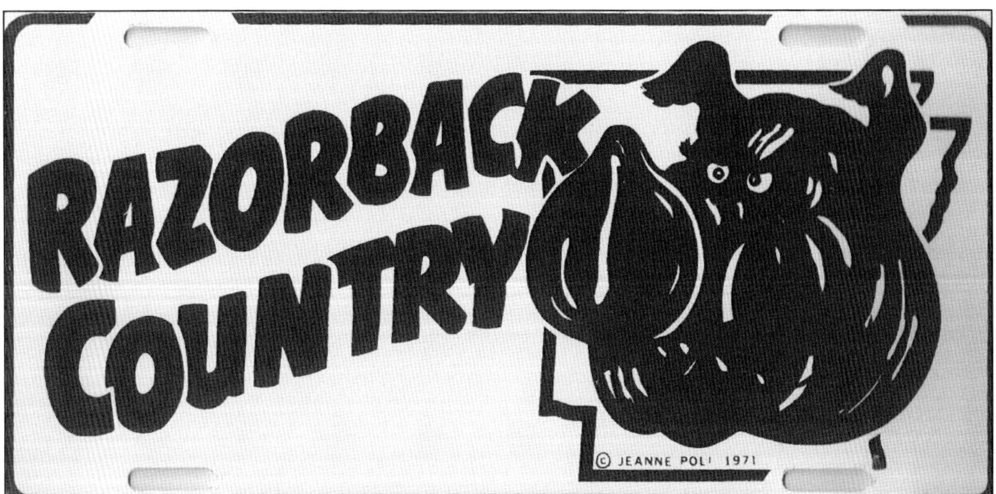

Jeanne is said to have been responsible for the design of one of the University of Arkansas Razorbacks logos and had this plate as a promotional item.

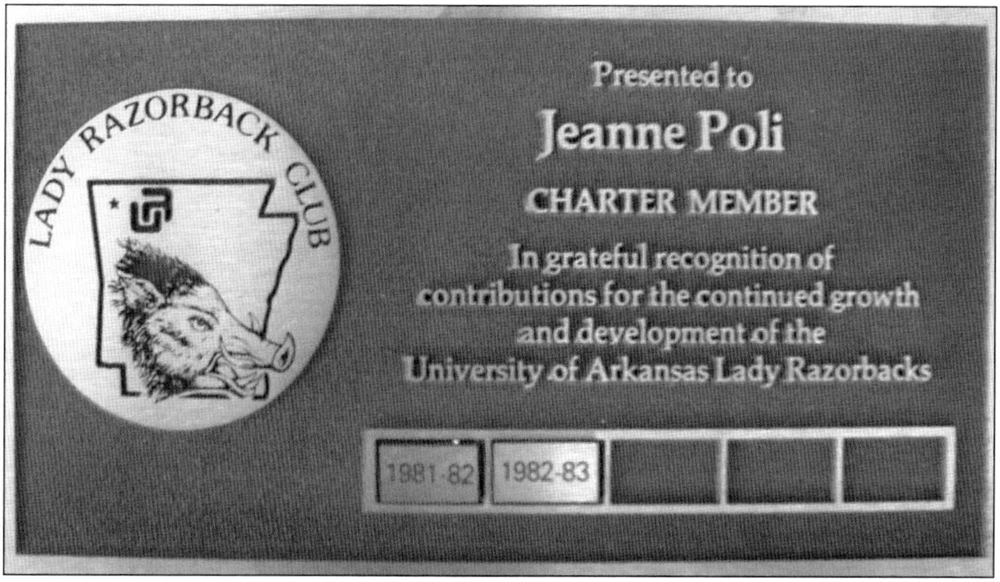

Fund-raising events at the university were well attended, drawing everyone's support, including that of then governor Bill Clinton. Jeanne Poli was a charter member of the Lady Razorbacks organization and was much appreciated, as this plaque suggests.

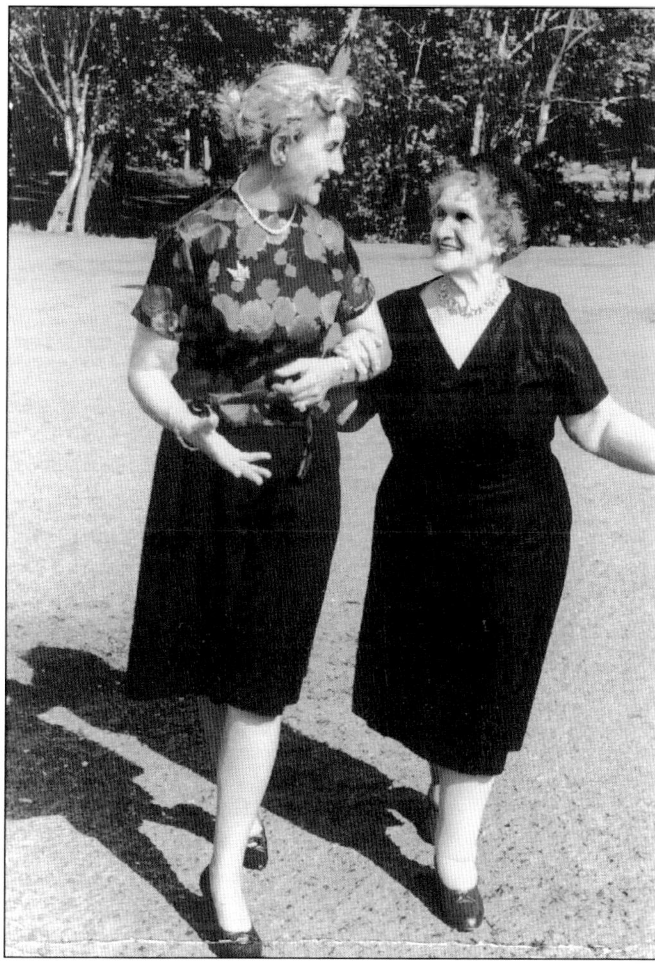

When Jeanne retired, she came back to her home in West Haven to enjoy her later years with her friend, Pauline Smith (right).

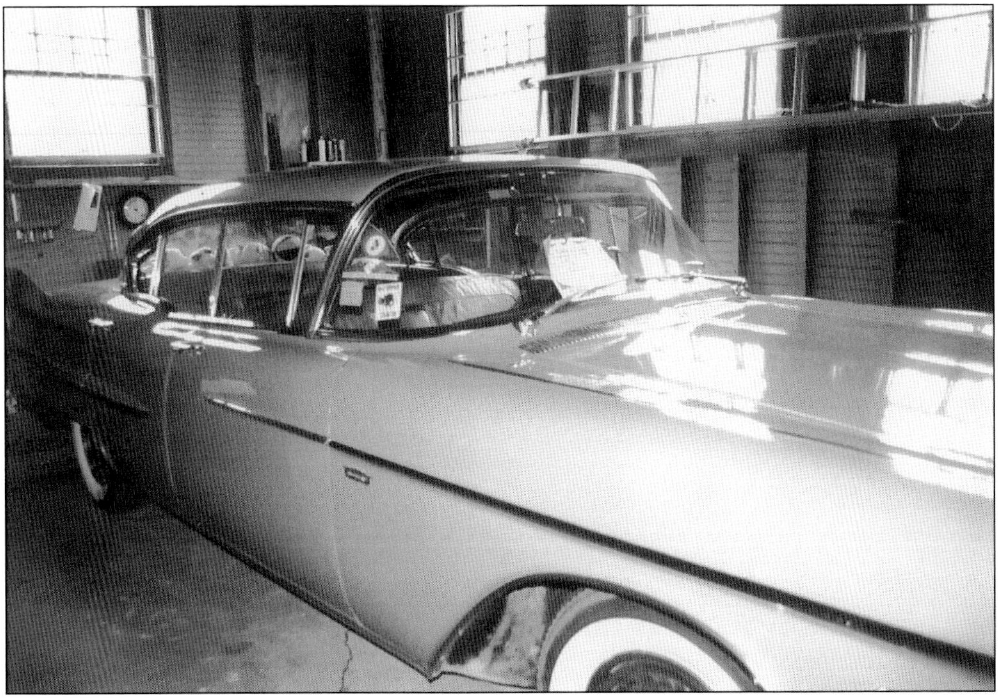

Whether the townspeople ever got to know Jeanne Poli personally or not, they always knew when she went out in her classic pink Cadillac with the mink-covered steering wheel. Her love of antique cars was evident in her collection.

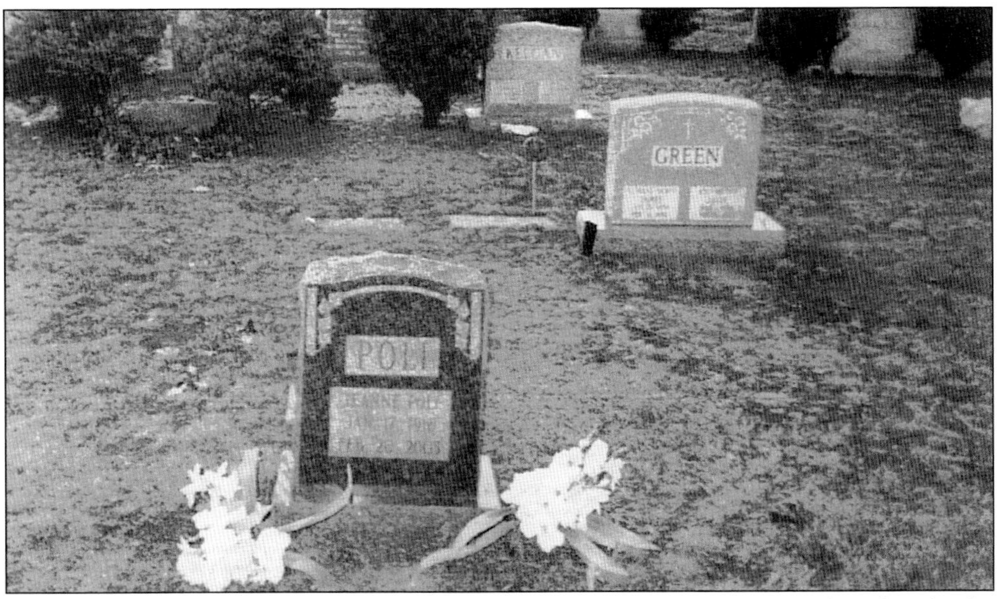

When Jeanne Poli died, she generously bequeathed large sums of money to her church, the public library, an animal shelter, and other charities. Her own grave site is inauspicious, unlike the family mausoleum.

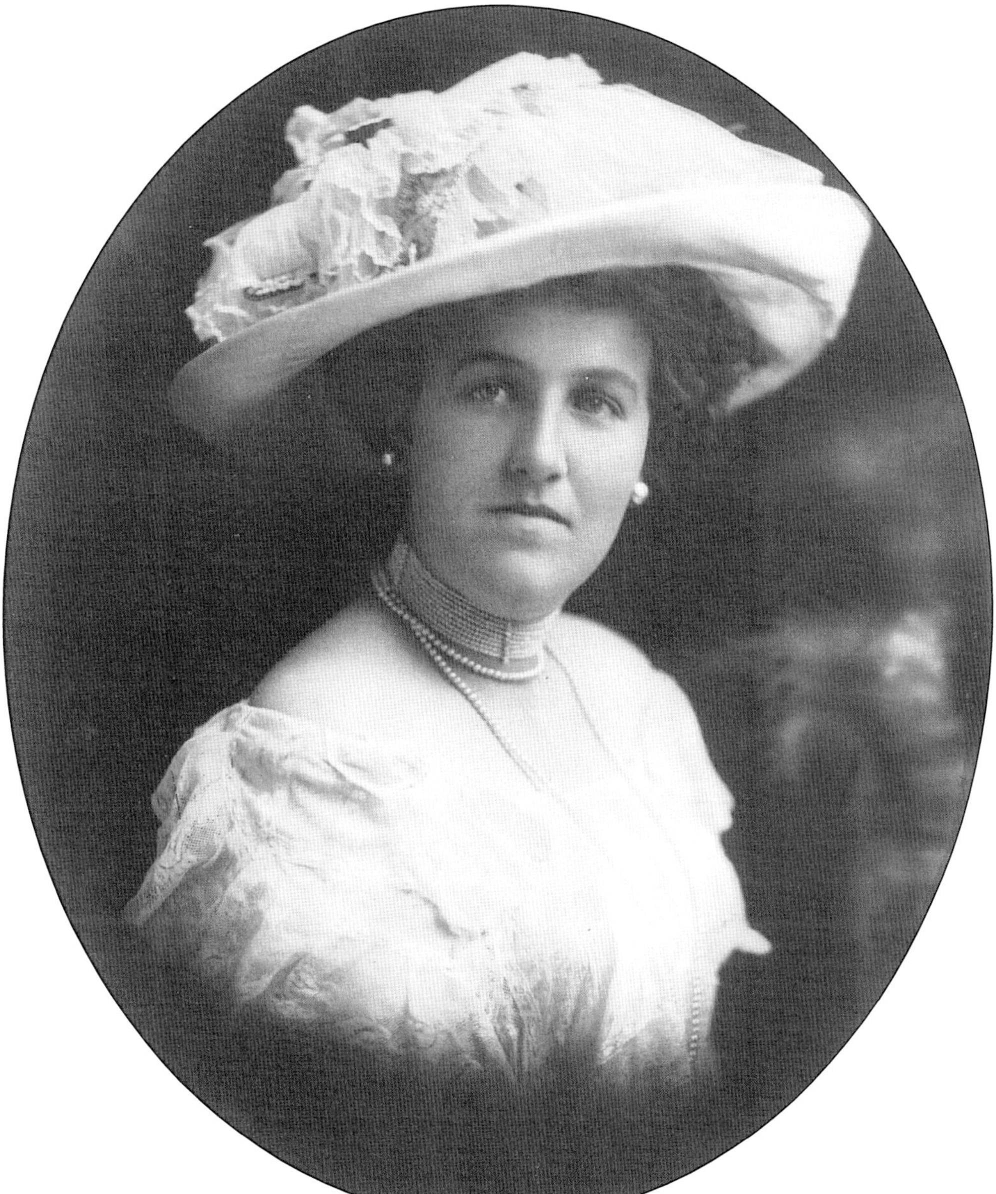

Grandmother Rosa Poli was truly the matriarch of this family whose name was associated with thousands of movie theaters in the northeast. She traveled with royalty, but expected everyone to put forth his or her greatest effort as an individual. She was a staunch supporter of her husband as he moved through life and a kind and generous person to needy causes.

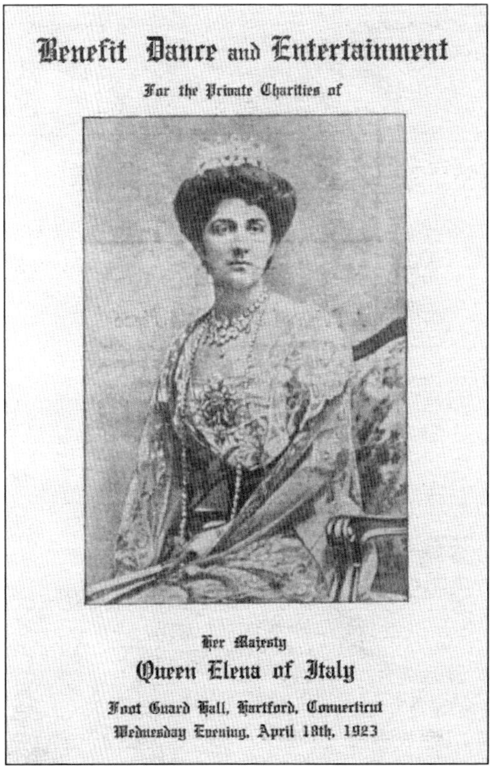

Rosa Poli, for whom the Italian villa compound was named, was honored at a dinner in Hartford where funds were raised to support the charities of Queen Elena of Italy. Rosa had met the queen, who was well known and well liked, at a private audience one year earlier.

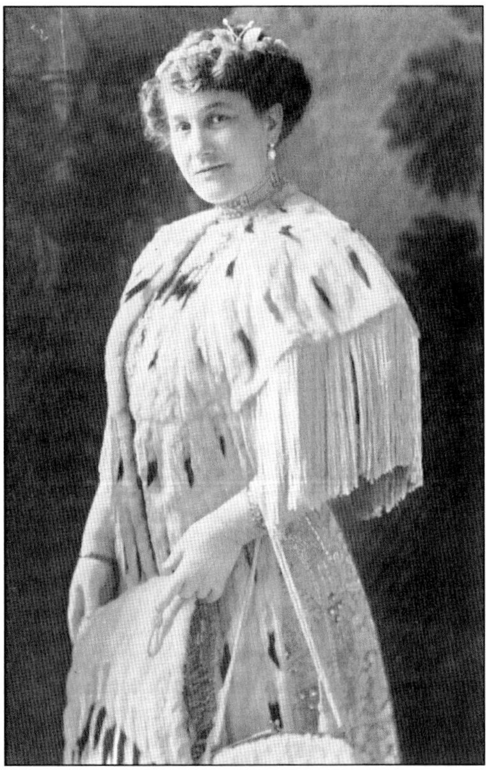

Rosa Poli wore an ermine stole to the event at which Connecticut governor Charles A. Templeton was a special guest.

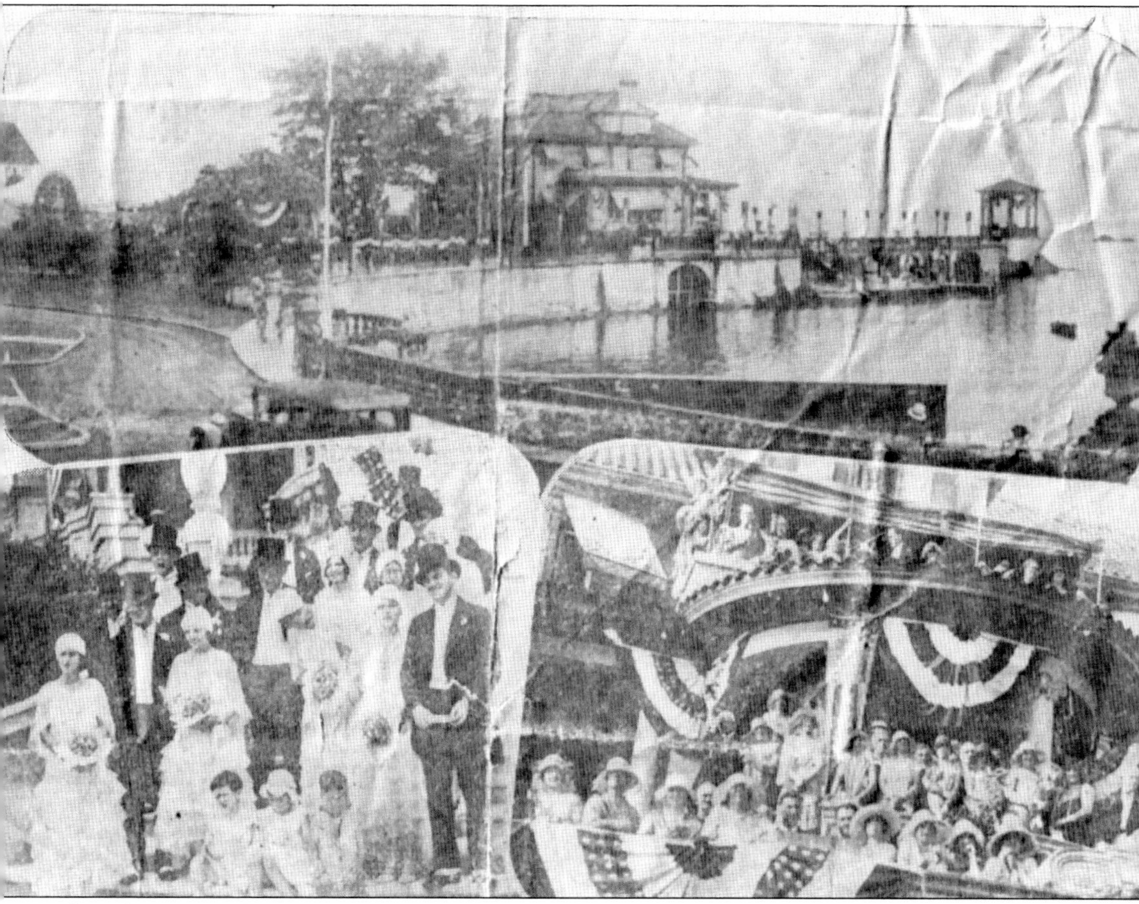

The July 1929 wedding of daughter Lillian Poli (Jeanne's aunt) to the Marquis Lippo Gerini of Florence was the event of the year. Elegantly dressed guests strolled the grounds of the Villa Rosa while fashionable attendants posed on the cascading staircases or in the gardens.

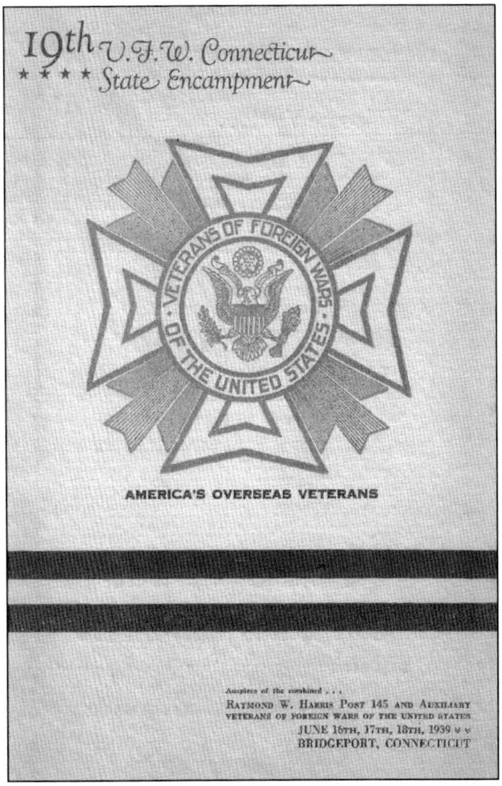

The Veterans of Foreign Wars organization was a recipient of Rosa Poli's generosity. She was honored with a plaque of appreciation by the group at the 19th-annual state encampment in 1939.

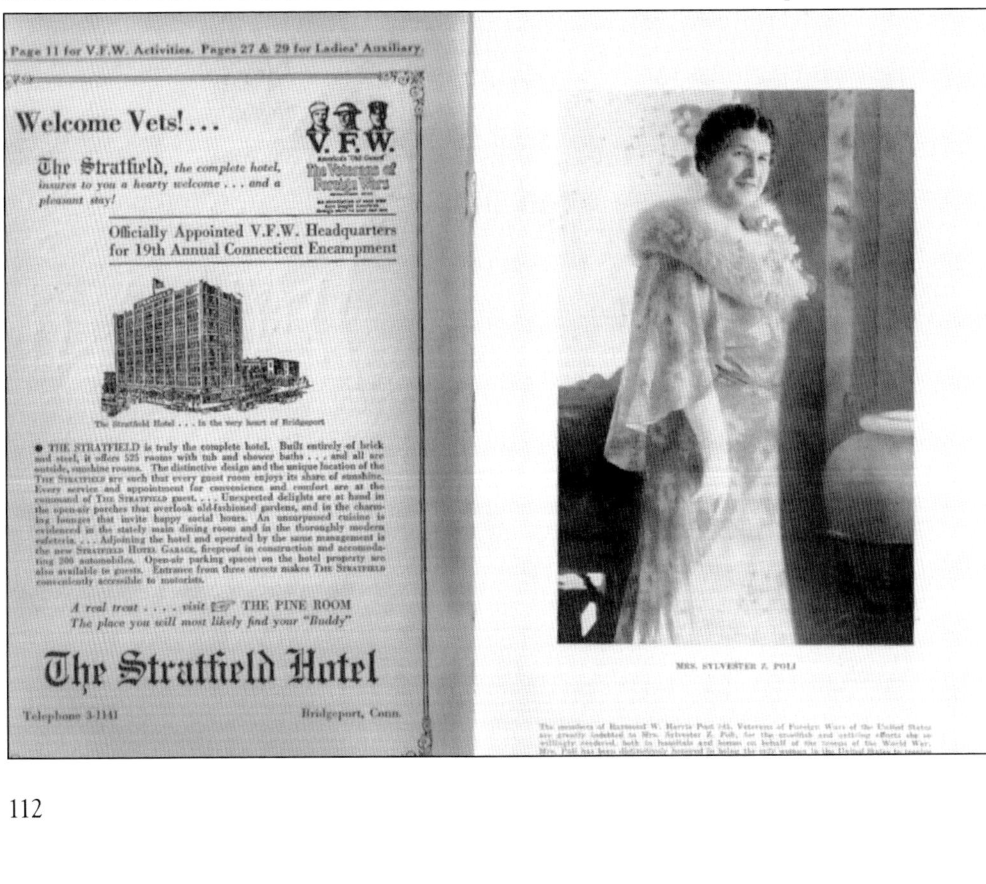

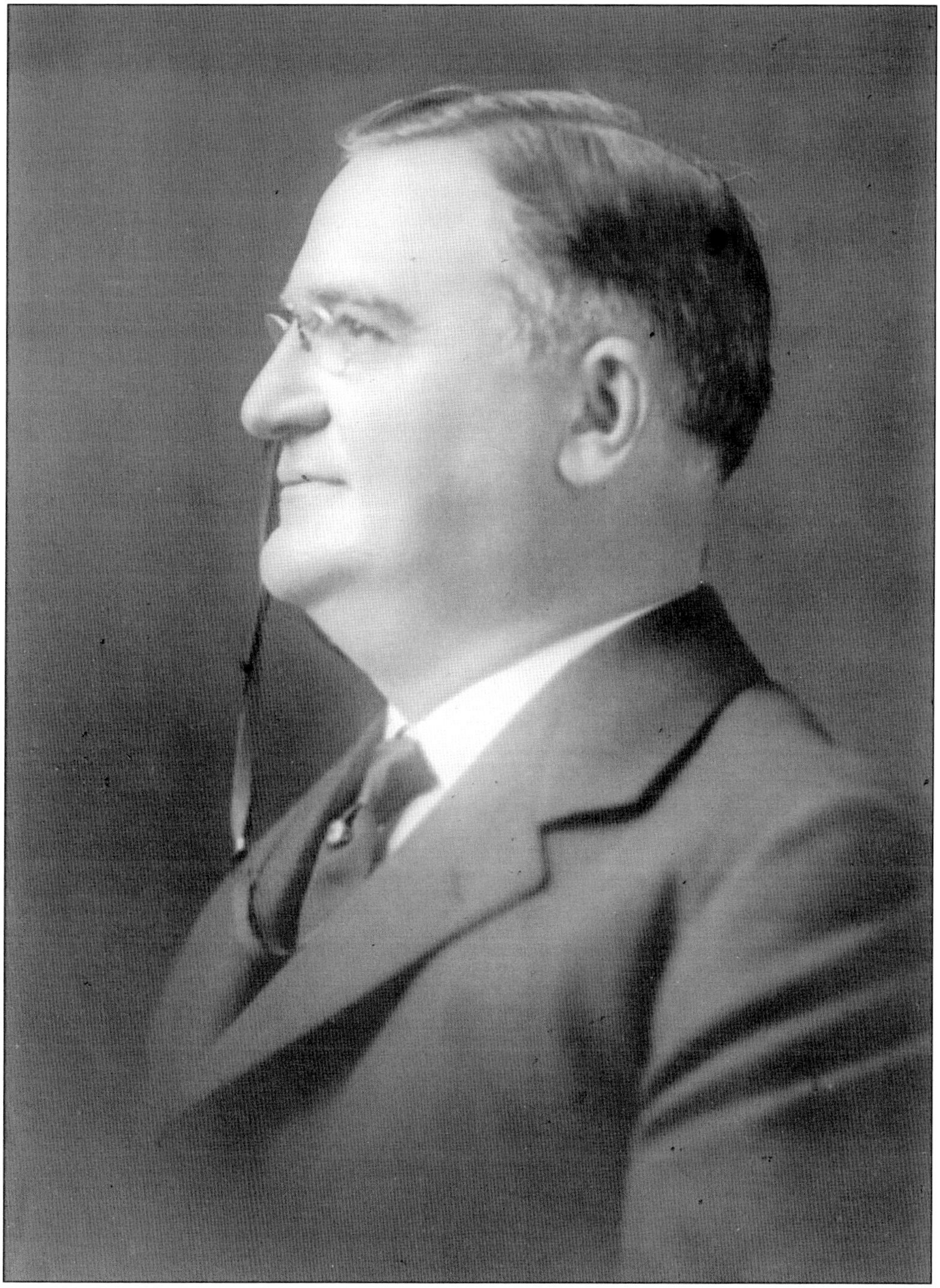

Grandfather Sylvester Zefferino Poli was best known as a talented artist, sculptor, entrepreneur, and philanthropist, yet he was a man who took the time to develop relationships and to care for his family. At age 13, a very talented Sylvester was sent to France to study sculpture, and he was hired by a wax museum in New York before he was 21. It was not long before Sylvester became interested in the design and development of theaters and began to work with the famous architect and designer Thomas W. Lamb.

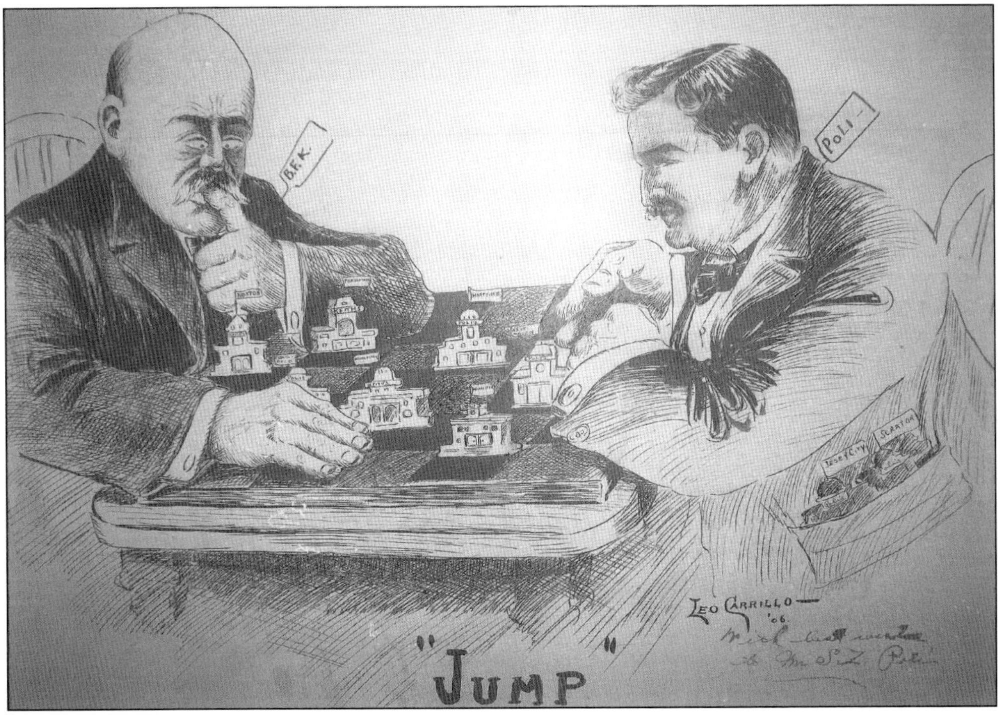

In 1904, the *New Yorker* carried this cartoon by Leo Carillo showing S. Z. Poli (right) playing a game of chess with his competitor B. F. Keith. They each have theaters in their pockets, and it appears that the decision as to whose move it is may be construed when comparing the look of satisfaction on Poli's face to that of consternation on Keith's.

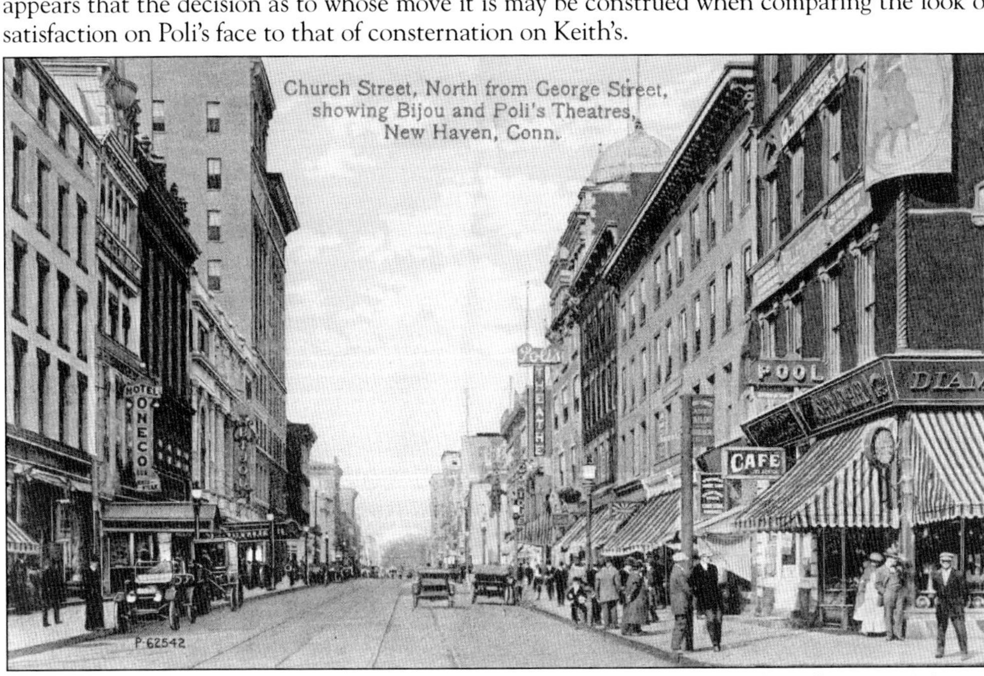

Long before television, New Haven had four major movie houses and several smaller ones. Sylvester Poli owned two across from each other on Church Street. Vaudeville created the need for theaters that would hold from 1,500 to 3,000 people. Shows could be filled two or three times a day.

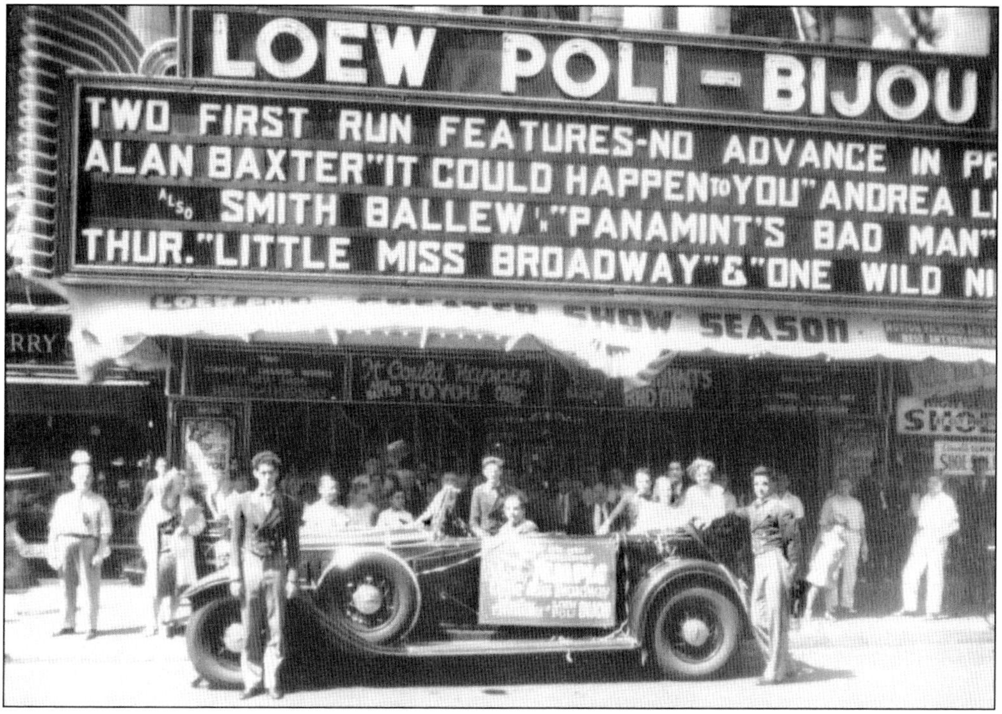

Jeanne Poli must have been influenced by her grandfather's role in theaters, as well as by some of his associates. New Haven movie houses owned by Sylvester Poli, and eventually the Loews Corporation, were only minutes from her home.

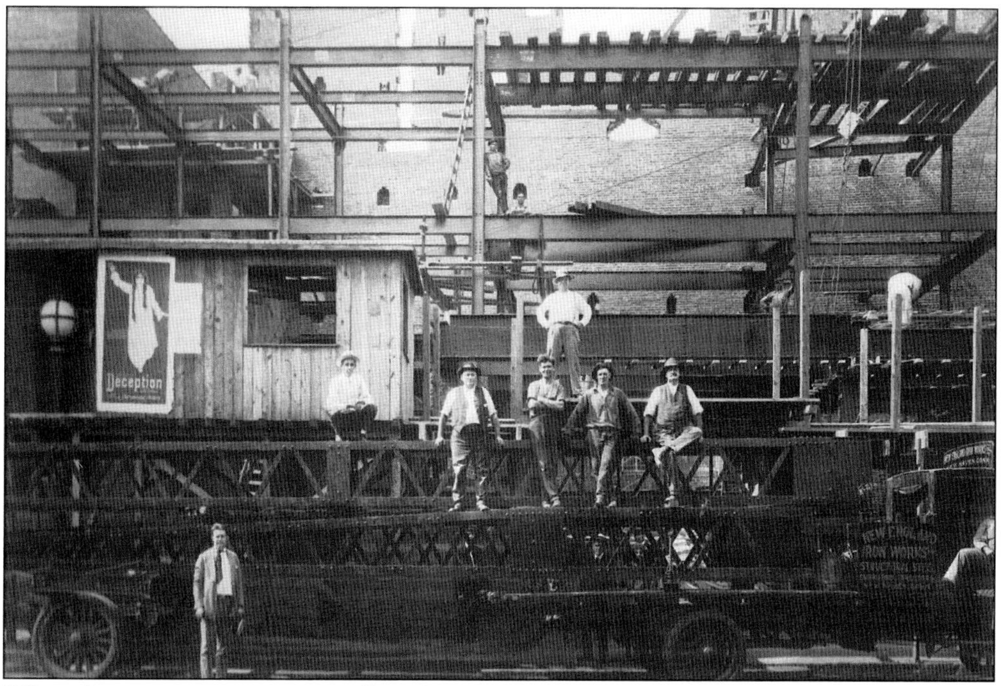

When theaters were going up rapidly, Sylvester wanted a hand in the action. He established the New Haven Iron Works, which he then turned over to his son-in-law, Walter Sheahan.

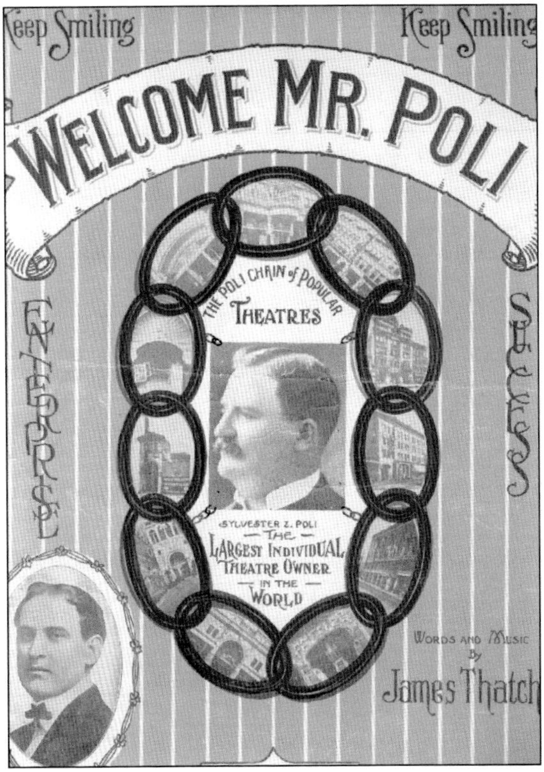

Whenever the opening of a Poli Theatre occurred, there was always local celebration. Sylvester Poli was greeted with a new song when he launched a theater in Scranton, Pennsylvania.

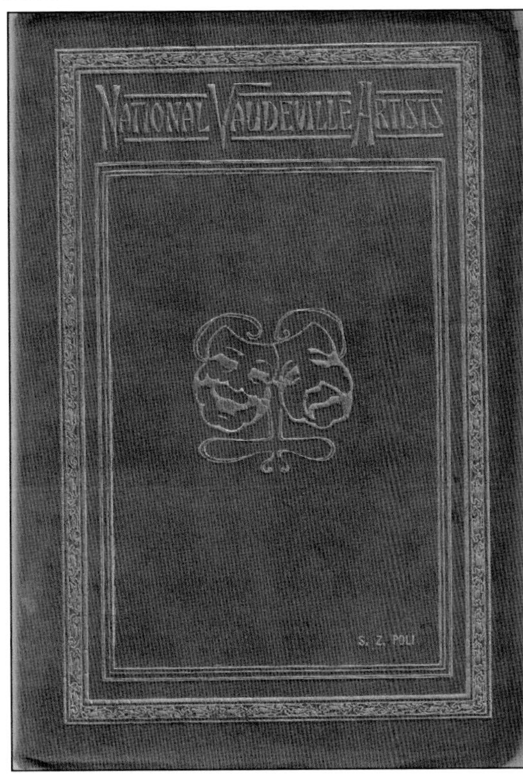

Sylvester Poli was concerned that his theaters carry only healthy, legitimate acts that would be appropriate for families, and he was instrumental in the creation of the American Vaudeville Association, aiding the careers of acts like Eddie Cantor, the Seven Little Foys, and many other great performers. Sylvester's influence in the American Vaudeville Association could be seen in this suede-covered, gold-lettered program dedicated in his name.

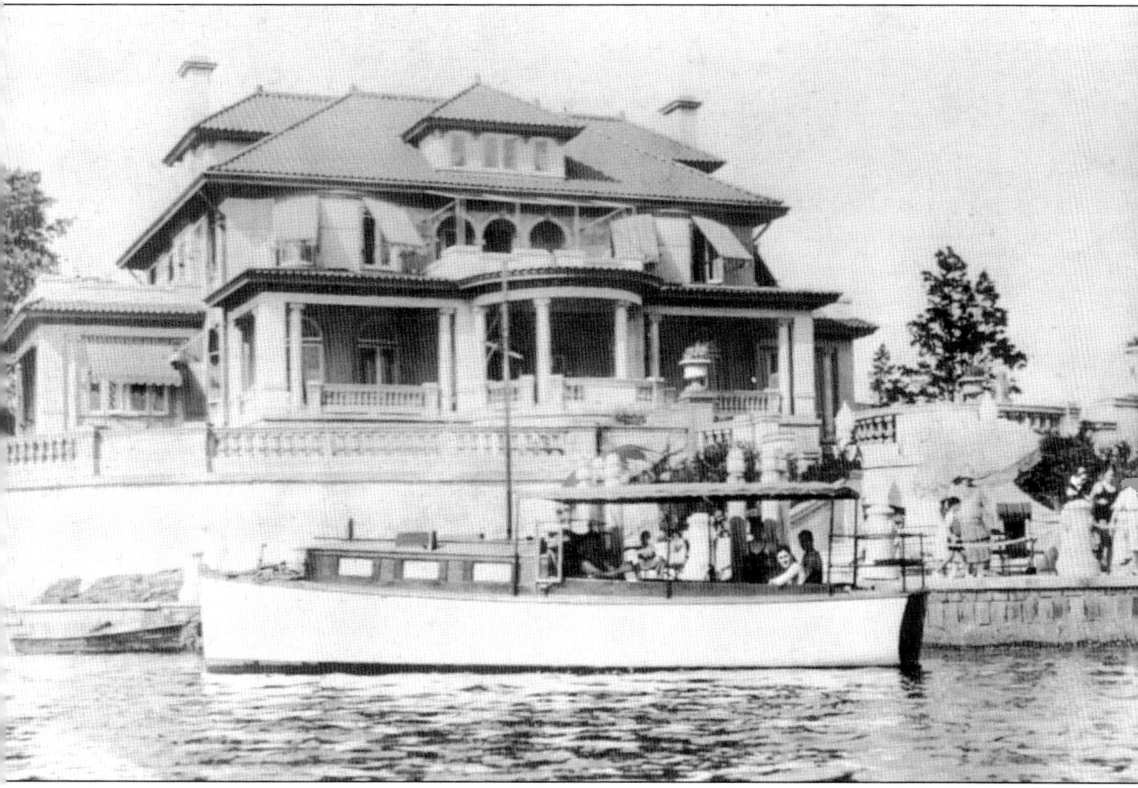

The Villa Rosa was the summer home of Sylvester and Rosa Poli. When Sylvester hosted the premier of the film *Top Hat* in his own home theater, guests arriving by launch were greeted by an orchestra on the lawn and a sumptuous meal. Local people were welcome to observe the festivities from their own boats, as long as they did not use motors that would create any noise.

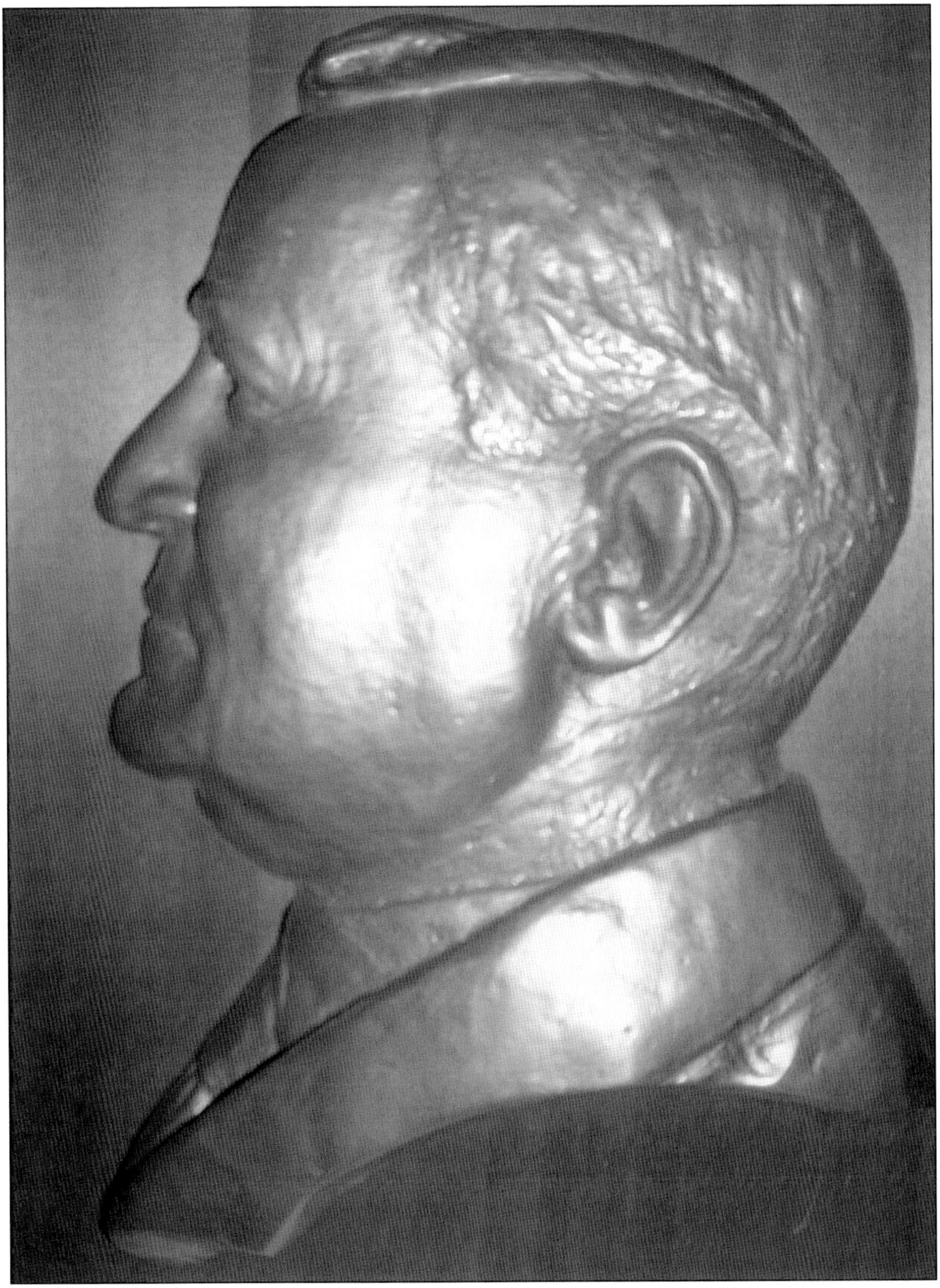

It is easy to forget that Sylvester Poli began his career as a sculptor. This self-portrait in bronze is a testimony to his personal skill and talent as an artist.

Eight

Occasions to Celebrate

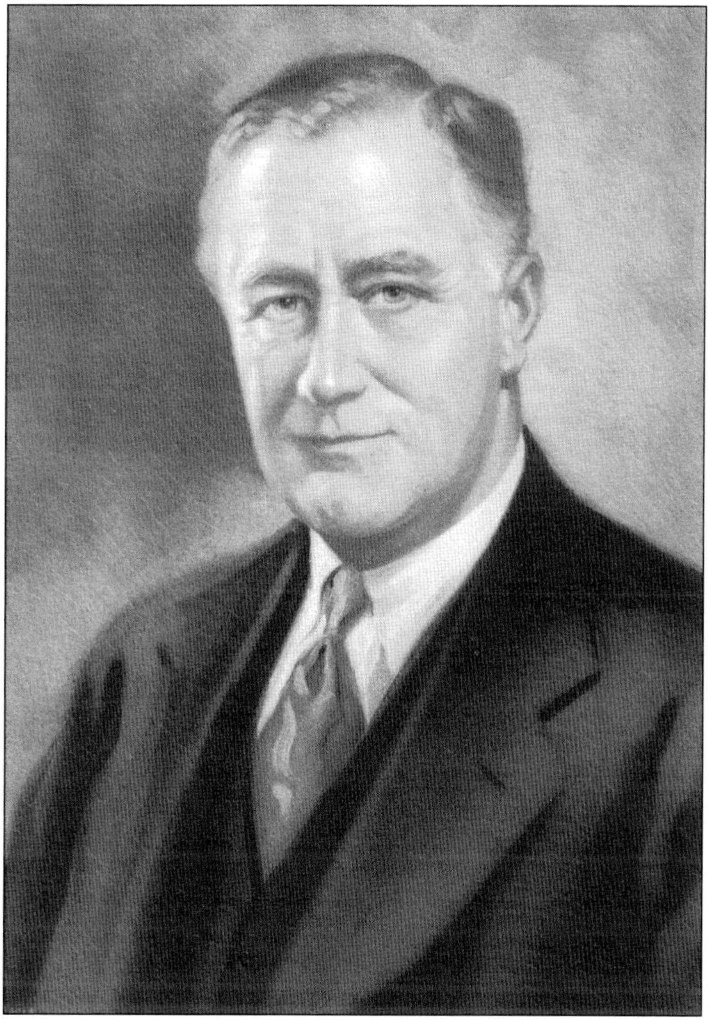

Over the centuries, the people of West Haven have celebrated with patriotic zeal and flag waving at events held for any number of reasons, including the birthday of Pres. Franklin Delano Roosevelt.

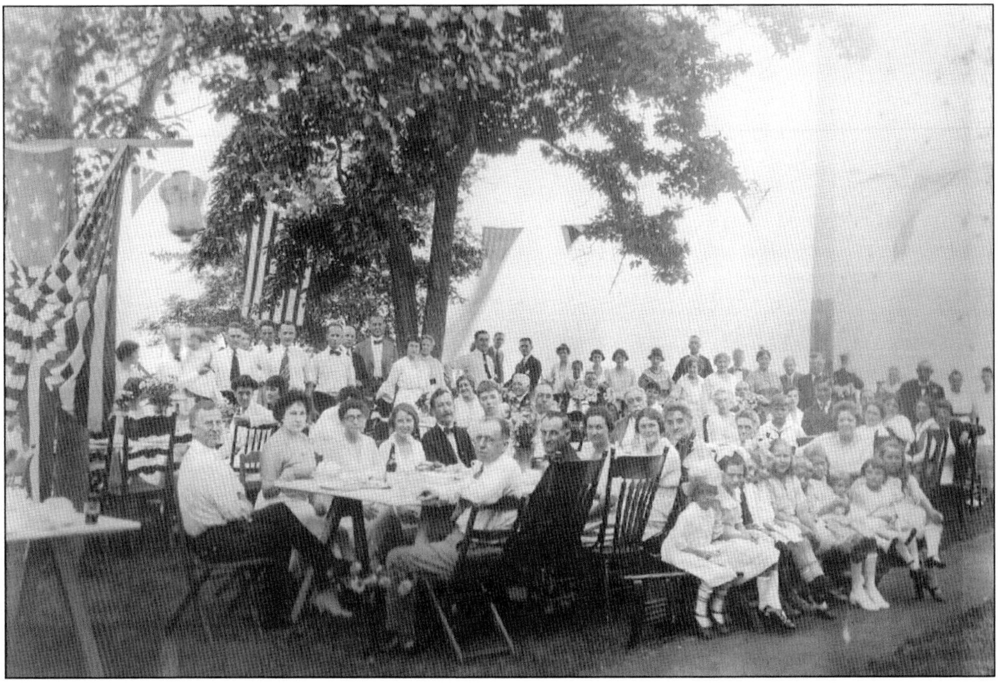

The shoreline was always a gathering place, and John H. Dillon and Louis Schmidt (seated across from one another at the end of the table, center front) decided that Woody Crest would be the perfect spot to host this dinner party on July 31, 1920. It was not unusual to have large parties at the shore, especially when one rented, or owned, a Victorian cottage for the summer.

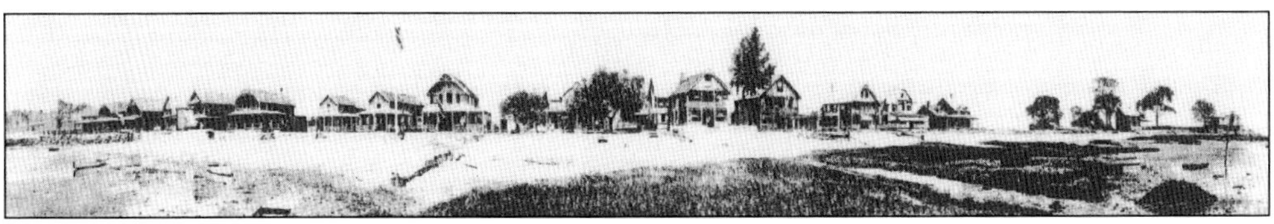

Bradley Point, located at the westernmost side of Savin Rock, attracted visitors to the Barnacle Coffee and Gift Shop or for a leisurely stroll. Eventually the point was lined with summer cottages, which were ravaged by the Great New England Hurricane of 1938.

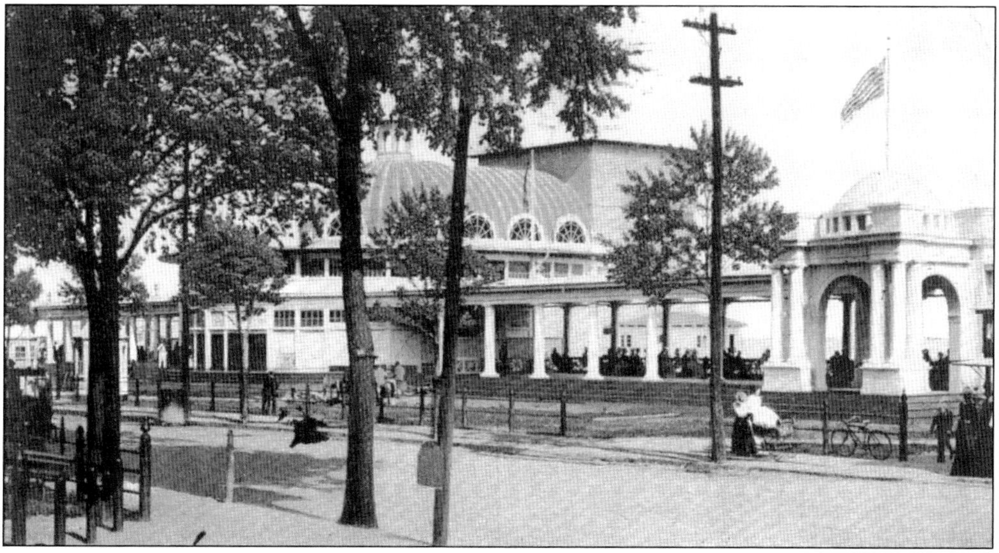

Gentle ocean breezes and a view of the ocean attracted diners to the fine shoreline restaurants of Savin Rock for almost 100 years. That tradition continues today, as several establishments continue to serve everything from hand-held grilled hot dogs or fresh-caught seafood to gourmet dinners.

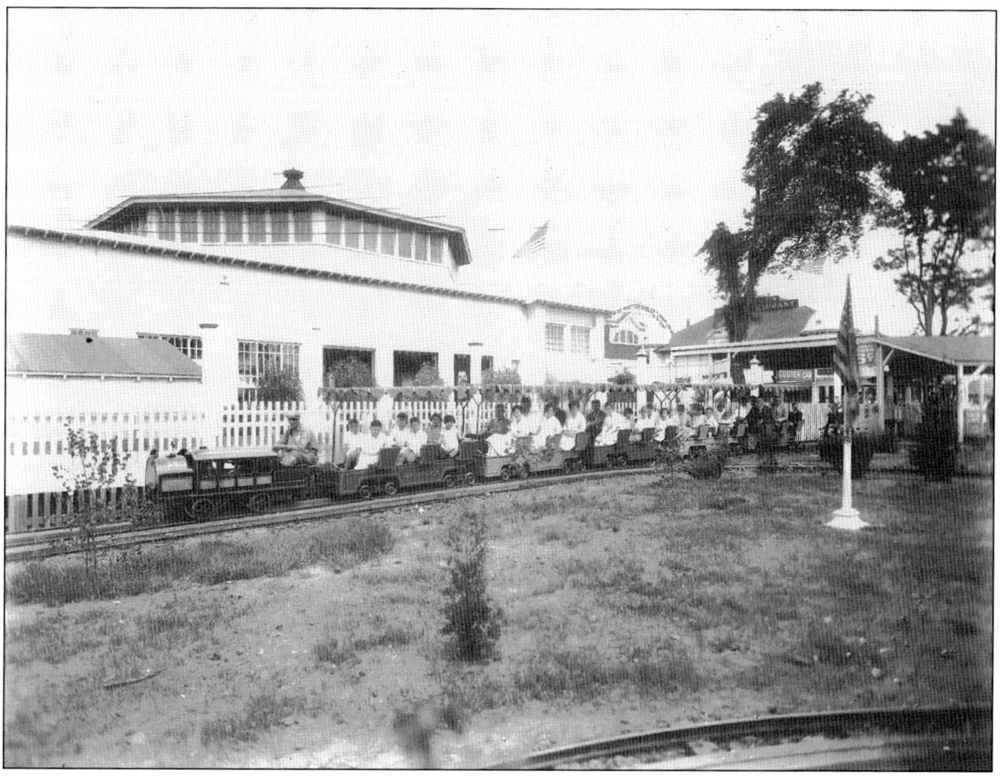

For those who preferred not to ride the roller coasters and chutes, there was a small train that circled through the Savin Rock Amusement Park.

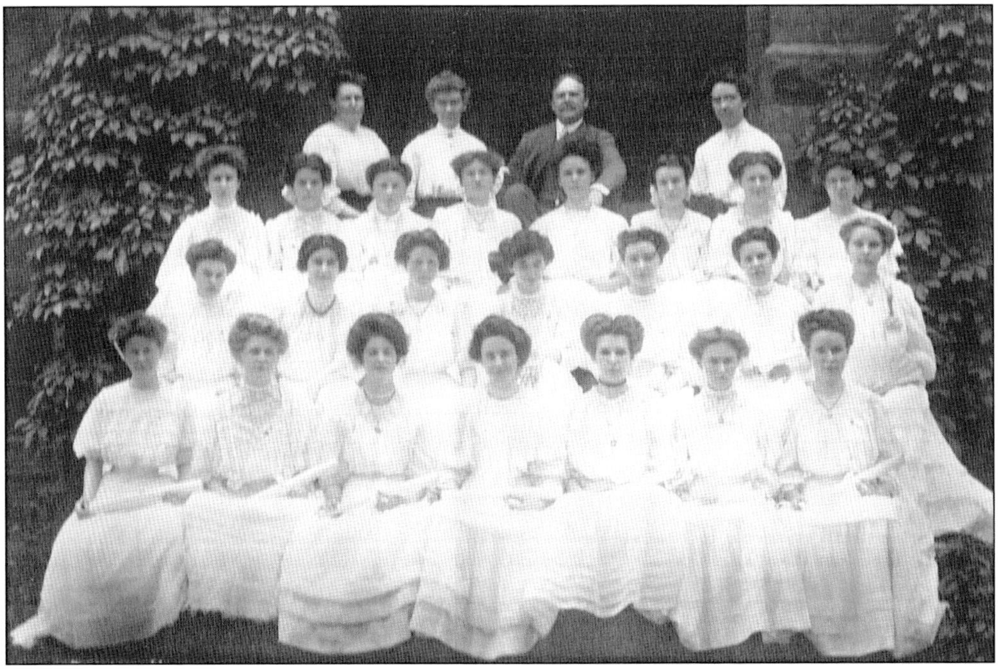

It was customary for graduating classes to spend a day at the Savin Rock Amusement Park, and chances are very likely that this Union High School Class followed this tradition in the early 1900s. Union School was West Haven's first high school. The handsome National Historic Landmark building now houses apartments for senior citizens.

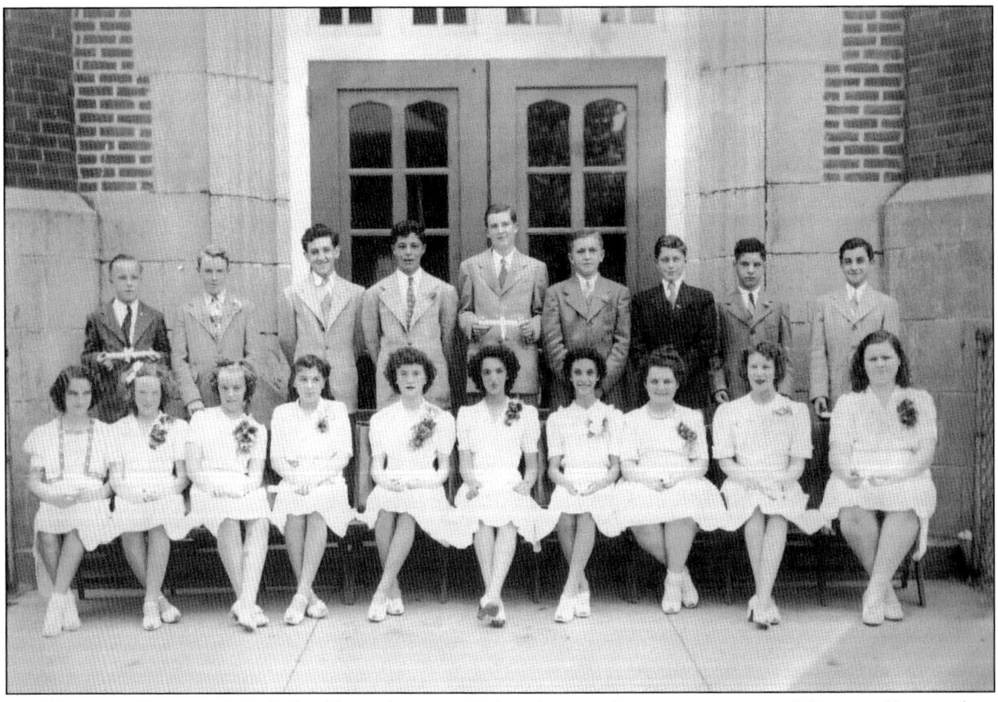

Students no longer attend the First Avenue School near the intersection of Spring Street, but their memory lives on in this picture of the class of 1940.

Nine

THE POWER OF AN EAGLE (SCOUT)

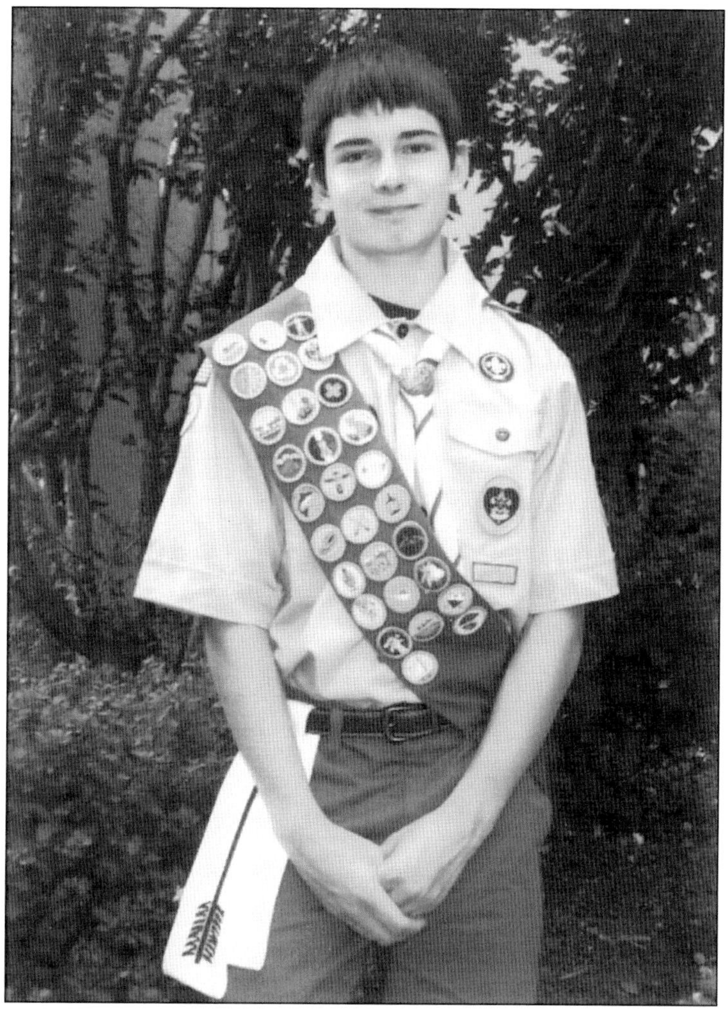

Eagle Scout candidate Matt King faced a daunting task when he elected to create the Archival Center in the West Haven Historical Society's new headquarters to earn his badge.

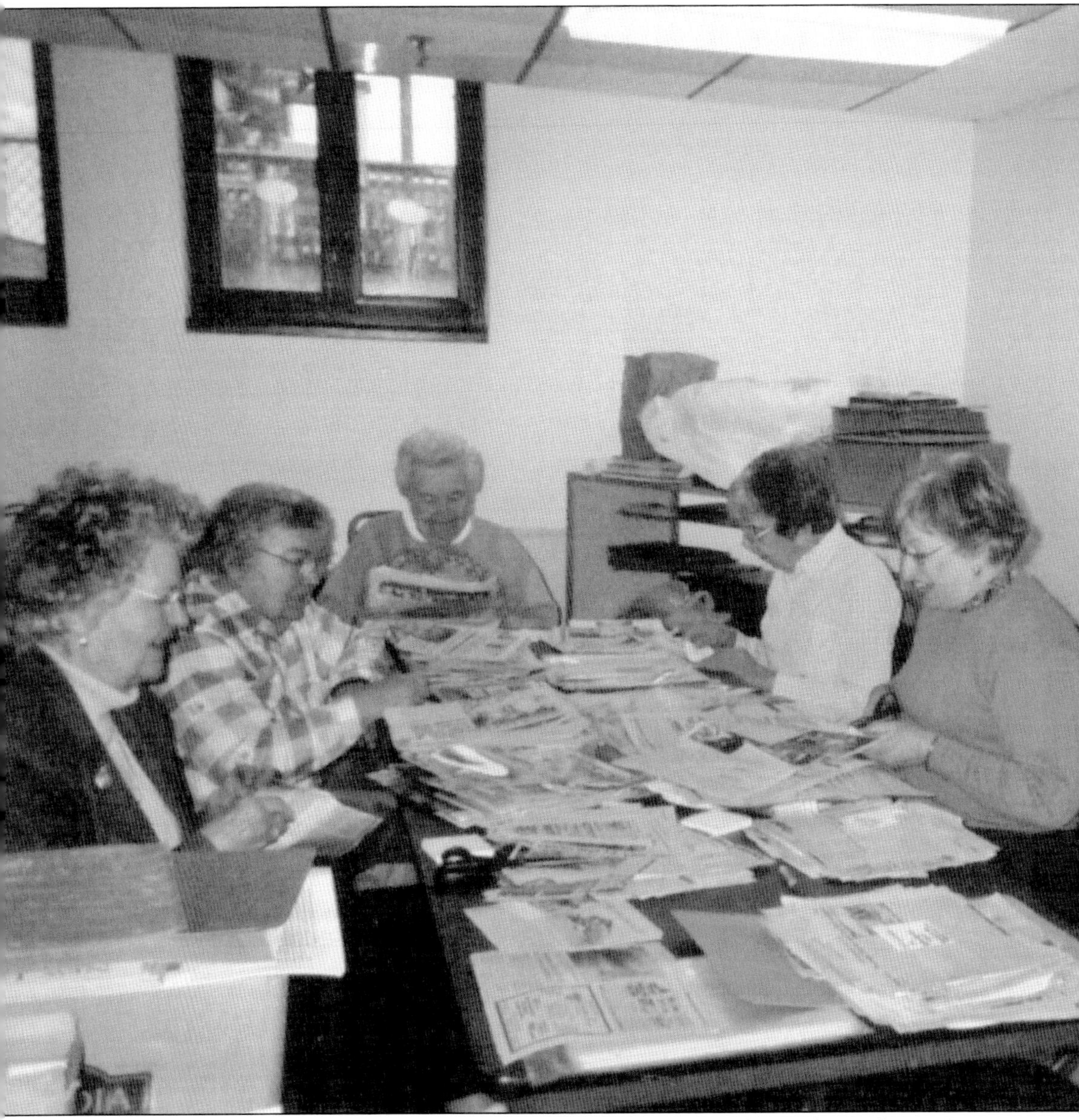

Hard at work organizing 50-plus years of news articles are, from left to right, archivists Lorraine Standish, Alice Butler, Eleanor Kandetsky, Violet Bornemann, and Carole A. Laydon McElrath. The diligent group, including Blanche Baldwin, Betty Roy, Diane Arduini, Marge Sodergren and intern Kari Burgess, a Southern Connecticut State University library science major, were professionally trained by Yale Divinity School international collections archivist Joan Duffy, who is a member of the historical society.

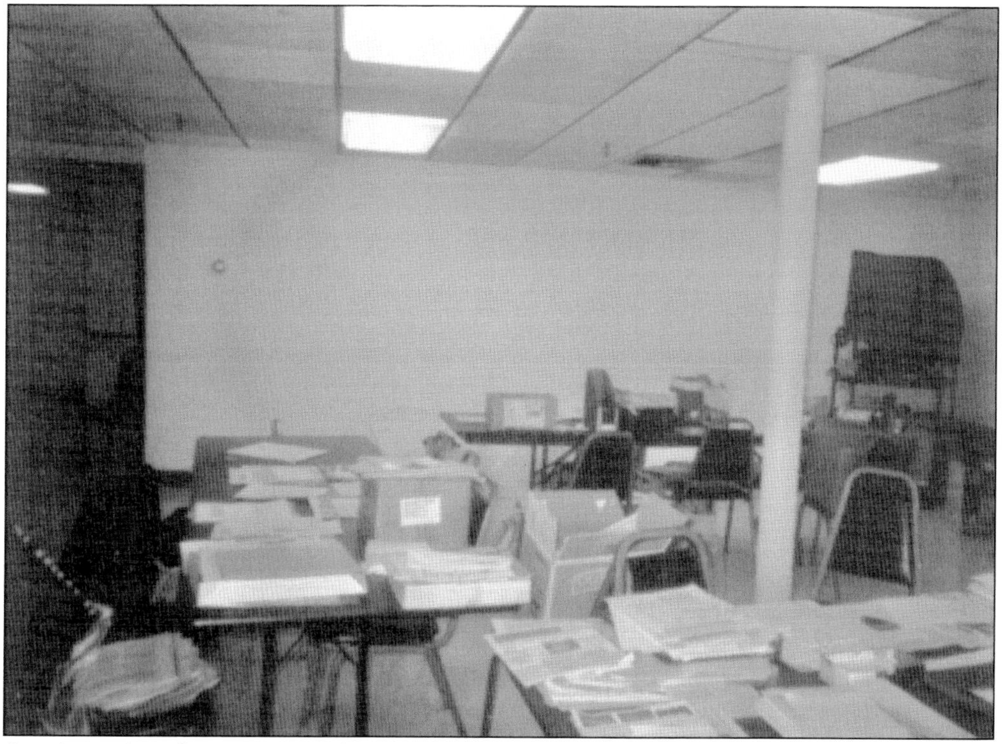

Articles and artifacts were sorted, often covering eight to ten 6-foot tables, as seen above. Once the ephemera was classified and the artifacts were recorded with museum precision, the team awaited the arrival of the archival storage boxes below. The final step was to put the sorted items into the acid-free folders and archival boxes in preparation for the move to the new Regional Archival Center on Savin Avenue.

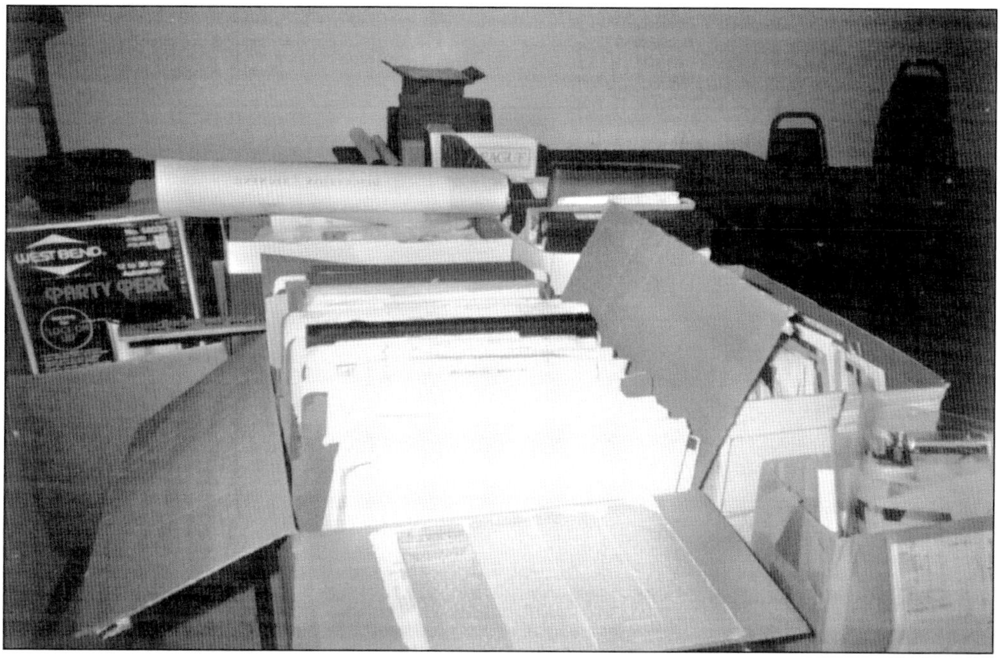

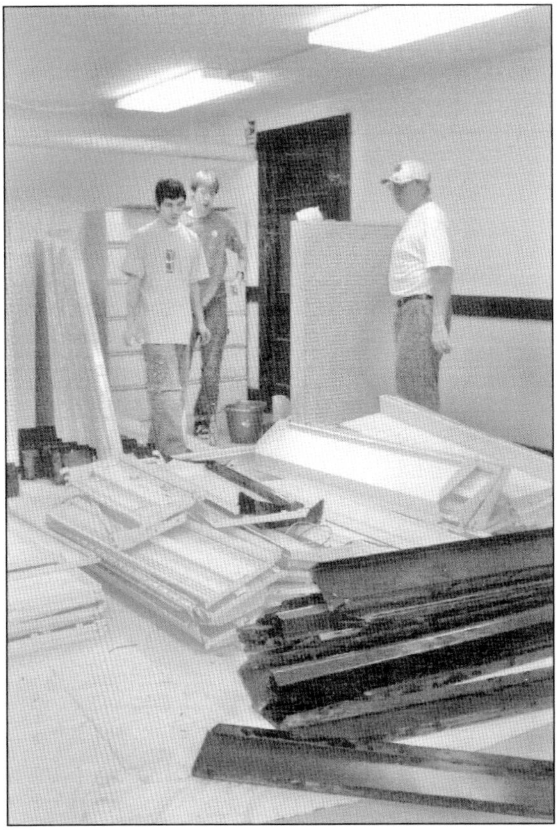

Matt King (left) faces his future as he surveys the dismantled shelving that would become the heart of the archival room. The shelving was made available through the generosity of local businessmen David and Scott Silver.

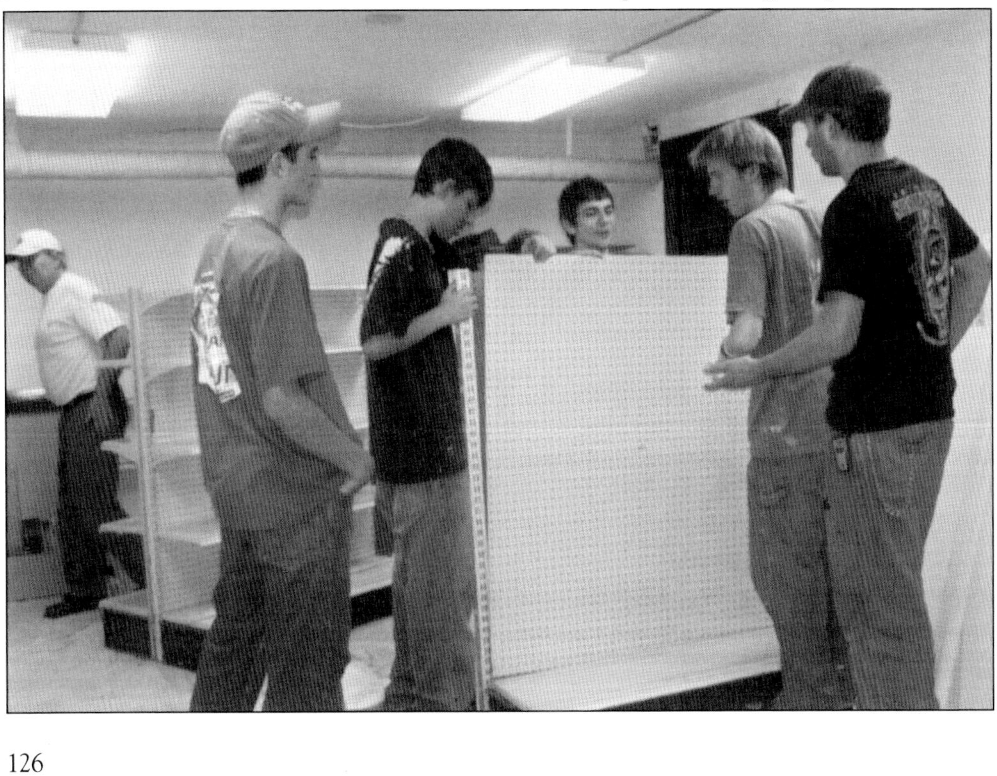

With the support and cooperation of his fellow scouts and leaders from Troop 202, Matt King (center, behind shelf) was able to sort through the pieces of this giant puzzle.

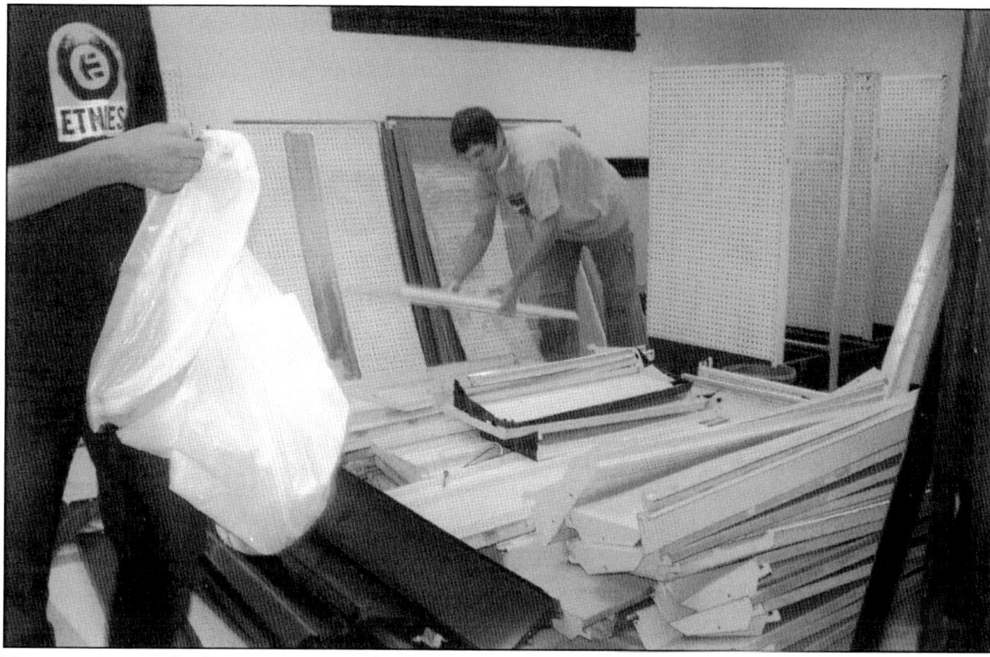

Teamwork was the key to securing the heavy pieces. As he put the last shelf in place, Matt King would have completed his requirements for his Eagle Scout petition, but he chose to continue on with the project by creating a database for every file, folder, and article that was stored in the new building. Today the archivists still meet regularly as a group, and everything remains in good order thanks to teen volunteers Keri Burgess and Matt King, who became involved in these most important tasks.

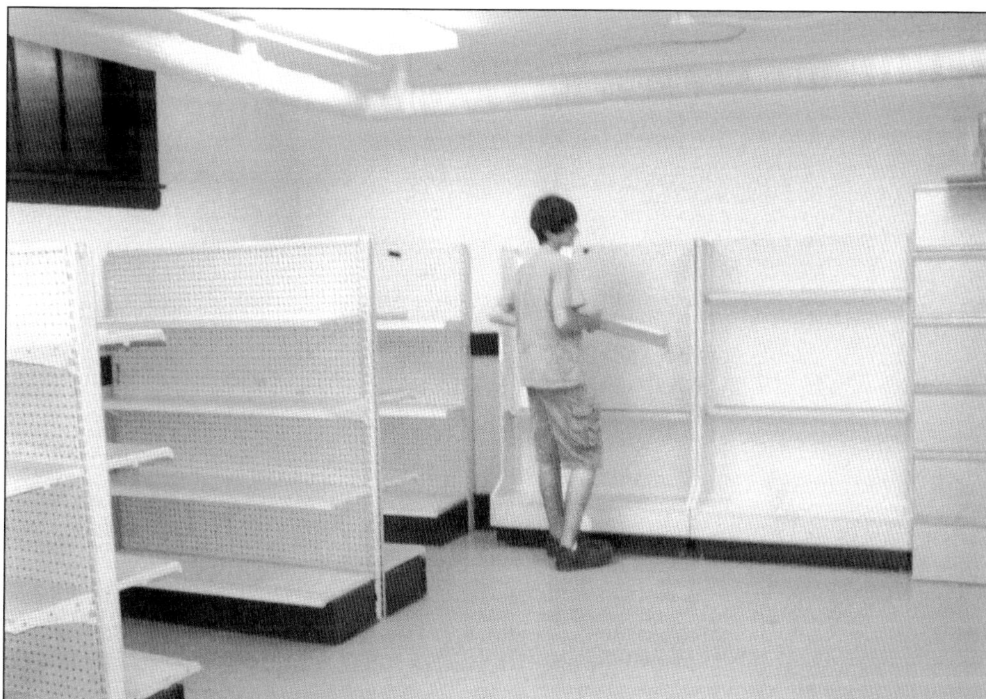